The Truth About the

Panama Canal

The Truth About the

Panama Canal

Denison Kitchel

ARLINGTON HOUSE·PUBLISHERS
NEW ROCHELLE, NEW YORK

Manufactured in the United States of America
10 9 8 7 6 5 4 3 2 1

Library of Congress Cataloging in Publication Data

Kitchel, Denison.
  The truth about the Panama Canal.

  Includes bibliographical references and index.
  1. Panama Canal. 2. United States—Foreign rela-
tions—Panama. 3. Panama—Foreign relations—United
States. I. Title.
JX1398.8.8K57   327.73'07287   77–16667
ISBN 0–87000–409–3

To N.D.K.

Contents

Foreword

SENATOR BARRY GOLDWATER

In the many years I have known Denison Kitchel, I believe the one thing that I have observed as the hallmark of everything he does is his complete dedication to the task at hand. In this book he has combined that dedication with a thoroughness of research and an incomparable writing style to shed light on one of the most complicated and emotional issues of this century.

A few years ago, he began talking with me about the Panama Canal because it was quite obvious even then that negotiations which had begun under the Johnson Administration would ultimately be completed and translated into a new treaty governing our relationships in the Canal Zone. This book is extremely important because it not only traces the history of the Panama Canal from the time when it was merely an impossible dream until it finally became the principal thoroughfare connecting the Atlantic and Pacific oceans, but because it brings that history right down to date. It does this with a precise attention to detail and to the prevailing sentiment of the American people and American officials at the times the various events that shaped this history were transpiring.

9

Many people have preconceived ideas of what the Canal problem is all about. Many of these ideas are based on sloppy historical conclusions. Mr. Kitchel has sought out and related the truth as he sees it. He has approached the problem from the standpoint of what is ultimately best for the United States, both in the immediate future and for years to come.

This is the perfect volume for people who want to thoroughly understand all of the intricacies of the Panama Canal problem. The book is easy to read and it's easy to understand.

Foreword

REPRESENTATIVE JOHN J. RHODES

One day during the spring of 1942 I was interrupted in my work as assistant adjutant at Williams Field, Arizona, by a young man in civilian clothes with a manila folder in his hands. He had in his folder orders from the War Department commissioning one Denison Kitchel of Phoenix, Arizona, a first lieutenant in the Army of the United States and ordering him to active duty as a "statistical officer" at Williams Field, an advanced-flying-training base. None of the headquarters personnel had heard of him, but because his papers were in order, I instructed him to raise his right hand and proceeded to administer to him the oath of office.

In a very few days Lt. Kitchel was fully uniformed and could salute well enough to get by in the Army Air Corps. Shortly thereafter, it became necessary for our commanding officer to prefer charges against a retreaded World War I flying officer of some note, a former member of the famous Lafayette Escadrille. He was the individual who during the Paris World War I victory celebration flew a fighter airplane through the Arc de Triomphe. After World War I he had flown for the Poles against the Russians, for the Greeks against the Turks, and then continued to operate as a flying soldier of fortune in various parts of the world. Unfortunately, he had deteriorated somewhat between wars and had developed a drinking problem that rendered him incapable of performing his duties. However, he refused to resign and therefore was court-martialed. In all, 29 charges of misconduct were filed against him. Because of his prominence, we all realized that he must be given a defense counsel who had the ability to do a thorough job.

At that time, anyone who appeared before a court-martial was presumed to be guilty or he wouldn't be there. The defense counsel usually was an officer who had been shanghaied into the job and merely wanted to get it over with. The commander of the field and I went through our officers roster very carefully and finally agreed that Lt. Kitchel was the man for the job. To make a long story short, Kitchel did such a thorough job of preparation and such an outstanding job presenting the evidence, bringing out the good side of his "client," that the officer was acquitted on 28 of the 29 charges.

The next day the base commander decided to have Kitchel on his side in future court-martial situations and named him post judge advocate. He also placed him in command of one of the crack school squadrons. Not long after that Lt. Kitchel was ordered overseas.

All of us, of course, were sorry to see Kitchel leave, but we recognized he had ability far beyond any of the administrative and legal positions we could give him.

He had a remarkable record in the Eighth and Twentieth air forces as an intelligence officer. After the war he came back to his law practice in Phoenix. About the same time, I was relieved from active duty and, having taken the Arizona bar examination during the war, was ready for the practice of law. When I had had my shingle out for a short period of time, I renewed acquaintance with Denison Kitchel, and we have been warm personal friends ever since.

Our longest period of close relationship came during the presidential campaign of 1964. Barry Goldwater, my good friend and colleague for many years, decided to become a candidate for president. He appointed as his "head honcho" my old friend, Denison Kitchel. He served as Barry Goldwater's campaign manager throughout that fascinating but ill-fated campaign. Though the campaign was not successful, everyone who came in contact with Kitchel was deeply impressed with his capabilities and energies. There can be no doubt in the mind of anyone who has been close to him through the years that he is endowed with the finest mental equipment the Good Lord has available.

I have known for some time that Kitchel was engaged in a study in depth concerning the Panama Canal. When he asked me to read his manuscript, I was pleased to do so, of course. He has done what I consider to be an outstanding job of presenting in highly readable form the background of the current controversy and the various considerations essential to its solution.

I have known few issues facing the people of this country that have aroused the depth of emotion provoked by the proposed Panama Canal treaties. Mr. Kitchel's calm, deliberate analysis of the problems involved comes as a welcome relief from the harsh and unproductive rhetoric that has come from both sides of the issue. He places the proposed treaties in clear perspective, and he does it well. Anyone who reads this book will be much better equipped to come to a rational decision regarding the proposed treaties than he previously was, whether or not in the final analysis he agrees with the conclusions of the author.

My good friend, Denison Kitchel, has performed a real service for his country, and for those of its citizens who are fortunate enough to read this very fine book. Those of us who know him would have expected no less.

Preface

Seldom thought of but long cherished as a part of our national heritage, a symbol of unique national accomplishment, the Panama Canal has suddenly become a national storm center.

Out of the blue, the American people are told that their leaders are committed to giving up the Canal, that we are going to get out of Panama, that we are going to pay Panama billions of dollars to take the responsibility for operating and defending the Canal off our hands, that these things *must* be done, that there is no other course. The average American is stunned and bewildered.

Two years ago, while studying the treaty negotiations between the United States and Panama, I became concerned that just such a situation would develop and that when it did millions of Americans, including myself, would be faced with a fateful decision we would be ill-equipped to make.

I knew my own instinctive feelings about the Canal. But I also knew that, aside from brief exposures to the Canal issue on two earlier occasions, I had no real understanding of the problem. I decided then to try and find out for myself, objectively and

15

thoroughly, what it was all about. As a result, my entire time for two years was devoted to that quest—research, study, inquiry, interviews, discussions—in the United States and in Panama, and to compiling the results. This book is the result of that effort.

In this project I had considerable encouragement and help from such friends as Senator Barry Goldwater, former Senator Paul Fannin, House Minority Leader John Rhodes, William J. Baroody, president of the American Enterprise Institute in Washington, D.C., and Dr. G. Warren Nutter of the University of Virginia, former assistant secretary of defense for international security affairs. In addition, I had the cooperation and assistance of officials in the National Security Council, the State Department, the Defense Department, and the Joint Chiefs of Staff.

My deepest debt of gratitude is owed to my beloved wife, Naomi, and to two friends of longstanding, Chester W. Dudley, Jr., and William A. Evans. Others to whom I am most grateful for assistance of varying sorts are Charles S. Burns, Howell S. Randolph, Frederic S. Marquardt, Susan Conway, and, most particularly, capable, dedicated Hazel Plowman. But for her this book would remain a mass of hieroglyphics on blue-lined paper.

A word about the title. From the outset and during most of the writing, it was, tentatively, "The Panama Canal Dilemma." But the distortions and omissions of fact that characterize the current debate have turned the resolution of that dilemma into a rhetorical brawl. The new title, *The Truth About the Panama Canal*, has been selected, not with any claim to omniscience, but in the hope that it will encourage a search for that truth in the consideration of this important issue.

Phoenix, Arizona   DENISON KITCHEL
November 1977

16

The Truth
About the
Panama
Canal

"*What's wrong with me? For thirty years I never gave a thought to the Panama Canal. Now suddenly I can't live without it.*"

1

The Panama
Canal Dilemma

During the past several years the Panama Canal has been referred to on many occasions as a time bomb. The basic facts about Panama, the Canal, and the United States are so simple that, at first blush, to talk about a dilemma, much less a time bomb, seems almost laughable.

Panama is a small Central American country with only two cities of any size and a population of 1.7 million. It has no military power. It has no developed mineral treasure. It has a mini-economy. Its one great natural resource is its geographic location, its superior suitability as the site for an interoceanic waterway.

In fact, the only thing Panama really has going for it is the Panama Canal, which splits it right down the middle and links the Atlantic and Pacific oceans. The Canal runs through what is known as the Canal Zone, a strip of jungle land and water 10 miles wide and 50 miles long, over which the United States exercises exclusive control, dividing the Republic of Panama into two completely separated halves.

The United States built the Panama Canal at a cost of some

$350 million to itself and no cost to Panama. Altogether, the U.S. now has an investment of about $7 billion in the Canal enterprise. The Canal is maintained and operated by the United States. The Canal is defended by the United States.

The United States did and does these things under a 75-year-old treaty with Panama that gives it the right to do them forever —"in perpetuity" are the treaty's words. For this right the United States made a down payment to Panama of $10 million. To keep it, it pays Panama $2.3 million a year. In addition, Panama derives some $250 million each year in indirect income generated by the Canal activity. This represents about a fourth of Panama's annual gross national product and a third of its annual earnings from foreign exchange.

What could be a better situation from Panama's standpoint? Or from ours? Where is the dilemma? Why a time bomb?

Well, Panama says she wants the Canal. And Panama says we had better give her the Canal, or else.

Or else what? This is nonsense. Tell them to forget it.

Unfortunately, at this stage of the game it is not that easy.

The main reason it is not that easy may come as a complete surprise to millions of Americans. It is just this: For the past 13 years, under four presidents—Johnson, Nixon, Ford, and Carter —the executive branch of our government has been committed to, and negotiating towards, the prompt return of the Canal Zone to Panama and the ultimate transfer of the Canal itself and the responsibility for its defense. In September 1977 the president of the United States and the chief of state of Panama signed two proposed new treaties accomplishing those very objectives—that is, if they are ratified by both countries.

Incredible? Probably so to many, because this policy and its implementation have been carried out over the years almost surreptitiously so far as the general American public is concerned. At least, no real effort has been made until very recently to tell the American people what was going on or to give them the reasons. This is one of the seeds of our dilemma.

It *is* incredible. Nevertheless, it is so. We are committed, not legally, but officially and perhaps morally. This is the number one reason why we cannot just tell a small, powerless nation like Panama to forget all about it. But there are many, many others.

Strangely enough, though this David-Goliath confrontation is easy to describe, the Panama Canal issue has become very complex. Complex because of the importance of the Canal itself and its location. Complex because the United States is a sensitive superpower and Panama is a small "developing" nation, a part of the strident Third World. Complex because the Panamanians are people, fundamentally no different than people of other nations: proud, acquisitive, nationalistic.

Complex because of a post-Vietnam revulsion in the United States against further involvement in armed conflict, curiously coupled with a post-Vietnam "don't-push-us-around" groping for national pride. Complex because of the difficulties of operating, maintaining, and defending the Canal in an increasingly hostile environment, a decreasing acceptance of our presence by the host country. Complex because of the nature of the present Panamanian government.

Complex because of Fidel Castro in nearby Cuba. Complex because of the never-ending contest for world power between East and West, the pervasive struggle for ideological supremacy.

Complex because of high hopes raised in Panama by rash U.S. commitments and excessive diplomatic zeal. Complex because of papered-over, basic differences between the U.S. military and the State Department concerning national security considerations.

Complex because of polarized points of view and blind convictions held widely by private American citizens and by members of Congress. And complex because of U.S. politics.

Complex is almost too mild a term.

In a 1976 issue of the *New Yorker* magazine there was a cartoon showing two corpulent, middle-aged U.S. city dwellers conversing at a bar. One is saying to the other: "What's wrong with me? For thirty years I never gave a thought to the Panama Canal. Now suddenly I can't live without it."

This depicts quite accurately the instinctive feeling of millions of Americans, probably a majority. The polls show it quite clearly: asked if they favor giving up the Panama Canal, more than 75 percent will reply with a resounding no.[1]

This instinctive feeling in the United States about the Panama Canal is another seed of our dilemma. Congressman Daniel J. Flood, the flamboyant liberal Democrat from Pennsylvania, long the leading spokesman in Congress of those who oppose any tampering with our rights and position in Panama, has described it in these words:

21

Everyone thinks the Panama Canal is as American as apple pie. This has been ingrained in them, they believe this all through their lives, and they just don't give away something that's as close to them . . . which they feel is an American thing. . . . The average American feels this so very deeply that . . . it's over my dead body, that kind of thing. . . . This is the feeling. You can't reason with it. It's ingrained and deep, deep-dyed in their hearts.[2]

Historically the subject of the Panama Canal has lain submerged in American public consciousness, surfacing only when large-scale violence in Panama hit the headlines, as it did in 1959, and again in 1964. It has received scant public attention, even when Congress gave indications of strong opposition to the "giveaway" course of action that has been so doggedly pursued by the executive branch of our government.

For example, it was scarcely noted in the press when, in 1974, 37 U.S. senators, 4 more than necessary to block a new treaty, cosponsored a resolution stating "that the government of the United States should maintain and protect its sovereign rights and jurisdiction over the Canal and Zone, and should in no way cede, dilute, forfeit, negotiate or transfer any of these rights."[3] Or in 1975 when the number cosponsoring such a resolution rose to 39 senators.[4]

Nor was there much publicity or excitement when, in 1975, the House, exercising its constitutional responsibility with regard to appropriations and the disposition of U.S. property, voted 246 to 164 to forbid the use of any funds "to negotiate the surrender or relinquishment of the United States' rights in the Panama Canal."[5]

Each of these congressional expressions was a strong reaction to some new development in the continuing U.S.-Panama negotiations for a new Canal treaty. Each was a recognition by Congress of that feeling "back home," the subterranean rumblings signalled by the few who are instantly alert when the Panama Canal nerve is touched. But, by and large, the American consciousness was on none of those occasions correspondingly aroused.

The subject finally surfaced in 1976. Why was this? What made the man at the *New Yorker* bar suddenly feel that he couldn't live without the Panama Canal? Apparently it was the rhetoric of the 1976 presidential campaign.

In the spring of 1976 Republican presidential contender Ronald Reagan discovered that the Panama Canal issue was a vote-getter. He harshly criticized the Ford Administration for its Panamanian policy. Immediately his campaign for the nomination came alive, and the race for convention delegates began to veer in his direction. The subject of Panama caught hold. Soon the voices of politicians and pundits were heard throughout the land, declaiming over Panama, pro and con. Feature articles in newspapers and magazines mushroomed across the nation.

Reagan had touched America's Panama Canal nerve: "We should tell Panama's tinhorn dictator just what he can do with his demands for sovereignty over the Canal Zone. We bought it, we paid for it, and they can't have it."[6]

This was a dramatic expression of the instinctive national feeling. Some call it the "knee-jerk" reaction.

If Reagan and the man at the *New Yorker* bar speak for a majority of Americans, how can the United States' position on Panama be otherwise? Where does the United States really stand on this issue? Which of two worlds, the world of officialdom or the world of instinctive American feeling, is the real one?

To determine the answer to this question it is essential to look briefly at the activities in the official world, to get at least a birdseye view of how far the United States has gone in its dealings with Panama over the Canal issue.

In December 1964, in the wake of that year's "Flag War" in Panama—the riots and invasions of the Canal Zone and the involvement of U.S. troops that cost the lives of 5 Americans and 20 Panamanians and produced a breaking off of diplomatic relations between the two countries—President Lyndon Johnson made a precedent-breaking policy announcement: "I have decided to propose to the Government of Panama the negotiation of an entirely new treaty on the existing Panama Canal."[7]

No fanfare. No real attempt at explanation. Just a press release.

Then, in September 1965, Johnson gave a report on the progress of the negotiations that he had thus initiated nine months earlier.[8] He reported that the United States had agreed to abrogate the 1903 treaty, to give up perpetuity, to recognize Panama's sovereignty over the Canal Zone, to place the Canal Zone under the jurisdiction and control of the Panamanian government, and to operate the Canal jointly with Panama.

Only the details remained to be negotiated. This was another momentous announcement, but, again, no fanfare, no real attempt at explanation. Just a press release.

That all occurred 13 years ago. The man at the *New Yorker* bar apparently did not hear about it. Ronald Reagan had not yet begun his quest for the presidency.

In 1967 three draft treaties were agreed upon and initialed by the negotiating teams. They covered, in complete detail, the Johnson announcement and commitments of '64 and '65 with regard to the 1903 treaty. They also covered the possibilities for a new canal and the matter of canal defense. The treaty covering the present Canal would terminate in 1999. Panama would then take over completely. The treaty concerning defense would terminate in 2004, with the relinquishment of all U.S. defense rights at that time.

There was no announcement at all by President Johnson of this historic wrap-up of the U.S.-Panama treaty negotiations. Just a State Department bulletin.[9] It took the *Chicago Tribune* to uncover the texts of the new treaties.[10] The Panamanian government was equally reticent.

The reason for the low-key bulletin and the failure to disclose details was obvious. Both the United States and Panama had presidential elections coming up in 1968. The administrations in both countries apparently deemed it the better part of political valor to be quiet about what they had agreed to do with the Panama Canal.

All this happened 10 years ago. The man at the *New Yorker* bar either did not hear or the news did not register. Reagan, serving his first term as governor of California, had no election pending.

The 1968 presidential elections brought about a political upheaval in Panama and a political change in the U.S. In Panama, Arnulfo Arias was elected president by an overwhelming popular vote. On October 11, 1968, only 10 days after he took office, Arias was ousted in a military coup staged by the Panamanian National Guard. A military junta, in which Lieutenant Colonel (now Brigadier General) Omar Torrijos emerged as the strong man, took over the government of Panama and has remained in control ever since. In the United States, Republican Richard Nixon was elected president. Neither the upheaval in Panama nor the change in the U.S. was in any way related to the Canal.

24

Two years later, in 1970, the Torrijos government notified the Nixon government that it rejected the 1967 draft treaties. So the negotiating teams went back to the drawing boards to start anew. The ensuing negotiations dragged. Under Torrijos, Panama moved the Canal issue into the international arena. In the fall of 1973, as a result of Torrijos' maneuvering, the United Nations Security Council got into the act and put the U.S. on the defensive.

In a scenario carefully staged by Panama and her many supporters, the United States, at a meeting of the Security Council held in Panama City, was forced to veto a resolution calling for a new Canal treaty that would "guarantee full respect for Panama's effective sovereignty over all of its territory."[11]

In the wake of this confrontation, the Nixon Administration placed the Panama Canal issue back on the front burner. The State Department's veteran of Vietnam diplomacy, Ellsworth Bunker, was placed at the head of the United States' negotiating team. He was told to get cracking. The pot began to boil again.

Substantial "progress" was made in only three months. With all the fanfare so carefully avoided on the previous occasions of startling new Canal developments, Secretary of State Henry Kissinger journeyed to Panama City, and there, on February 7, 1974, he and Panamanian Foreign Minister Juan Tack signed a Statement of Principles establishing eight guidelines for a new Canal treaty. New voice, same words and tune, only more so:

(1) The 1903 treaty would be abrogated and replaced by an entirely new treaty.

(2) The concept of perpetuity would be eliminated and the new treaty would have a fixed termination date.

(3) United States jurisdiction over Panamanian territory would be terminated promptly in accordance with the terms of the new treaty.

(4) The Canal Zone would be returned to Panamanian jurisdiction, with the United States retaining specified rights of use for the duration of the new treaty.

(5) Panama would have a "just and equitable" share of the economic benefits derived from the Canal's operations.

(6) Panama would participate in the administration of the Canal with a view to taking over full responsibility for its operation at the termination of the new treaty.

(7) Panama would share in the protection and defense of the Canal.

(8) The United States and Panama would agree on provisions for enlarging the capacity of the Canal.[12]

That was only three years ago. Certainly the message was loud and clear. Yet it still did not get through to the man at the *New Yorker* bar. Ronald Reagan, completing his last year as governor of California, had no election pending—just thoughts, perhaps, of 1976.

Six months after the Kissinger-Tack agreement, Vice President Gerald Ford became president of the United States. A year later it became clear that the Ford policy on the Panama Canal was a continuation of the Johnson-Nixon policy. Another revelation occurred that could have brought the Canal issue to the surface before the 1976 election, but did not.

In September 1975 Kissinger made a statement in Florida that angered the Panamanian government and made it suspect that perhaps the United States was reneging on the Kissinger-Tack agreement. Kissinger said: "The United States must defend the right, unilaterally, to defend the Canal for an indefinite future, or for a long future."[13] Apparently this blew the lid in Panama, for Panama immediately violated the agreement of secrecy regarding the negotiations and released the texts of three "conceptual agreements" that had already been reached in the talks, implementing major elements of the Kissinger-Tack Statement of Principles. The Ford Administration did not deny their validity and later quietly admitted their existence.

There could no longer be any doubt about what was going on in the official world of the Ford Administration regarding the Panama Canal. Again, the message was clear. But it apparently was still not loud enough for the man at the *New Yorker* bar to hear. Ronald Reagan had no doubt heard. He had already launched his race for the Republican presidential nomination.

During the spring of 1976, candidate Reagan became the Paul Revere of the Panama Canal, warning the American people in ringing terms of the "giveaway" program. The man at the *New Yorker* bar finally got the message. However, the official world continued on its unswerving course.

When Democrat Jimmy Carter won the 1976 presidential election, there was reason to expect that a change in U.S. policy would occur. During the closing days of the campaign, Carter had stated: "I would never give up complete control or practical control of the Panama Canal Zone."[14] Nevertheless, only a few days after he took office President Carter gave the negotiation of a new treaty with Panama, *on the basis of the Kissinger-Tack agreement of 1974,* top priority in his foreign relations program. Less than nine months later, Carter signed the two proposed new treaties that now face the U.S. Congress and the American people.

Here, then, are the two worlds: a clear indication, on one hand, that a majority of the American people is instinctively opposed to giving up our rights and position in Panama—call it the world of U.S. public opinion—and on the other, in the official world, an even clearer indication that those rights and that position are going to be given up.

Both worlds are real. They are on a collision course. When the collision occurs, one would assume that public opinion will triumph over official policy. Theoretically at least, Congress will not approve a new treaty with Panama that is not acceptable to the American people.

This is the Panama Canal dilemma.

What should be done under the circumstances? The simple solution would seem to be to reverse our official policy of the past 13 years and tell Panama to forget the whole thing; we are standing pat.

Such a solution raises two immediate questions. First, can the United States realistically reject the many promises and commitments made by its executive department to Panama, even though they are not constitutionally binding in the absence of congressional approval? Second, what would be the practical consequences of such a step?

It will be easy for some to answer the first question: Our foreign policy has for too long catered to world opinion. Why should the United States give up the Canal just because Panama wants it? If we cave in to the Third World, we will be playing right into the hands of the Communists. Now is the very time when a firm stand by the United States will restore our prestige and, in the long run, command the respect of all nations, large and small, developed and undeveloped. Reject the proposed treaties out of hand.

Others will have doubts. They will wonder whether the United States can maintain its position of world leadership, much less leadership in the Western Hemisphere, if it goes back on its publicly and officially proclaimed commitments to Panama. The fact that Panama is a small nation heightens the problem. The USSR could get away with this kind of thing. But a major ingredient of the United States' influence and power in the world is its respect for people and the morality of its policies.

Thus, of the doubters, some will quickly conclude that we must honor all of our nonbinding commitments to the letter, no matter how wrong they may be, no matter the consequences. As far as failing to think things through is concerned, that conclusion is about on a par with its opposite, the forget-all-about-it conclusion.

Most thinking people will spurn the simple answer. They will want to determine for themselves first whether there are valid considerations that compel some change in our official policy with regard to the Canal. If they find none, they will favor the ratification of the proposed new treaties without change. If, on the other hand, they find that there are such valid considerations, if they find that considerations of national security, or foreign relations, or economics, or combinations of all three, require something different than the pending proposals, they will want changes made in them—constructive changes. They will look for alternatives.

Obviously, when it comes to answering the first question, the question of whether or not, at this stage of the game, we can, or should, reject many of our nonbinding promises to Panama, there are many basic things to be considered. They are very important, very complex. To consider them wisely requires knowledge and understanding. The American public has to date been denied both. This book is intended as a contribution toward filling that void.

As to the second question, the question of the consequences of rejection, it is perhaps helpful to listen first to a few voices, some measured, some shrill:

Ambassador Ellsworth Bunker: "Unless we succeed, I believe that Panama's consent to our presence will continue to decline. . . . Some form of conflict in Panama would seem virtually certain—and it would be the kind of conflict which would be costly for all concerned."[15]

Secretary of State Henry Kissinger: "Our concern with the Panama Canal issue is to avoid a situation in which the United States is drawn into a confrontation with all of Latin America, in which American military force will have to be used to fight a guerrilla war in the Western Hemisphere. . . ."[16]

Former U.S. Ambassador to Panama Jack Vaughn: "Another Vietnam."[17]

Brig. Gen. Omar Torrijos: "Patience has limits. We are now following the peaceful route of Gandhi. We are also prepared to follow the Ho Chi Minh route if necessary. That means terrorism, guerrilla operations and sabotage in a national-liberation war to regain our territory."[18]

"If there were any uprising, if there were terrorism, I, as commander of the National Guard, would have two options: to crush them or lead them. And I can't crush them."[19]

A "senior Army Department" negotiator: "For those of us who really care about the Army, My Lai was an awful blow. We know what that's done to our reputation. The last thing in the world we want now is to be ordered to start shooting into a crowd of Panamanians."[20]

A conservative, pro-American Panamanian citizen: "If we don't get a new treaty, the United States is going to have a canal full of bodies. You'll provide the bullets, and we'll provide the people."[21]

These statements can be taken with varying amounts of salt. But at least they indicate that if we fail to arrive at new treaty arrangements that are satisfactory to both the U.S. and Panama, one consequence could be conflict and bloodshed in Panama.

Just what form it might take, or how far it might go, is not so certain. That there would be street riots, vandalism, and sorties into the Canal Zone by bands of Panamanian civilians, mostly students at the outset, armed with no more than sticks, stones, Molotov cocktails and an occasional rifle or pistol, is almost a foregone conclusion. Once these started they would become more intense and incessant as Panamanian police failed to restrain—in fact, encouraged—them. The use of firearms would increase. U.S. forces would probably have to intervene to protect American citizens and property. The loss of Panamanian lives could become heavy. Martyrs could proliferate. Some American lives could be lost. This could keep up until the United States either sued for peace to stop the bloodshed or used sufficient force to restore and maintain order, if necessary augmenting the troops stationed in the Zone.

In addition to civilian violence, there is a remote possibility of harassing guerrilla operations against U.S. civilian installations within the Zone, carried out by the small, U.S.-trained combat force of not more than 1500 men within the Panamaian National Guard. This force could conceivably be supplemented by a few regulars from Cuba and a smattering of irregulars from other Latin American countries.

It is most unlikely, however, that any conflict and bloodshed in Panama would involve any regular troops from other Latin American nations, with the possible exception of Cuba. In the main, these countries do not have adequate forces trained in guerrilla warfare to take part in such operations. Equally important, they would not be inclined to support Panama to the extent of armed intervention.

This latter fact leads to another possible consequence of our failing to achieve a satisfactory new treaty arrangement with Panama. Latin America will support Panama in many ways other than armed intervention. Throughout Latin America, in varying degrees, there could be economic, physical, and diplomatic retaliation against the United States in support of Panama. This could take various forms: expropriations of American business enterprises, economic boycotts, student attacks on American embassies, terrorist activities against U.S. diplomats and businessmen, and severance of diplomatic relations. These activities would cause considerable economic hardship to the Latin American nations themselves because they would stop the flow of U.S. economic aid and U.S. purchases. And, unfortunately, Moscow would be standing by to fill the void.

All of this sounds like blackmail. Blackmail it is. Neither Panama nor any other Latin American nation can threaten us in any other fashion. Our military power is too great. Blackmail is the only weapon they have against us.

So the question narrows down to whether or not the United States can be blackmailed into capitulating to Panama's "aspirations." Must we accept conflict and bloodshed in Panama? Must we accept various forms of retaliation throughout Latin America? Are these consequences inevitable? What are the stakes? What are our options?

This is our dilemma. Perhaps even our time bomb.

2

The Impossible Dream: Canal Beginnings

The impossible dream began four and a half centuries ago. On a misty, dripping morning in September 1513 Vasco Núñez de Balboa, the bold Spanish explorer, looked southward out over the vast Pacific Ocean from a tangled Panamanian hilltop. For more than a month he and his sturdy band of conquistadors had been inching and sweating their way from the Atlantic shore, through dense jungle, across treacherous swampland, up and down abrupt hills choked with tropical rain forest. Behind them lay 50 miles of unbelievable agony. But now Balboa learned for all his world that this humid, tangled land mass was in fact a narrow isthmus linking two continents, dividing two mighty oceans.

This was the beginning of the impossible dream, the dream of a waterway that would someday divide the continents and link the oceans. Over the years this dream came to be shared by countless men of many nationalities.[1] It was to cost tens of thousands of lives. It was to produce feats of heroism and scientific achievement that were miracles of their times.

Alvaro de Saavedra, a Castilian engineer in Balboa's group,

31

was perhaps the first to have the dream. He urged that a search be made along the isthmus for a strait connecting the two oceans and suggested that if one could not be found, "yet it might not be impossible to make one."[2] In the years that immediately followed, Saavedra, serving on an expedition under Cortes, made that search and produced a study of four potential routes, one across Mexico at Tehuantepec, one across Nicaragua by way of Lake Nicaragua and the San Juan River, one at the center of the Isthmus of Panama near the site of the present canal, and one in the eastern part of the Isthmus, known as Darien, where he had crossed with Balboa.

Similar searches and surveys were made by the Spaniards during the next 50 years, but nothing came of them. Efforts by others were very limited. All of Central and most of South America were under the tight control of Spain. In 1567, after a particularly discouraging report on chances for a waterway, Philip II of Spain decreed that since God had not seen fit to divide the land, for man to do so would be a sacrilege. At the same time he decreed that the established land route across Panama was the only legal means of crossing the Isthmus.[3]

This decree put a damper on the dream for almost three centuries. In the early 1800s it was revived by two factors, the Industrial Revolution and the demise of the Spanish empire. The former brought development of the machinery and tools that would make the digging of a canal feasible. The latter allowed others to become bold and take steps toward a canal beginning.

As the Latin American countries began to break away from Spain, other European powers cast covetous eyes in their direction. This prompted the United States, itself just emerged as a power to be reckoned with, to proclaim the Monroe Doctrine in 1823, warning against any efforts by outsiders to gain new territory or establish new colonies in the Western Hemisphere. At the same time the new Latin American nations began to give collective consideration to their own destiny.

In 1826 Simon Bolívar, the great liberator of South America, convened the first inter-American conference. Bolívar at that time was the president of Gran Colombia, a large nation comprised of New Granada (now Colombia and Panama), Venezuela, and Ecuador. He had long indicated an interest in an isthmian canal. Significantly, U.S. Secretary of State Henry Clay gave these instructions to the two U.S. delegates to the conference:

A cut or a canal for the purpose of navigation somewhere through the isthmus that connects the new Americas, to unite the Pacific and Atlantic oceans, will form a proper subject for consideration of the Congress [conference]. If the work should ever be executed so as to admit of passage of sea vessels from ocean to ocean, the benefits ought not to be exclusively appropriated to any one nation, but should be extended to all parts of the globe upon payment of a just consideration or reasonable tolls.[4]

With these words the United States officially joined the dreamers, at the same time giving the dream an altruistic, universal cast.

For 50 years the U.S. as a nation and many of its enterprising private citizens became increasingly active in efforts to develop an isthmian canal. The interest shifted back and forth between Panama and Nicaragua as the two most suitable areas. Then came the strong impetus of the 1848 gold strike in California and the opening up of the Oregon Territory. These developments made it imperative that the journey between the eastern part of the United States and the West Coast be made faster and easier.

At that moment prior events favored Panama. Two years earlier, in 1846, the United States had entered into a treaty with by-then-independent New Granada (Colombia including the Isthmus of Panama) known as the Bidlack-Mallarino Treaty, whereby the U.S. guaranteed the sovereignty of New Granada over the Isthmus of Panama and agreed to preserve the neutrality of the area. On its part, New Granada agreed that U.S. citizens were to have free transit across the Isthmus, on the same basis as citizens of New Granada, "whether by road, railroad, or canal."[5]

Shortly after that treaty was signed, a group of New York financiers had acquired a charter from New Granada to build either a railroad or a canal across the Isthmus of Panama. Work on the railroad had commenced. The rush to the West, supplemented by U.S. subsidies to two steamship lines, one running from New York to the mouth of the Chagres River on the Atlantic side of Panama, the other from Panama City on the Pacific shore to San Francisco, insured the success of this enterprise. Thousands of gold and land seekers were deposited on the Atlantic side knowing that ocean passage from the other side on was available if they could just cross the Isthmus. The railroad, completed in 1855, became a gold mine in its own right. But while this was going on in Panama, a keen rivalry was developing between the U.S. and England in Nicaragua. For many years the British had been active in Central America, particularly in Nicaragua and Honduras. Whether this activity stemmed from their own dream of a canal or merely a desire to gain a foothold from which to await and exploit future developments is not clear. At any rate, many people in the United States believed that the navigable waters of the San Juan River and Lake Nicaragua and the short land passage from there to the Pacific presented by far the most feasible route for an isthmian canal. Members of the U.S. Congress seemed to favor the Nicaragua route. But there, athwart their aspirations, were the British, with gunboats and troops. A physical confrontation became a real possibility.

Out of this situation—our concern, on the one hand, over Britain's intentions and position in the Nicaragua-Honduras area, and the British concern, on the other, over American progress in Panama—came a curious compromise. In 1850 a treaty, known as the Clayton-Bulwer Treaty, was negotiated between the two nations. Under its terms any canal developed by either nation, or by both acting in concert, would be placed under the joint patronage of the two countries. The canal was "to be open to the citizens and subjects of the parties on equal terms." It was to be neutral. No fortifications were to be allowed. Neither country was to assume or exercise any dominion over any territory in Central America through which a canal might pass, or obtain new colonies there. While the Clayton-Bulwer Treaty pointed toward Nicaragua as the most likely place for the building of a canal, its terms were extended to any "canal or railway across the isthmus which connects North and South America."[6]

This was indeed a curious agreement. It created a highly unworkable partnership for the possible development of an undefended, uncontrolled waterway. Perhaps both nations were merely buying time. The British never became active in any canal endeavor; they probably never intended to. The treaty assured them of the benefits of any ultimate effort by the United States. That is very likely all they wanted—that and the avoidance of a confrontation with the United States. As for the United States, the extension of British influence and power in Central America by the construction of a British canal had been forestalled. But at the same time its own independent, and far more important, effort had been severely handicapped. One can only say that either U.S. Secretary of State John M. Clayton had been no diplomatic match for Lord Bulwer, or the thwarting of Britain's ambitions in the Western Hemisphere was, at the moment, of paramount importance to the U.S. To make way for a U.S. canal, Clayton-Bulwer had to be scuttled half a century later.

As it turned out, the United States interest in a canal became diverted soon after Clayton-Bulwer. The clouds of a great civil war were looming on our national horizon. That sad chapter in United States history, with the pangs of the Reconstruction period that followed, sidetracked the American canal effort for two generations.

It was during this lull that the French had their dream. It turned out to be a nightmare. But by any name it was a bold, magnificent try, the only real one that preceded the American success of the twentieth century. The expenditure of more than $250 million, the excavation of some 80 million cubic yards of earth, and the loss of over 25,000 lives in the end brought total disaster to the French enterprise. A faulty concept, that of a sea-level canal, was perhaps at the root of this tragedy. But in all fairness to the French, it is unlikely that, given the states of engineering technology and medical knowledge at the time of the undertaking, others in their stead would have fared much better.

Because the Panama Canal of today was built over substantially the same route as that attempted by the French in the 1880s, it is interesting to note some of the features, and difficulties, that faced the French in their task.

Panama has four formidable lines of defense against the building of an interoceanic canal. First, its physical contour, the hills rising steeply in irregular patterns. Beneath the surface of these hills lies a geologic horror of volcanic cores, faults, dikes and sills, no two areas alike in structure or composition. Second, the ground cover. Panama, lying nine degrees north of the equator, has an average rainfall of 105 inches and an average temperature of 85 degrees, the perfect environment for almost impenetrable jungle growth. Third, the constant flooding of the multitude of rivers that course through the jungle terrain, wild, raging torrents caused by the heavy rainfall and the precipitous slopes of the hills. Finally, the defense line of death, the twin killers, malaria and yellow fever.

To the task of surmounting these awesome obstacles came a man who was neither engineer nor doctor, the famous Ferdinand de Lesseps, the 80-year-old hero of the Suez Canal, which had been completed in 1869. De Lesseps' name was legendary. What he lacked in technical skill and medical knowledge, he made up for with a vengeance in energy, inspirational leadership, enthusiasm, and confidence. As it turned out, these characteristics, even in such great abundance, could not crack Panama's natural defenses. Suez had called for a mighty shoveller. Panama called for a highly skilled, painstaking engineer who could do a lot more than dig.

Turn back for a moment. In 1878 Lieutenant Lucien Napoleon Bonaparte Wyse, an officer in the French navy, having spent two years on the Isthmus surveying canal possibilities, secured personally from Colombia (New Granada changed its name to Colombia in 1863) a 99-year concession for the construction of an interoceanic canal across Colombia's province of Panama. Wyse also obtained from the Panama Railroad Company a concession to build the canal along the line of the 1855 railway, assuming, in return, the obligation to buy out the railroad at a future date. These concessions to Wyse became the foundations of the Panama Canal of today. At the time they were acquired they were but parts of an impossible dream.

Wyse's rights were taken over for $10 million by a private French company formed by de Lesseps, La Compagnie Universelle du Canale Interoceanique de Panama. Before he had even seen a detailed survey of the proposed canal project or set foot on Panamanian soil, de Lesseps set out with supreme confidence to raise $100 million through public subscription. Before he was through he had carried out a series of such promotions, bringing in a total of $275 million put up by men and women all over the world on the strength of de Lesseps' reputation and his zeal for the project.

This sounds like, and was, a huge financial promotion. But it was far more than that. It produced a massive effort to build a canal. In initial charge of construction, de Lesseps placed a French firm of civil engineers that had vast experience, including Suez, and a worldwide reputation. During the first year and a half of excavation they brought to the job more, and some say better, equipment than the Americans did in a similar period 20 years later: 32 steam shovels versus 8; 3300 flatcars and trucks versus 560; 49 locomotives versus 35; 169 drills versus 390 (maybe there is some significance here); 14 dredges versus 7; 92 boats, barges, tugs, lighters, etc., versus 48; 80 miles of railway track versus 6; 96 pumps versus none.[7] All these items were of the best quality and highest performance standards that the technology of the day could produce. The living quarters built for the workers, the hospitals, dispensaries, convalescent homes, warehouses, repair facilities, structures of all sorts, were built solidly, some magnificently. Thousands of laborers were brought in, principally from the West Indies. Hundreds of skilled workers came from France and elsewhere. By midsummer of the second year excavations were under way at five points along the proposed canal route, including the famous, and calamitous, Culebra Cut through the Continental Divide. Work had begun on the terminal channels at both the Atlantic and Pacific ends. De Lessups' "second Suez" was off to a glorious, grandiose start.

But from the second year on, everything started to fall apart. Workers died like flies from malaria and yellow fever. Benefiting from hindsight we know the reasons: no insect screens in the living quarters and hospitals and inadequate sanitation. Excavations were swept away in torrential floods. Hindsight reason: no master plan to harness the rivers, particularly the mighty Chagres. Digging became fruitless in some places, impossible in others, because of slides, cave-ins, or impervious ground. Hindsight reason: inadequate knowledge of the geology of the route. Rail haulage of supplies and waste material became hopelessly inefficient. Hindsight reason: lack of coordination resulting in multi-gauge track and rolling stock.

One could go on at length listing the things that went wrong and the reasons why. But it would all boil down to the same thing: Panama's four horsemen, terrain, jungle, floods, and pestilence, were too much for the planning and technology of the French.

Good money by the millions was poured in after the bad. For seven long years the struggle continued. Finally the money-well went dry. In 1888 de Lessups' company failed, the work ground to a halt.

The nightmare was over. The dream seemed more impossible than ever.

3

A Volcano Erupts:
The Canal Route War

The French nightmare in Panama, what appeared to be a complete engineering fiasco in the face of insurmountable odds, had a profound effect on opinion regarding the best location for an isthmian canal. As a result, during the last decade of the nineteenth century, almost all eyes were on Nicaragua.

Although those same eyes ultimately turned back and became fixed on Panama, no thorough consideration of the contemporary Panama Canal issue can overlook Nicaragua, past, present, and future, as a possible canal site. For, had it not been for some extraordinary last-minute happenings, some contrived, some natural, the canal in operation today would probably be one traversing Nicaragua, with Panama still just a jungle province of Colombia. Furthermore, and perhaps more important in light of current talk about the need for a new canal and the ever-increasing tensions in U.S.-Panama relations, many of the eyes now searching for solutions are again turning toward Nicaragua.

It is worthy of note that during the first 80 years of the nineteenth century—up until the start of the massive French effort to build a canal in Panama—interest and activity centering on an eventual Nicaragua canal were just as prevalent as those looking toward a waterway across Panama. Surveys, promotions, negotiations, conspiracies, even revolutions, all related somehow to canal expectations, were equally commonplace in both areas.

Anticipating a canal, by mid-century both routes were competing aggressively for the trans-isthmian traffic generated by the great trek to the west coast of North America. The Panama Railroad, completed in 1855, had the advantage of the shortness of the overland distance from sea to sea. But the sea routes between the major Atlantic and Pacific coast ports and the isthmus were considerably shorter by the Nicaraguan land-water crossing.

Taking the Nicaraguan way, the westbound voyager made a multi-vehicular journey under the auspices of the Accessory Transit Company, owned by the ubiquitous New York financial wizard "Colonel" Cornelius Vanderbilt. Vanderbilt also owned the steamship lines that plied between New York and the isthmus, on the east, and the isthmus and San Francisco, on the west. At the Caribbean port of San Juan del Norte, which the British at that time called Greytown, the traveler went aboard a small riverboat. This little steamer struggled 122 tortuous miles up the winding, shallow San Juan River, at times forcing its way against seething rapids. At Fuerte de San Carlos, on the eastern shore of Lake Nicaragua, the traveler transferred to a larger steamboat for a 55-mile lake trip. During that crossing he passed close by one of the many volcanic peaks that would later plague the promoters of a Nicaragua canal. He disembarked at the lakeside port of La Virgen. The remainder of the journey was a bumpy, 15-mile stagecoach ride down to San Juan del Sur on the Pacific coast.

If all went well, the entire trans-isthmian passage took less than three days, a time span that did not eat up the traveler's seatime savings credits against the Panama route. But it was far more expensive. In 1853, 10,062 emigrants arrived in San Francisco by way of Nicaragua, as compared with 15,502 by way of Panama.[1]

All of the plans for a canal across Nicaragua involved use of Lake Nicaragua as the main passageway, with a series of locks at each end of the crossing. It is interesting to note that the surface of Lake Nicaragua is 107 feet above sea level, 22 feet higher than the surface of manmade Gatun Lake, a part of the present Panama Canal.

A substantial attempt to build a Nicaragua canal commenced even before the last French gasp in Panama. In 1887 a group of U.S. financiers formed the Maritime Canal Company of Nicaragua, capitalized at $250 million. Attempts to get the U.S. government to participate financially failed, but negotiations with both Nicaragua and Costa Rica, in which a portion of the proposed route was located, produced the necessary rights to build a canal.

Six million dollars in cash was raised, and construction got under way. Workshops and a hospital went up at San Juan del Norte. A breakwater was built at the mouth of the San Juan River. Using equipment leased from the French in Panama, canal digging began. When the money ran out, a canal 280 feet wide and 17 feet deep had been dug. Unfortunately, it was only three-quarters of a mile long. The story had the same ending as the one in Panama. The money-well went dry.[2]

The failure of the American effort in Nicaragua was not as spectacular as that of the French in Panama. Far less money, far less world attention, and far less accomplishment were involved. But it was, after all, another failure. It demonstrated with great clarity how difficult a task a Nicaragua canal would be under any circumstances. But more significantly, it served as further evidence of the necessity for the expenditure of money in any trans-isthmian canal venture, wherever located, apparently beyond the capabilities of private capital.

The situation developed by the two failures has been well described in these words:

Thus by the end of the century the two great rival canal projects had come to grief. In Nicaragua work had stopped altogether; in Panama excavation continued under French direction but at a slow pace and on a small scale. At both locations private enterprise had proved inadequate to the gigantic task. The only remaining hope for ultimate completion of either canal lay in its ownership, construction, and operation by the United States government.[3]

And so the impossible dream faded in the gloom of a second failure. Conniving went on and diplomatic probes continued, in both Nicaragua and Panama, but in a desultory, never-never fashion. A canal seemed unattainable to most people. The only work being carried on was that continued by the French in Panama, just enough to keep their concession from Colombia alive so that, if a miracle should happen, the French owners would have a saleable commodity, a bail-out potential.

Suddenly the miracle began to develop. The Spanish-American War broke out. The small United States Navy became the key to the outcome of this far-flung venture. On March 18, 1898, just a few weeks after the opening of hostilities, the battleship U.S.S. *Oregon* steamed out of San Francisco harbor headed for the Caribbean. She was needed urgently. The world, and particularly the people of the United States, followed her progress with rapt attention. Thirteen thousand miles she had to go, around the Horn—68 days, while the world watched and waited. If only she could cut across the Central American isthmus and head straight for Cuba—her voyage cut in half, the outcome of the war perhaps decided!

The *Oregon* steamed into Santiago Bay just as the war was ending. Spain capitulated, and the United States emerged as a world power. The time to dream about a canal was again at hand. But the voyage of the U.S.S. *Oregon* had made two things quite clear. This time the dream had to come true. And this time the dream had to be a U.S. dream, the canal, a U.S. canal.

Almost immediately Congress went into action. The French debacle in Panama still loomed large. Nicaragua was the congressional favorite, its advocates led by the dedicated, aggressive Senator John Tyler Morgan of Alabama. Morgan had been pushing for a Nicaragua canal for more than 10 years. His preference for Nicaragua stemmed from his Southern roots: the sailing time between the Gulf ports and the Pacific coast by way of Nicaragua was considerably shorter than by way of Panama. In the Democrat-controlled Senate, Morgan was the chairman of the Committee on Interoceanic Canals, a powerful position from which to guide legislation.

Morgan developed two obsessions: one, a national one, that there must be a trans-isthmian canal at any cost, the other, a sectional one, that the canal must, if at all possible, be across Nicaragua. He fought hard to achieve both goals, so much so and so well that when he and the Nicaraguan route were, in the end, going down to defeat, his colleague, Senator John C. Spooner of Wisconsin, a leading proponent of the Panamanian

41

route, said of him, "Upon whatever route an isthmian canal shall be constructed, the Senator from Alabama will forever stand in the memory of the people as the father of the isthmian canal."[4]

But at the outset of the canal route war Senator Morgan had it all his way. In 1897 President William McKinley had appointed a commission, known as the First Walker Commission, for the sole purpose of executing a survey of the Nicaragua route and making a final recommendation. The next year Morgan introduced a bill calling for the construction, operation, and fortification of a Nicaragua canal by the United States government. Early in 1899, in the wake of the U.S.S. *Oregon's* 13,000 mile journey around the Horn, the Senate passed that bill by an overwhelming vote of 48 to 6. Shortly afterwards the Walker Commission reported favorably on a definite Nicaragua canal route. The Nicaragua bandwagon was rolling at a seemingly relentless pace.

But when the Morgan bill arrived in the House of Representatives roadblocks had been set up to slow it down. The obstruction engineers were two men who were to play the major behind-the-scenes roles in the unfolding drama of the canal routes, both in and out of Congress. One was William Nelson Cromwell, a well-known, high-priced lawyer, partner in the prestigious New York law firm of Sullivan and Cromwell. Cromwell had been hired by the French to protect their Panamanian interests. The other was a resourceful young French engineer, Philippe Bunau-Varilla, an ardent disciple of de Lesseps. At the age of 27 Bunau-Varilla had been, briefly, in complete charge of the gigantic French canal effort in Panama. He also had invested heavily in the project. Now he had become a one-man crusade to salvage the honor of France and the fortune of Bunau-Varilla.

These two men disliked each other intensely and operated quite independently of one another throughout the four-year struggle over a canal site. But their objective was the same: a Panama canal with the French interests bought out by the U.S. The clever, and, at times, diabolical manipulations that each was able to contrive and carry out on his own combined to direct the course of history.

When the pro-Nicaragua Morgan bill reached the House there were two immediately retarding influences in its path. One was the personal ambition of Representative William Peter Hepburn of Iowa. Hepburn, although a proponent of the Nicaraguan route, was determined that the canal legislation that finally emerged from Congress should bear his, not Morgan's, name. As chairman of the House Committee on Interstate and Foreign Commerce he was able to hold things up while he got his own bill into position for passage.

The other, and obviously more complex, brake on any canal legislation was the 1850 Clayton-Bulwer Treaty between the United States and England. Until this treaty could be either modified or abrogated, any scheme for a fortified totally U.S. owned-operated canal would be in violation of our commitments to Britain.

The behind-the-scene manipulators made the most of these and every other obstruction. A whole year elapsed while Representative Hepburn, having stalled the Morgan bill, fathered one of his own, a pro-Nicaragua Hepburn bill, and sent it over to the Senate by the substantial House vote of 224 to 36. But by that time the Senate was considering the ratification of a new treaty with England, the Hay-Pauncefote Treaty, designed to clear away the obstacle of Clayton-Bulwer. Accordingly, the Senate deferred action on the Hepburn bill. In the meantime Congress had established a new commission to study the canal route question, this time with directions to include Panama, as well as Nicaragua, in its deliberations. This was known as the Second Walker Commission. The Nicaraguan band wagon, temporarily at least, was bogged down.

However, in the closing months of 1901 Nicaragua surged ahead again. The Hay-Pauncefote Treaty was ratified by the Senate, giving the United States clearance to build, fortify, and operate a trans-isthmian canal on its own. The Second Walker Commission came in with a preliminary report favoring Nicaragua over Panama. Representative Hepburn, striking while the iron was hot, sent another pro-Nicaragua Hepburn bill over to the Senate, this time by the astounding vote of 308 to 2. The Nicaraguan band wagon was not only rolling again, it was almost home.

Suddenly there was another reversal. The Second Walker Commission reported a switch in its position. It now favored Panama. With this the pro-Panama forces made their first affirmative move, putting a bandwagon of their own on the road, a bandwagon labeled the "Spooner Amendment."

On January 28, 1902, Senator Spooner came forward with a startling proposal to amend the pro-Nicaragua Hepburn bill in the Senate by authorizing the president of the United States to purchase the French interests in Panama for $40 million and to acquire by treaty from Colombia the necessary territory for the construction of a Panama canal. The Spooner proposal also had a "kicker" in it to speed things up and make it more palatable. It provided that if things could not be worked out with the French and Colombia "within a reasonable time and upon reasonable terms,"[5] the president should negotiate the necessary treaty for a Nicaragua canal. For the first time in the legislative war, the Nicaraguan route was placed on the defensive. If the Spooner Amendment were adopted, obviously Nicaragua would be relegated to second place.

The pro-Panama forces were now on the move. Their leader was the powerful Marcus Alonzo Hanna, senator from Ohio. Hanna had great influence in the White House, in the Congress, and in the dominant Republican Party. Although he died before the contest in 1903 over the ratification of the Hay–Bunau-Varilla Treaty with Panama, the final battle of the canal route war, he, probably more than any other member of Congress, was responsible for the pro-Panama legislation that gave birth to that treaty.

The collision between the pro-Nicaragua forces led by Morgan and the pro-Panama forces under Hanna, triggered by the offering of the Spooner Amendment, became a classic in the annals of congressional warfare. The Nicaraguan route still had the edge, but it was so close that, as often happens in the case of major conflicts, a seemingly irrelevant event could have a profound effect on the final outcome. And in this instance one did.

The presence or absence of volcanic craters capable of erupting and producing earthquakes had always been recognized as a matter to be at least noted in comparing the relative merits of the two canal routes. Nicaragua has them, Panama does not. But the point had never received much emphasis. Now Mother Nature got into the act. The sequence of events is interesting.

On March 13, 1902, Morgan's Senate Interoceanic Canal Committee voted seven to four to reject the Spooner Amendment and to send the pro-Nicaragua Hepburn bill, unamended, to the floor of the Senate for final action. This was another abrupt tilt of the see-saw, and a signal triumph for Morgan. The final debate was scheduled to commence on June 4.

On May 18 Mont Pelée on the little East Caribbean island of Martinique, almost a thousand miles from Nicaragua, erupted with such violence that it wiped out the entire town of St. Pierre and killed 40,000 people.

Overnight the American people became volcano-conscious. The press, encouraged by the pro-Panama forces, took up the hue and cry. Mt. Pelée became Nicaragua's waterloo.

The debate in the Senate, where the Hanna forces were bent on resurrecting the Spooner Amendment, began on schedule. For two weeks the battle of words raged. Much was said about volcanoes, but Nicaragua consistently denied that any of its craters had erupted in recent times. The outcome of the final vote was anyone's guess.

Bunau-Varilla, as an engineer and canal expert, had long stressed the point about volcanoes. Now he decided that the Mt. Pelée disaster would have to be moved closer to Nicaragua. But how? He had a fortunate flash of recollection. He made frantic visits to stamp dealers in Washington and New York. Then, on the morning of June 16, three days before the final vote in the Senate, there appeared on the desk of each senator a beautiful scenic postage stamp, issued by the Nicaraguan government two years before, portraying a volcano in full eruption with Lake Nicaragua in the foreground.[6]

On June 19 the Spooner Amendment was adopted by the Senate. The vote was 67 in favor, only 6 against. A week later the House retreated from its pro-Nicaragua position. The Spooner Act went to the White House, where it was quickly signed by President Theodore Roosevelt.

Maybe it was the volcano, maybe it was not. More than likely the volcano was merely a timely spash of color in the course of conscientious congressional deliberation that would have led, in any event, to a correct decision on the merits. At any rate, the die was cast. Now all eyes turned to Panama, or, more accurately, to Colombia, of which Panama was the most westerly province.

4

Gunboat Diplomacy: Birth of a Nation

The Panama all eyes turned to in 1902 had been the neglected foster child of Colombia for more than three-quarters of a century. When the shackles of Spain were cast aside in 1821, the people of the Panamanian Isthmus, after a short period of independence, chose of necessity to be included in Gran Colombia, the new composite nation put together at that time by Simon Bolívar. One of the terms of that initial affiliation was the right of secession.

In 1830 Gran Colombia split up into the three separate nations of Venezuela, Ecuador, and New Granada (Colombia). Panama elected to stay with New Granada. But, separated from the other provinces and the Colombian capital by an impenetrable, mountainous jungle, accessible from the east only by boat, and constantly ignored by the government in Bogota, Panama was always a rebellious child, a child with runaway tendencies. She had a long history of civil disorders, including six full-fledged revolutions. One, in 1840, resulted in over a year of complete independence.

Thus, in 1902, the idea of ultimate separation from Colombia and existence as an independent nation was fundamental to the people of Panama. An economic basis for such an existence, a canal, was the missing element.

This foster-parent, independence-oriented relationship between Panama and Colombia should be kept clearly in mind when reviewing, and judging, the kaleidoscopic events of 1903 that produced the new Republic of Panama. It has often been overlooked by historians and is intentionally played down by those who seek to condemn the United States for the part it played in those events.

Nor can there be a proper review and evaluation of the events of 1903 without an awareness of the unique relationship that existed between the United States and Colombia during the 57 years preceding those events, particularly with regard to coping with civil disorders and revolutions in Panama and the protection of the Isthmian crossing. That relationship goes back to the Bidlack-Mallarino Treaty of 1846 mentioned earlier.[1]

At mid-century conditions for crossing the Isthmus of Panama were not greatly improved over what they were when Balboa struggled across in 1513, nothing more than a makeshift, at times impassable, unpaved roadway. Following the practice initiated by Philip II of Spain 300 years before, Colombia was charging, with rampant discrimination, whatever tolls it could extort from those wishing to make the arduous transit. And, of course, there were thousands of captive customers, because the westward trek was in full swing and the voyage around the Horn required three or four additional months of travel. Hope for an eventual canal sprang eternal, but it was a dim one. The United States urgently needed to make things easier for its traveling citizens and its intercoastal commerce.

Out of this situation came the 1846 treaty. Basically it was a run-of-the-mill, commercial arrangement designed to benefit both nations. Article 35, however, was a highly significant innovation. In that article Colombia guaranteed to the United States and its citizens "the right of way or transit across the Isthmus of Panama upon any modes of communication that now exist or that may be, hereafter, constructed." In exchange, the United States guaranteed to Colombia the neutrality of the Isthmus, "with a view that the free transit from one to the other sea may not be interrupted or embarrassed in any future time." It also guaranteed Colombia's "rights of sovereignty" over the area.[2]

As far as the Isthmus of Panama is concerned, the relationship between the United States and Colombia created by this treaty was, in effect, that of guardian and ward. While recognizing and guaranteeing Colombia's basic sovereignty over the Isthmus, the United States assumed the obligation, and acquired the right, to preserve the neutrality of the area against all comers and to keep open whatever transit way across it there might be, roadway, railway, or waterway.

This role of protector of another nation was an entirely new one for the United States. It was one that many Americans at the time feared was the type of "entangling alliance" George Washington had warned against 50 years before.

The arrangement with Colombia also created a new concept in official U.S. canal policy—the idea of a canal under exclusive U.S. control. This policy was to receive a slight setback in the Clayton-Bulwer Treaty signed with England just four years later, but it would ultimately prevail as the only canal policy that the United States was willing to pursue.

It was on the basis of this 1846 treaty with Colombia that American citizens built the highly successful Panama Railroad across the Isthmus. And it was on the basis of this treaty that, on nine different occasions during the period 1856–1902, United States armed forces intervened in Panama to quell disorders that threatened transit across the Isthmus. Thus, for over 50 years before the events of 1903, United States warships had been steaming in and out of Colombia's Panamanian harbors and U.S. troops had been landing at Colombia's Panamanian ports in the legitimate fulfillment of U.S. treaty obligations.

Anyone who was surprised in November 1903 when two U.S. warships and a small force of Marines showed up in the harbor of Colon during the first few days of a widely heralded Panamanian revolution either had failed to observe past events, or had forgotten them.

These, then, were the two essential features of the backdrop behind the 1903 stage setting: the constant, historical goal of the Panamanian people to achieve independence from Colombia, and the repeated, Colombia-sanctioned interventions by U.S. military forces to preserve order in Panama.

The setting of the stage moved rapidly with the passage of the Spooner Act in June 1902, directing the president of the United States to negotiate a canal treaty with Colombia. Negotiations initiated by Colombia the year before were, as a matter of fact, already in progress. However, nothing beyond some rather clumsy diplomatic maneuvers and misunderstandings had developed. But when the clock began to tick on the "reasonable time" allowed by Congress for the making of a treaty with Colombia, things speeded up. On January 22, 1903, U.S. Secretary of State John Hay and Colombian Minister Tomas Herran arrived at an agreement and signed a treaty.

The United States was, of course, all geared up and ready to go. Get a treaty fast, get it ratified, close a deal with the French, and start building a canal. Full speed ahead! These, in effect, were the orders of President Roosevelt. They reflected the mood of the American people.

In fairness to Colombia, when one judges what happened, or, rather, what did not happen, in Bogota after the Hay-Herran Treaty was signed, it should be observed that the framework for getting something done in Colombia was just the opposite of what it was in the United States. A crash effort, involving something as basic to Colombia's economic and political structure as the reality of a trans-Isthmian canal, could not have taken place at a more inopportune time. The Colombian government was reeling under intense political pressures, some bordering on revolution. The economy was in dire straits. Contention for political power and compulsion to exact from the U.S. the maximum amount of money for a canal treaty put the process of arriving at an agreement on a treaty and then ratifying it in about as difficult a setting as could be imagined.

Under the terms of the Hay-Herran Treaty,[3] the United States would have been authorized to build a canal across the Isthmus of Panama through a zone 10 kilometers wide. Colombia's retention of sovereignty over the canal zone would have been recognized. The United States was to protect the canal if Colombia failed or was unable to do so. Colombian courts, U.S. courts, and joint tribunals, depending on the litigants involved, were to function in the zone.

The United States was to pay Colombia $10 million in cash and $250,000 a year. The latter figure was the amount Colombia received annually from the Panama Railroad Company. Under the treaty Colombia would release to the United States its financial interest in the railroad concession. Colombia was also to relinquish any claim of indemnity against the French that might arise out of the contemplated $40 million sale by the French to the U.S. of the rights and property of the French canal company. The grant to the U.S., referred to as a lease, was to be for a period of 100 years, renewable indefinitely at the option of the U.S.

Ratification of the treaty by the United States Senate, for all Roosevelt's zest to get on with the canal project, was no hasty affair. A month of heated debate took place, with Senator Morgan leading the opposition and proposing some 60 amendments to the treaty, all of which ultimately failed. It is interesting to note that even Senators Hanna and Spooner, ardent advocates of a Panama canal, favored an amendment granting the U.S. complete sovereignty over the proposed canal zone. That amendment also failed. There was considerable awareness of the strong resistance to the treaty in Colombia, and it was feared that any change whatsoever would invite rejection by the Colombian Senate. On March 17, 1903, the U.S. Senate ratified the treaty by a vote of 73 to 5.[4]

The fight for political power in Colombia and the drive to hold the United States up for more money combined to sink the treaty in Bogota. While the people of the United States—along with the people of Panama, whose economic hopes were at stake—watched impatiently, the pulling and hauling in the legislative halls, the political backrooms, and the public forums of Colombia went on interminably. They did end, however, for all practical purposes, on 12 August 1903, when the Colombian Senate voted 24 to 0 to reject the treaty.[5]

The next day a resolution was adopted setting up a new Colombian committee to draft a new treaty for submission to the United States, a feeble attempt to keep the door open. But nothing of significance developed. By mid-October it became obvious that Colombia was not going to make a deal with the United States until Colombia's political affairs settled down. It was equally obvious that that time was a long way off.

It is not unlikely that if the United States had, during the eight or nine months of Colombian indecision, upped the ante by some $10 or $15 million, agreement could have been reached. But that was not in the cards. The strong, pro-Nicaragua forces in the U.S. Congress were waiting eagerly for the "reasonable time" clock to count Colombia, and Panama, out—and Nicaragua in.

Much went on in both the United States and Panama during those eight or nine months. This was natural because, from the outset, most interested and informed people realized that the chances of the Hay-Herran Treaty being ratified by Colombia were very slim.

50

The leaders in Panama saw in Colombia's recalcitrance nothing but disaster for their hopes for a canal and the economic birth of the Isthmus. Nicaragua was lurking in the wings. They realized that if the worst happened, rejection of the treaty by Colombia, which seemed almost inevitable, they would have to do something on their own, then or never.

Although Cromwell and Bunau-Varilla, in their separate ways, did all they could to bring about acceptance of the treaty in Bogota, they both were eyeing other means of salvaging the French interests in Panama. Nicaragua was a sword of Damocles over their heads. The clock was ticking. Their pro-Panama machinations were constant.

President Roosevelt, the leader and, to a certain extent, moulder of United States thought, was not only determined, in his inimitable way, to get a canal built; he was also sold on the idea that Panama was *the* spot for the canal.

Here was a strange, unallied triumvirate of forces—Roosevelt and his administration in the United States, the political leaders on the Isthmus of Panama, and the ever-active Cromwell and Bunau-Varilla, the estranged Castor and Pollux of French interests in Panama—three separate forces with a common objective, all working toward the same end. Each operated in its own way to produce the final events and the final outcome, an outcome not necessarily inevitable, but certainly one not unlikely.

Many accounts about what took place have been written. The known facts and those assumed for a particular purpose have been reconstructed to produce any conclusion desired, times and places have been altered, heroes and villains interchanged.

One version, that of the pro-Colombians, the pro-Nicaraguans, and the anti-Rooseveltians, tends to establish that the United States, as the moving party, planned, incited, managed, and successfully completed the Panama revolution.

Another version, that of many pro-Panamanians, and of the Panamanians themselves, tends to establish, to the contrary, that Panama gained her independence in spite of the United States and without any help, but was swindled by the U.S. in the process. Panama's history books use this version.

A third version, that of Americans who feel required to defend the United States, tends to establish that the U.S. was not only innocent of any wrongdoing, but actually was unaware of what was going on, that the independence of Panama and the ultimate canal treaty just fell from heaven.

All three versions are biased in accordance with their source —and quite fallible.

A fourth version probably comes closest to the truth. It is one that recognizes the realities of turn-of-the-century diplomacy. It is one that is aware of the absence of pristine international standards for the recognition or nonrecognition of revolutionary governments. And it is one that bears in mind the backdrop features of the 1903 setting: Panama's goal of independence from Colombia and the history of U.S. military intervention in Panama.

This fourth version takes the known facts and concludes from them: (1) that Panama was the prime mover in her own reach for independence and for the essential economic element, a canal, that would make that independence viable, (2) that the United States, fully aware of Panama's aspirations and intentions, as well as many of her plans, was in a position to play a crucial role in either thwarting or encouraging the Panama move, and (3) that the United States, acting in her own best interests, took advantage of the situation presented as a welcome alternative to waiting indefinitely for Colombia or turning to Nicaragua.

Those who accept this version point no fingers, award no medals, wear no hairshirts. However, they raise their eyebrows sharply at Bunau-Varilla's treaty-making antics.

The principal facts can be reviewed briefly. As was stated earlier, the hope for ratification by Colombia of the Hay-Herran Treaty died officially on August 12, 1903. Roosevelt's state of mind and intentions at that time are best gleaned from a letter he wrote a week later to his secretary of state, John Hay:

> [I have decided] to do nothing at present. If under the treaty of 1846 [with Colombia], we have a color of right to start in and build the canal, my off-hand judgment would favor such proceeding. It seems that the great bulk of the best engineers are agreed that that route is best; and I do not think that the Bogota lot of jack rabbits should be allowed permanently to bar one of the future highways of civilization. Of course under the terms of the [Spooner] Act we could now go ahead with Nicaragua and perhaps would technically be required to do so. But what we do now will be of consequence centuries hence, and we must be sure that we are taking the right step before we act.[6]

Roosevelt's reference to "color of right" to go ahead with a canal under the 1846 treaty with Colombia stemmed from an opinion to that effect by Professor John Bassett Moore, a highly respected authority on international law.[7] Roosevelt's letter to Hay, though evidencing characteristic impatience, reflects both calmness and wisdom under extremely frustrating circumstances. Certainly it gives no hint of a diabolical plot for a Panamanian coup d'etat.

There can be no doubt, however, that such a plot was already in the making in Panama, a plot conceived and developed by Panamanians, some of them participants in previous breaks for freedom from Colombia. In 1901, before the Hay-Herran agreement was reached, Colombia's minister to the United States, Martinez Silva, had warned his government that failure to make a canal treaty with the United States could lead to the secession of Panama.[8] In June 1903, before the final rejection of the treaty in Bogota, both Cromwell[9] and Bunau-Varilla,[10] in their separate efforts to stave off that rejection, were trumpeting a revolution by Panama if Colombian ratification did not materialize.

When Colombia rejected the treaty, the plot quickened. On September 1, 1903, as the representative of a revolutionary committee in Panama, Dr. Manuel Amador, later to become the first president of the Republic of Panama, arrived in New York from Colon. He had come to survey the possibilities of political and financial assistance. Cromwell was his natural first contact, but that shrewd gentleman, fearful at that juncture of being caught by Colombia supporting a Panama break-away and thus of jeopardizing the continuation of the French canal concession, avoided him—in fact, fled to France to prove his righteousness. Apparently by mere coincidence, Amador then fell into the clutches of Bunau-Varilla, just arrived in New York from France, eager to play the game of nation building.

After learning from Amador all about the plan afoot in Panama, Bunau-Varilla went immediately to President Roosevelt and Secretary of State Hay and advised them of the Panamanian scheme. Some time later Roosevelt wrote to a friend about this meeting with Bunau-Varilla:

> Of course, I have no idea what Bunau-Varilla advised the revolutionists . . . but I do know . . . that he had no assurance in any way, either from Hay or myself, or from anyone authorized to speak for us. He

53

is a very able fellow, and it was his business to find out what he thought our Government would do. I have no doubt he was able to make a very accurate guess, and to advise his people accordingly.[12]

As a result of his meetings with Roosevelt and Hay, when he saw Amador off for Panama a few days later, Bunau-Varilla assured him that the United States would look favorably on the revolutionary movement. At the same time Bunau-Varilla promised the revolutionists $100,000 (presumably his own money), gave Amador a code to use in future communications with him, and even furnished him with a proposed declaration of independence and a constitution for the new republic. To top it all, he presented Amador with a flag for Panama made by Mme. Bunau-Varilla.[13]

Before leaving for Panama, Amador agreed that the moment independence was declared in Panama, a telegram would be sent to Bunau-Varilla by the provisional government designating him as Panama's "Minister Plenipotentiary in order to obtain the recognition of the Republic and signature of Canal Treaty." Even the date for the revolution was selected: November 3.[14]

Dr. Amador sailed for Panama on October 20 and arrived in Colon on October 27. At that time the United States had two warships standing close by, the U.S.S. *Nashville* at Kingston, Jamaica, and the U.S.S. *Dixie* at Guantanamo, Cuba. On October 29 Amador cabled Bunau-Varilla that Colombian troops were being sent by ship from Cartagena to Colon to suppress the expected revolution. He pleaded for help. Making a shrewd guess from news dispatches in the United States and a remark made to him by the assistant secretary of the navy in Washington, Bunau-Varilla wired back on October 30 that the *Nashville* would arrive in Colon on November 2.[15]

The *Nashville* did, in fact, arrive the afternoon of November 2. At about midnight of the same evening the Colombian gunboat *Cartagena* also steamed into Colon Harbor with 474 Colombian troops aboard under the command of a General Tovar. The captain of the *Nashville*, having received no special instructions and having no knowledge of the expected revolution, made no effort to prevent General Tovar and his troops from landing the next morning, November 3.

But the revolutionist group had not been idle. Anticipating the arrival of the Colombian troops, they had arranged that all but two or three cars of the Panama Railroad's rolling stock would be inconveniently positioned at the Panama City end of the line. When the Colombian force came ashore and asked for transportation across the Isthmus, General Tovar was offered immediate transit for himself and his officers, with the assurance that the troops would be sent along as soon as enough cars could be assembled for them. Tovar fell blithely into this courteous trap. He and his officers had a comfortable trip across the Isthmus and were jailed when they arrived in Panama City. The one Colombian officer remaining with the troops in Colon was bought off for $8000. On the morning of November 4 he and his command boarded the Royal Mail steamer *Orinoco* and headed back for Cartagena.

On that same day in Panama City, while General Tovar languished in jail, Dr. Amador and his revolutionary associates proclaimed the Republic of Panama. The "armed forces" of the revolutionary government at that time consisted of 300 young men organized into a "fire brigade," the Panama police, a detachment of Colombian regulars commanded by a member of the revolutionary junta who had been promised $50,000 for his cooperation, and the Colombian gunboat *Padilla* in Panama Bay, whose captain had agreed to hand over the ship and its crew for $35,000.[16] Small and makeshift as it was, this "force," with the departure from Colon of the Colombian troops aboard the *Orinoco*, placed the provisional government in control of the Isthmus, all that was needed as a basis for the de facto recognition of the new republic given by the United States two days later, on November 6.

In the meantime, on November 5, the U.S.S. *Dixie* had arrived in Colon Harbor from Guantanamo with 47 Marines aboard. The Marines went ashore to protect the railroad right of way, pursuant to the 1846 treaty with Colombia.

The revolutionary "war" was over. The only "shot heard round the world" in that revolution was a salvo from the Colombian gunboat *Bogota* in the Bay of Panama. Six shells were fired into the heart of Panama City, killing one person and one donkey.

For several months efforts were made in Bogota to declare war against the United States and to send adequate military forces to Panama to suppress the insurrection. These failed because of the same political disunity that had thwarted Colombia's ratification of the canal treaty. It should be noted that while there was still any chance that Colombia might intervene militarily in Panama, forces of U.S. warships were built up off Panama City and Colon.[17]

In Washington, Bunau-Varilla lost no time. As soon as he received them, he presented to President Roosevelt his credentials as Panama's first ambassador extraordinary and minister plenipotentiary. Immediately following that presentation, on November 13, the United States granted full recognition to the new republic.

Bunau-Varilla was aware that three days earlier a commission consisting of Dr. Amador and two other Panamanian revolutionists had sailed from Colon to join him in Washington. He had good reason to suspect that upon their arrival he would be subjected to their direction and control, that he might even be deprived of his diplomatic authority. He therefore repeatedly urged upon Secretary of State Hay the necessity for speedy action on a treaty between the United States and the Republic of Panama. His urgings bore fruit.

On November 15 Hay presented to Bunau-Varilla a draft of a proposed treaty. Its terms did not differ greatly from those of the ill-fated Hay-Herran Treaty with Colombia. Bunau-Varilla worked feverishly that night and all the next day preparing his own draft of a treaty. On November 17 he returned Hay's draft along with his own version, indicating that he was willing to sign for Panama whichever of the two Hay preferred. That was on the same day that Amador and his associates arrived in New York.

In the late afternoon of November 18, while the Panamanians were en route by train to Washington from New York, Hay and Bunau-Varilla met in Hay's office. Hay immediately stated his preference for the Bunau-Varilla treaty draft, with one change —the phrase "leases in perpetuity" in Article II was to be changed to read "grants to the United States in perpetuity the use, occupation and control." At 6:40 P.M. they signed the Bunau-Varilla version with the suggested change.

At 9:40 P.M. Amador and his companions were met at Washington's Union Station by Bunau-Varilla, signed treaty in hand. To say that they were surprised and shocked would be an understatement. According to Bunau-Varilla, Amador "nearly swooned on the platform of the station."[18]

The signed treaty was a *fait accompli*. Amador and his associates knew that any change in the U.S. policy of recognition and support occasioned by objections to the treaty on their part could lead to disaster. Everything they had gained by the revolution could be lost. Their hands were tied. The provisional government ratified the treaty, without amendment, on December 2.

In the United States Senate, Morgan and his pro-Nicaraguan forces did not go down without a fight. But Bunau-Varilla by his clever draftsmanship had spiked their guns. All the objections raised in the earlier battle over the Hay-Herran Treaty with Colombia had been anticipated and resolved in the new treaty with Panama. Ratification took place on February 23, 1904, by a vote of 75 to 17.

By the terms of the Hay–Bunau-Varilla Treaty,[19] the United States acquired far more in the way of rights and privileges for canal purposes than it had ever demanded of Colombia. The Canal Zone was to be 10, rather than 6, miles wide. Instead of the renewable 100 year lease it had been willing to accept from Colombia, the United States acquired the use and control of the zone "in perpetuity."[20] It even got the right to expropriate any additional land or water areas it might need later on *anywhere in Panama*.[21] It got the right to intervene and supersede the Panamanian authorities with regard to water, sewage, and health matters in Colon and Panama City, both of them outside the Canal Zone.[22] And it was given the right to intervene outside the Canal Zone to preserve or restore order.[23]

In the Colombian treaty the United States had recognized Colombia's sovereignty over the Canal Zone. In this new treaty, except in the preamble, no mention was made of Panama's sovereignty. Panama "granted" to the United States "all the rights, power and authority within the zone . . . and within the limits of all auxiliary lands and waters . . . which the United States would possess and exercise if it were the sovereign of the territory . . . to the exclusion of the exercise by . . . Panama of any such sovereign rights, power, or authority."[24]

In exchange for all these concessions, the United States agreed to guarantee the independence of Panama.[25] The money payments to Panama were identical to those contained in the Colombian treaty: $10 million down and an annual payment of $250,000.[26]

There never was such a one-sided treaty. If it had been written at the conclusion of a war between the United States and Panama and the money payments had run the other way, it would have served as a document of unconditional surrender.

Secretary Hay, who "negotiated" it for the United States, had this to say of it at the time: "We have here a treaty very advantageous to the United States and, we must admit with what face we can muster, not so advantageous to Panama."[27]

Bunau-Varilla, the French "negotiator" *for Panama*, described his feelings at the time the treaty ratifications were exchanged by Hay and himself in this way:

> The two signatures once appended we shook hands and I left him simply saying: "It seems to me as if we had together made something great."
>
> I went on, having at last unburdened my heart of the load which had so long weighed on it.
>
> I had fulfilled my mission, the mission I had taken on myself; I had safeguarded the work of the French genius. I had avenged its honour; I had served France.[28]

But had he served Panama? That is the question that sparks today's controversy between the United States and Panama.

Apparently most Panamanians feel that Bunau-Varilla did not serve Panama, that he betrayed her. But did he? If one looks at the Hay–Bunau-Varilla Treaty in the context of the time at which it was signed, it served Panama well. Not only served, but saved her. Perhaps no one but Bunau-Varilla would have had both the wisdom and the temerity to contrive it. Panama was a nation two weeks old. Her government was scarcely established. Her ability to preserve law and order, much less her independence from Colombia, was negligible. She could only continue to exist and develop as a nation if the United States were willing to build a canal across her territory and protect her. Within the United States there were powerful forces bent on having the canal built across Nicaragua. Those forces had to be thwarted at any price if Panama was to become the canal site. It is doubtful that a treaty less favorable to the United States would have sufficed.

Looked at from the United States viewpoint at that time, it is highly questionable whether a less favorable treaty, a treaty that went no further in making concessions to the United States than the Colombian treaty did, would have been realistic. With Colombia, the United States had been dealing with a nation three-quarters of a century old, a nation with an established, albeit shaky, government, a nation with a military force at least capable of keeping the peace. Building and operating a canal under treaty arrangements with such a nation obviously did not require the broad assumption of governmental responsibilities and corresponding rights, the assurances of stability, even the assurance of mere continued existence, that were needed in dealing with the Panamanian embryo.

On balance, regardless of Bunau-Varilla's selfish and French-devoted motives, the Hay–Bunau-Varilla Treaty, at the time it was entered into, was the treaty needed by both Panama and the United States. Unfortunately, it contained the seeds of ultimate dissatisfaction on the part of Panama as a developing nation. Unfortunately, on the other side of the coin, it encouraged U.S. entrenchment and assumption of authority in Panama to become so extensive and so institutionalized that attempts later on to diminish U.S. rights under the treaty would be considered, by many Americans, as a national affront. But as of that time, as of November 17, 1903, it was perhaps the only recipe for success for both countries.

Following that same line of reasoning, what may now appear in hindsight to Panamanians and others to have been the taking of undue advantage, even a gross immorality, was, in fact, both justifiable and necessary. But by the same token, now that Panama is three-quarters of a century old, the same age that Colombia was in 1903, now that Panama has an established government, now that Panama has the ability to preserve law and order, maybe what was once right is now wrong. At least the basis for arguing that it is, is perfectly clear.

Eight years after the revolution in Panama, and two years after he left the White House, Theodore Roosevelt made a most unfortunate, though typically braggadocio, statement: " . . . I took the isthmus, started the canal and then left Congress not to debate the canal, but to debate me."[29]

That utterance was not only boastful; it was incorrect. "Teddy" Roosevelt did not "take" the Isthmus—he merely recognized the revolutionary government of Panama, one of several in Panamanian history, and made a very advantageous treaty with it. Putting 47 Marines ashore was hardly a taking. He had not "started the canal" before Congress had a chance to debate it. The debate had been going on in Congress for four years and had already ended in favor of Panama as the site for a canal. Furthermore, the debate over the canal treaty was so voluble and extensive that it has been aptly described as "one of the most bitter struggles in the history of the Senate."[30] The Canal was not started until the Congressional debate over it had ended. And finally, it was not the Congress that was left "to debate me," that is, to debate the merits and demerits of Roosevelt's actions. That debate was left to the press and to the historians. It went on for years. It goes on today.

Roosevelt's statement was unfortunate, because it has been used against the United States ever since. It was used by Colombia to bolster its claim that the United States was responsible for the insurrection in Panama and therefore for Colombia's loss of the Isthmus and the prospect of a canal—used so successfully that in 1922 the United States paid Colombia an indemnity of $22 million.

It was, and is, used by Panama to bolster her claim that the United States acquired sovereign rights over the Canal Zone in perpetuity by fostering a betrayal of Panama's national interests—used so successfully that a great many nations accept and support that claim.

It was, and is, used by a great many people in the United States, primarily in intellectual circles and in the State Department, to bolster their claim that the U.S. role in Panama was conceived in a sin for which there must be complete atonement —used so successfully that today self-indictment gravely weakens our ability to arrive at a satisfactory and salutary solution to the Panama Canal issue.

Whatever one may think of the events of 1903, they made dramatic and lasting history, and as a result of them, the United States crossed the threshold of the impossible dream. This time her own dream. Her own canal.

5

The Dream Comes True: Building the Canal

The dream did come true. The United States performed a miracle. The story of that magnificent achievement has been told many times, by historians, by engineers, even by novelists. The details of it have no particular significance in relation to today's dilemma. But recalling briefly some of its principal features may etch into the contemporary scene the basis for the instinctive, enduring national pride that the building of the Panama Canal engenders in most Americans. This is something to be recognized and reckoned with, for this instinctive pride of accomplishment, pride to the point of unyielding possessiveness, is one of the roots of our dilemma: the conflict between American public opinion and U.S. official policy.

It took 10 long, difficult years to make the dream come true. During that period, particularly in the early stages, there were times when failure was a distinct possibility. Only the will and wisdom of a few outstanding leaders, the persistence and ingenuity of hundreds of unsung heroes, and the steady plodding, the toil and sweat, of tens of thousands of workers averted that tragedy.

The project got off to a dismal start, primarily because of the type of organization Congress created to run it, a top-heavy, seven-member, Washington-based commission. The first chief engineer assigned to the job, John F. Wallace, was given far too little authority and far too little latitude. By the end of the first year both the organization and the project were hopelessly bogged down in red tape. Although the work force in Panama had been rapidly built up to number some 7000 workers, most of them were engaged in excavation work that was part of no basic plan—a futile effort to "make the dirt fly" in response to President Roosevelt's exhortation and the mood of the American people.

The only real accomplishment during that first year was the transfer of the French property in Panama to the United States for $40 million, as provided for in the enabling legislation. For this sum, the United States acquired some excellent maps and surveys, many buildings, a somewhat decrepit but extremely valuable one-track railroad across the Isthmus, a great deal of machinery and equipment, mostly in poor condition but much of it salvageable, and, as far as the rudiments of a canal were concerned, the results of the excavation by the French of 50 million cubic yards of material on the Continental Divide. This excavation, the so-called Culebra Cut, was the only part of the French canal that became an integral part of the ultimate American structure.

In 1905 Roosevelt took matters into his own hands. Circumventing congressional strictures, he streamlined the commission so that Panama became the center of activity and responsibility rather than Washington. But it was too late for Wallace. Frustrated, and reportedly fearful of yellow fever, he resigned.

This turned out to be a blessing. The man who took his place as chief engineer was to become one of the trio of superb leaders that was primarily responsible for the ultimate success of the Canal. He was John F. ("Big Smoke") Stevens, a railroad engineer and executive of extraordinary ability and drive. He had been one of the conquerors of another frontier, one of the pioneers who pushed the railroads across the parched deserts and rugged mountains of the western United States.

Stevens went to Panama, took a quick look around, and brought all excavation work to a standstill. He insisted that there had to be a basic canal plan and that there had to be some thorough preparation along four essential lines before further excavation could be undertaken—no more wasted motion. When the job rolled again it had to be on a path of assured success.

The basic plan of the French was for a sea-level canal. Stevens, after six months in Panama and careful observation of flooding conditions, became firmly convinced that a lock canal was the only feasible approach. He made Roosevelt a powerful ally in this conviction. But there were many who believed strongly in a sea-level canal. Finally, on June 29, 1906, two years after the signing of the treaty with Panama, Congress decided the matter in legislation calling for a lock canal.[1]

Since most of the talk today about the possibility of a new isthmian canal, in Panama or elsewhere, presupposes a sea-level canal, it is not amiss to wonder why, 70 years ago, the decision was made to go the lock canal route. The ostensible reasons were cost and time: it was estimated that a lock canal would cost $150 million and take nine years to build, as compared with a sea-level canal at double the cost and three more years of construction.[2]

The great disparity in the two items stemmed primarily from one thing, the difference in the amount of excavation through the Continental Divide required by the two plans. That difference was 85 feet in depth along a 10-mile stretch. Beside the extra time and cost of merely removing more material, each additional foot in depth for the sea-level canal would require a compensating increase in width and in drainage facilities to equalize the increased risk of slides. As it turned out, flood-induced slides became the name of the game even under the finally adopted lock-canal plan. In either case the Chagres and its tributaries would have to be harnessed to the same extent, and that harnessing, in the case of the lock canal, would produce both the water and the power needed to operate the locks. And finally, the sea-level canal would require a tidal lock at the Pacific end to cope with the 20-foot difference in the tidal movements of the two oceans.

On the other hand, it was obvious that the cost of operating and maintaining a sea-level canal would be far less than that of a lock canal and that a sea-level canal would be less vulnerable from a defense standpoint. These sea-level pluses, both advanced at the time the decision was being made, indicate that the underlying reason for the choice of a lock canal 70 years ago was that excavating methods and flood control techniques had not, at that time, reached a point where a sea-level canal across Panama could be successfully built.

63

By the time the decision was made, Stevens had a plan for a lock canal ready. It was both simple and grand. The course of the canal was plotted from the entrance in Limon Bay on the Atlantic side through a dredged sea-level channel almost 8 miles long to a massive earthen dam, Gatun Dam, which would harness the Chagres River, up three flights of locks a height of 85 feet to Gatun Lake, to be the largest manmade lake in the world, across the lake a distance of 22 miles, then 10 miles through the Continental Divide via the Culebra Cut (now known as Gaillard Cut in honor of the man who directed its construction and gave his life for it) to Pedro Miguel, down 31 feet by one flight of locks, 5 miles across another manmade lake to Sosa Hill, down 54 feet by two flights of locks (later on, for defense and terrain reasons, the Miraflores Locks, 4 miles to the west, were substituted for those planned at Sosa Hill and the second artificial lake eliminated), and out to the Pacific through a dredged sea-level channel 6 miles long, for a total distance of about 51 miles.[3]

George Goethals, who became Stevens' successor, aptly described this plan as not calling so much for a canal as for "a bridge of water consisting of lakes, locks, and sea-approaches."[4]

In addition to insisting on a basic canal plan to which the work to be done could be geared with precision, Stevens also insisted that before any further excavating could be undertaken there had to be thorough preparation in four essential areas. These were: (1) the eradication of yellow fever and malaria, the dread diseases that were taking a horrible toll in lives, working time, and morale, (2) the construction and arrangements necessary to adequately house, feed, and care for the work force, an ultimate payroll of more than 40,000, plus some dependents, a total of as many as 100,000 people, (3) the restructuring of the entire transport system of the Isthmus by establishing adequate terminals at each end, realigning and double-tracking the main line of the railroad, and building spur lines and sidings so that excavated material could be disposed of quickly and efficiently, and men, equipment, and supplies moved wherever necessary in an orderly, expedited manner, and (4) the development of a program for acquiring the right equipment in the right amounts for every task that lay ahead and assuring its availability in serviceable condition at the appropriate times and places. These were large orders, but by the time the decision on the type of canal was made, all four were well under way.

The most spectacular of these tasks, the disease eradication program, has become part of American folklore; most American school children at some time become acquainted with *Aëdes calopus* and *Anopheles*, the two species of mosquitoes that were, respectively, the carriers of yellow fever and malaria. The man who conceived and directed the program was Major William C. Gorgas, a mild-mannered, dedicated Army doctor. His persistence in pressing for what he believed was right, the community cooperation he generated, and the thoroughness of his program finally overcame the prejudices and inertia that had characterized all earlier efforts to solve the problem. Gorgas ranks with Stevens as one of the three outstanding leaders responsible for the success of the Canal venture.

The results of Gorgas' efforts were astounding. It is impossible to determine with any accuracy how many lives were lost to disease during the French operation, but the indications are that they were in the tens of thousands, maybe as many as 30,000. In only two years Gorgas was successful in completely eradicating yellow fever, the principal killer.[5] Malaria, which is less of a killer but more of a disabler, was never eliminated entirely, but in the first two years, Gorgas cut the incidence of malaria in the work force almost in half, from 84 percent in 1905 to 43 percent in 1907. By 1913 it was down to less than 8 percent.[6]

The American work force was much larger than the French. The total number of deaths from all diseases during the period 1904–1914 was 6630. Gorgas is reported to have estimated that 78,000 would have died if the sanitary conditions under which the French worked had prevailed during the American period.[7] That seems rather high. The safer estimate is that if Gorgas had not succeeded the Canal would never have been completed at all.

By the spring of 1907, all four of Stevens' preparatory programs had been completed. The time had come to start building the Canal. At that point, to everyone's surprise and disappointment, Stevens resigned. He apparently had accomplished all that he had set out to do—to set the project on a path bound to lead to completion.

Having lost two chief engineers by resignations, Roosevelt decided to choose the next one not from private life but from the Army Corps of Engineers. Whoever it might be would have to stay on the job until relieved of duty by the commander-in-chief. The man he chose was Major George Washington Goethals. It turned out to be an excellent choice. Goethals has long been acclaimed as the "builder" of the Panama Canal. That he was, and he deserves great credit for it. But the achievements of Stevens and Gorgas had paved the way for him. All three men were primarily responsible for getting the job done. Nor should Roosevelt be forgotten when the palms are being passed out.

The Canal was built by the Corps of Engineers, not by private contractors as originally contemplated. Whether it could have been done as well by private enterprise, there is no way of knowing. But the key to Goethals' success, aside from the great organizational ability and leadership he brought to the task, was probably the vast amount of authority Roosevelt gave to him. He wore three hats at the same time, chairman of the commission, chief engineer of the project, and president of the railroad.

The size of the work force, far greater than had been contemplated at the outset, is indicative of the dimensions of the project. The average number on the payroll each year during the period 1907–1914 was 47,308, with a peak of 56,654 in 1913, the year of the final assault on the Culebra Cut. The majority of the unskilled workers were blacks from the West Indies, though there were many European whites. The skilled workers were mostly Americans.[8]

Never before in the history of engineering had there been such a stern test of skill, coordination, and endurance. The creation of Goethals' "bridge of water" was a series of engineering triumphs in the various phases of the enterprise: dredging the approach channels, clearing the Chagres valley, building the massive earthen dam at Gatun, forming the record-size lake, building and installing the locks, developing the water, power, and drainage systems, and finally, the most difficult of all, completing the cut through the Continental Divide.

When, on August 15, 1914, the S.S. *Ancon* made the first official transit of the Canal, the American people had every reason to be proud. Unfortunately, just 12 days before, World War I had started and global attention was centered on Europe. Nevertheless, the impossible dream had come true.

The building of the Panama Canal has often been referred to as the moonshot of its era. For those who thrilled to the exploits of the Apollo program in the 1960s and 1970s it is perhaps difficult to compare the two achievements. Engineering science, all science, has moved forward so rapidly that what were once fantastic feats of accomplishment now seem commonplace. But by any measure, the building of the Panama Canal, almost three-quarters of a century ago, was a miracle of its age.

66

6

A Rose
By Any Other Name:
Sovereignty

And so, in a somewhat low key because of the onset of World War I, the Panama Canal was opened to the commerce of the world. The impossible dream had come true. Everyone will concede that since that great day the United States has maintained and operated the Canal effectively for the benefit of all nations.

Panama has benefited from it most of all, for it is difficult to visualize what Panama would be today if the Canal had not been built. It probably would not even exist as a nation.

The United States, too, has reaped great rewards. Not in direct monetary benefits, because the Canal has never been operated as a profit-making enterprise. But from a commercial standpoint the availability of the Canal to U.S. and world shipping has, over the years, stimulated trade and cut costs beyond all measure. Even more important, the Canal has played a vital role in the defense of the United States through two world wars and two subsequent large-scale military conflicts in the Far East.

Why then is there a Panama Canal issue?

On that great day, August 15, 1914, the future of the Canal, the future of Panama, and the future of the relationship between the United States and the newborn republic, all seemed dazzlingly bright. And the foundation from which all that brightness emanated, the 1903 treaty, seemed sound and solid. Yet that very treaty is the reason for the Panama Canal issue.

No one can attempt to understand the Panama problem without first becoming reasonably conversant with the major provisions of the 1903 treaty.[1] There never had been a treaty like it before, dealing with a continuing relationship between two nations. Solid it was for certain. Nothing could be more solid, more immutable, more durable, than ties that bind "in perpetuity." Nothing could be more solid, more certain, than granting one nation sovereign rights, as distinguished from mere use and occupancy, over the soil of another. And solid it is today, convincingly so from the viewpoint of most Americans, overwhelmingly and frustratingly so from the viewpoint of most Panamanians.

At the time it was signed, the treaty was probably sound as well as solid. The granting of sovereignty rights by Panama to the U.S. in perpetuity was the "open sesame" to a speedy agreement, the means of ending further bickering, a way of getting the show on the road. But whether or not it is still sound is the question that goes to the heart of the present controversy.

Sovereignty, if it were not so in 1903, quickly became the blemish, later the festering sore, in the relationship between the United States and Panama. Again, unless one understands this, one cannot understand the Panama problem.

There are many definitions of the term *sovereignty*, but they boil down to this: *Sovereignty* is the supreme, absolute, and uncontrollable power by which any independent state is governed.[2] The word stems from the days when monarchies were the usual form of government. It carries with it connotations of national honor, national pride, the trappings that go with man's nationalistic instincts. It is the source of national power and authority, even though that power and authority may, under varying circumstances, be separated from it. It is, therefore, most meaningful as a national symbol.

The matter of sovereignty as regards the Panama Canal, and particularly the Canal Zone, has created more self-made lawyers than are good for any issue of public policy. In discussions about the Canal the word is bandied about with such glibness that it serves as a clincher for both sides of the argument. It is used interchangeably, and quite incorrectly, with other technical, legal terms. By using the word *sovereignty*, throwing in some "titles" and "jurisdictions" here and there, and being very ardent, many people quickly become authorities on the Panama Canal.

The time has long since come when this confusion should be dispelled, when people who are sincerely concerned should look dispassionately at the words of the 1903 treaty, learn them, admit that they say what they do in fact say, and then, most important of all, place this whole matter of sovereignty in proper perspective. If this is done, the myths disappear, and sovereignty emerges in its true light as the essence of the problem, not because of legal niceties, but because of its symbolism.

The key phrases in this regard appear in the preamble to the 1903 treaty and in Articles II and III, its basic provisions. The preamble recites that the United States and Panama are eager to have a canal constructed across the Isthmus, that the president of the United States has been authorized by Congress to acquire "the control of the necessary territory" for that purpose, and that "the sovereignty of such territory" is "vested in the Republic of Panama."[3]

The congressional authorization referred to is, of course, the Spooner Act, described earlier. So far as sovereignty is concerned, the purpose of the preamble was merely to state officially that newborn Panama had acquired the sovereignty of its predecessor, Colombia, over the land to be covered by the treaty and was, therefore, in a position to act with regard to it. Nothing was said about passing that sovereignty on to the United States. On the contrary, if the preamble has any significance at all in this respect, it lies in the fact that it refers only to the acquisition by the United States of control of the necessary territory—not sovereignty over it.

Moving into the body of the treaty, we find that in Article II Panama "*grants* to the United States *in perpetuity the use, occupation and control* of a zone of land and land under water for the *construction, maintenance, operation, sanitation and protection of said Canal.*"[4] (Emphasis added.) The zone described is 10 miles wide and, roughly, 50 miles long. No reference is made at all to sovereignty, only to "use, occupation and control." Even a nonlawyer knows that you can acquire that much in the way of rights and power over land as a mere tenant under a lease. So, clearly, no intention to pass sovereignty from Panama to the United States is manifested in this article.

Furthermore, under Article II, the perpetual right to use,

occupy, and control the territory involved is limited to a single purpose, "said Canal." If the United States had not proceeded with the building of the Canal, or, having built it, had for some reason abandoned it, it obviously would have forfeited that right. The same is true today. Many experts say the Canal is obsolete, or fast becoming so. If this is true, and the United States at some future date discontinues Canal operations and commences using the Canal site as, say, a tourist attraction, the right to the "use, occupation and control" of the Canal Zone would *automatically* terminate under the language of the treaty. That is a far cry from sovereignty.

Finally we arrive at Article III. This is the part that triggers the sea-going lawyers. In it Panama "grants to the United States all the rights, power and authority within the zone . . . which the United States would possess and exercise *if* it were the sovereign . . . to the entire exclusion of the exercise by the Republic of Panama of any such sovereign rights, power or authority."[5] (Emphasis added.)

For some reason many people, primarily those who are avidly opposed to any change of the U.S. position in Panama, become undiscerning when they read this language, and they do not see the all-important word, *if*. And, flying directly in the face of it, they tell you with apparent sincerity that the language they read gives the United States complete sovereignty over the Canal Zone.

One highly respected diplomat, Spruille Braden, former U.S. ambassador to several Latin American countries, refers to "the strict terms of the 1903 Hay–Bunau-Varilla Treaty" as "giving the U.S. sovereignty in perpetuity over the Canal Zone."[6] This simply is not so.

In spite of the big "if," other experts on the Panama Canal equate our position in Panama with two well-known territorial acquisitions by the United States. Senator Strom Thurmond of South Carolina puts it in these words: "The legal position of the United States as sovereign of the Canal Zone is as unassailable as it is on Alaska and the Louisiana Purchase."[7] Dr. James Lucier, chief legislative assistant to Senator Jesse Helms of North Carolina, states that "There is no more reason to give this territory to Panama than to give the Louisiana Purchase back to France, or Alaska back to the Soviet Union."[8] Dr. Lucier may be right from a practical or political standpoint. That is beside the point at this juncture. But both he and Senator Thurmond are in error, legally, on the basic question of sovereignty. A look at the language of the Louisiana and Alaska acquisitions will confirm this.

In Article I of the 1803 Louisiana Purchase treaty with France it is stated that "the First Consul of the French Republic . . . doth hereby *cede* to the United States . . . forever and *in full Sovereignty* the said territory with all its rights and appurtenances. . . ."[9] (Emphasis added.) By the terms of the 1867 Alaskan purchase treaty with Russia the emperor agreed "to *cede* to the United States . . . all the territory *and dominion* [*dominion* means *sovereignty*[10]] now possessed by his Majesty on the continent of America" and declared the "cession of territory *and dominion* herein made . . . to be *free of any reservations.*"[11] (Emphasis added.) In both these treaties it was provided that the inhabitants of the ceded territories should have U.S. citizenship bestowed on them. Nothing of that nature is contained in the 1903 Panama treaty. It is also worth noting that in both the Louisiana and Alaska transactions the territories involved were *ceded* to the United States, a term common to international conveyances of sovereignty. In the Panama treaty the word *grant* is used, and the only thing granted is the "use, occupation and control" of certain territory, not one acre of territory itself.

Another interesting legal fact that is often noted in discussions of the nature of U.S. sovereignty over the Zone is that children born in the Zone to non-U.S. citizens—in most instances Panamanians—do not automatically become U.S. citizens, as they would if they were born in the United States.

No legal training is necessary to perceive the significant differences in language between the Louisiana and Alaska transactions on the one hand, and the Panama transaction on the other. Those differences are there for all to see who care to see.

There is probably no better way to determine what particular language was intended to mean than to consult the person who wrote it. In the case of treaties that is not usually possible. But the unique wording of Article III of the 1903 Panama treaty was composed by one man. Neither lawyer nor diplomat, he was the wily French engineer, Philippe Bunau-Varilla, commissioned by the provisional government of Panama as its envoy extraordinary and minister plenipotentiary to the United States. He knew exactly what he was doing. Bearing in mind the earlier debates over the Spooner Act and the Hay-Herran Treaty between the U.S. and Colombia, he wanted treaty language the U.S. Senate

71

could not possibly reject.[12] And here is what Bunau-Varilla said later on of his intentions regarding sovereignty:

> The United States *without becoming the sovereign* received *the exclusive use* of the rights of sovereignty, while respecting the sovereignty itself of the Panama Republic.[13] (Emphasis added.)

Bunau-Varilla is a bad word in Panama, but this explanation of his is of particular significance to Panamanians. Obviously it could not be more authoritative. Putting it in less technical terms, the Bunau-Varilla language seems to say quite clearly that Panama owns the crown, as recited in the preamble of the treaty, but the United States is entitled to wear it in the Canal Zone for certain purposes. A nice distinction, but important if you happen to own the crown and want it back someday.

Secretary of War William Howard Taft, later to become president and then chief justice of the United States, explained the situation to President Theodore Roosevelt in 1905 in this way:

> The truth is that while we have all the attributes of sovereignty necessary in the construction, maintenance and protection of the Canal, the very form in which these attributes are conferred in the treaty seems to preserve the titular sovereignty over the Canal Zone in the Republic of Panama.[14]

And this has been the official position of the United States ever since, one recognizing, or "respecting," as Bunau-Varilla put it, the titular or residual sovereignty of Panama over the Zone.

As indicated earlier, the exponents of complete U.S. sovereignty, those who reject the Bunau-Varilla–Taft concept, often use the term interchangeably with other technical terms to bolster their position. For example, they point out that after the 1903 treaty was signed the United States acquired the title to all the privately owned land in the Canal Zone by purchase from the owners. Then they go on to equate the title thus acquired with sovereignty. But there is no essential relationship between title to land and sovereignty over it. A private citizen owning land, that is, having title to it, does not have sovereignty over it. The sovereignty over that land resides in government. The same is true of a foreign government that buys land in another country.

It acquires title to the land, it owns it, but the host country retains sovereignty over it.

The complete sovereignty advocates also point out that the United States exercises jurisdiction over the Canal Zone by passing laws to govern it and enforcing them through a U.S. federal court. True, jurisdiction, or, literally, the right to dictate, is an element of sovereignty, and the exercise of jurisdiction is the exercise of a sovereign right. But jurisdiction is not the same as sovereignty. It stems from sovereignty.

This all may sound quite trivial, a mere quibble over words. But it is not. Not when it comes to gaining an understanding of the Panama Canal issue. It is crucially important because sovereignty has become *the* symbol of national interest to the antagonists in this controversy, both Americans and Panamanians.

We say, or at least many of us do, that we have complete sovereignty over the Canal, that that was decided many years ago, that regardless of its geographical location the Canal Zone is an integral part of the United States, that you can talk about other things, canal operations, annual payments, hiring practices, etc., as much as you want, but not about that, not about sovereignty.

On the other hand, the Panamanians say, with seeming unanimity, that we did not acquire complete sovereignty over the Canal Zone. They say that all we got was the right to exercise sovereign rights for one particular purpose, the Canal, that the Canal Zone is an integral part of Panama, that because of its geographical location it is a barrier to Panama's national entity, Panama's nationhood, and that the continued exercise of sovereign rights by a foreign nation in the middle of their country is what they want most to talk about, not other things.

This is not to say that there is nothing to this whole problem besides the matter of sovereignty. Far from it. Maybe, generally speaking, as far as Panama is concerned, that is all there is to it. But not so for the United States. For us there are far more difficult aspects to the problem—foreign relations, international and domestic commerce, and, above all, national security—all to be considered at length in the chapters ahead. These are aspects that from our standpoint, at least cumulatively, far outweigh the single issue of sovereignty. But it cannot be repeated too often that to understand the Panama Canal question one has to understand the sovereignty aspect. You have to know the words and the tune to understand the play. Musical comedy it may be to some Americans, but it is tragedy to most Panamanians.

In discussing the Panama Canal issue, Panamanians often put forward a hypothetical situation. Suppose, they say, that at the time of the American Revolution, in exchange for French help against the British and the payment of $10 million, the United States had given France in perpetuity the control of the Mississippi River as a waterway and the exclusive rights of sovereignty over a zone five miles wide on each side of that river and running for its full length, from the Gulf of Mexico to Canada. At that time, 200 years ago, the Mississippi River was way out in the western hinterland of our newborn republic, so it would not have made much difference. How, they ask, would the people of the United States feel today if their country was divided completely in half by such a French zone? How would the American people feel today if every time a U.S. citizen wanted to go from east to west or west to east in his own country he had to pass through that zone and, while passing through, be subject to French laws, French police, French courts, even French jails?

Except for the fact that the United States built the Panama Canal where there was none, while the Mississippi is a natural waterway, the analogy thus presented is not inept. It serves a real purpose in helping a conscientious, patriotic American put himself in the position of a conscientious, patriotic Panamanian. Of course, it is a plea to the emotions. But emotion is a major element of nationalism. And nationalism is a reality, everywhere.

If it were not so important from the standpoint of national attitudes and national symbolism, the argument over sovereignty could really be written off as a draw: both sides are right, each has sovereignty in the sense each understands the term. But from the Panamanian viewpoint we have more than they would like us to have.

The Americans who feel so strongly about the Canal, the exponents of complete U.S. sovereignty, can be charged with overkill. They really do not have to keep repeating, "We bought it. We paid for it. It is ours." That is legally incorrect. We can't sell the Canal. We can't even give it away. But, regardless of what is correct, it still is an unnecessary stretching of a point. For, both in fact and in law, what we bought, what we paid for, and what is ours is the use, occupancy, and control of the Panama Canal Zone for Canal purposes for as long as we want it for those purposes, *plus* the privilege of exercising all rights of sovereignty necessary for the accomplishment of those purposes. We have, therefore, everything we need in the way of rights; our position in Panama, legally, is unassailable. The we-bought-it, we-paid-for-it, it-is-ours syndrome is rhetorical gloss.

The Panamanians are equally right from a legal standpoint, so far as sovereignty is concerned. Panama has sovereignty over the Zone. Theirs is the source of the rights we are privileged to exercise in the Zone for Canal purposes. But so long as we care to exercise them for that purpose, Panama cannot exercise them. That is where the trouble lies.

So whether or not the United States has complete sovereignty is beside the point. She has the privilege of exercising sovereign rights in perpetuity. "A rose by any other name would smell as sweet." But while the United States sniffs that rose, she must be ever mindful that to Panamanians the scent is tantalizing—and highly provocative.

7

Pressure Cooker:
Two Generations of
U.S.-Panama Relations
1913–1965

A problem involving sovereignty surfaced at the very outset of
the relationship between the United States and Panama under
the new treaty. It involved the applicability of U.S. customs laws
to goods entering the Canal Zone. Inherent in this problem was
the fact, not often noted by historians, that the two principal
ports of Panama, Cristobal on the Atlantic side and Balboa on
the Pacific, were cut away from Panama and included in the
Zone. The two major Panamanian cities, Panama City and Colon,
adjacent to these ports and dependent on them, did not have
adequate shipping facilities of their own. As a result, practically
all ocean shipping to and from Panama entered or left the Isthmus via the Canal Zone. This is still true to a major extent.

In June 1904 a new U.S. tariff law was made applicable to the
Canal Zone. This meant that while all goods coming into the Zone
from the United States were duty free, the high duty rates of the
recently enacted Dingley Tariff Act had to be paid on everything
coming into the Zone from foreign nations, including Panama.
The Panamanians became greatly concerned over this, because
it obviously limited Panama's access to the one real market in

the area, the burgeoning Canal construction community in the Canal Zone. United States Secretary of War Taft called it "an unfortunate mistake in our policy."[1]

Another matter involving sovereignty, one regarding postal service, also created friction at an early date. While it cost five cents to send a letter from Panama to the United States, from within the Canal Zone it cost only two. Naturally, many residents of Panama City and Colon walked into the Zone to mail their letters to the United States at this three-cent saving, and Panama's postal revenue suffered accordingly.

These and many other problems were getting the relationship between the two countries off to a bad start. In October 1904 President Roosevelt sent Taft to Panama to straighten things out. Taft carried with him certain "instructions" from Roosevelt, of which the following portion, in the light of subsequent developments and even the current situation, is of particular interest:

> There is no ground for believing that in the execution of the rights conferred by the treaty, the people of Panama have been unduly alarmed at the effect of the establishment of a government in the canal strip by the commission [the Isthmian Canal Commission]. Apparently they fear lest the effect be to create out of a part of their territory a competing and independent community which shall injuriously affect their business, reduce their incomes, and diminish their prestige as a nation.
>
> The United States is to confer on the people of Panama a very great benefit by the expenditure of millions of dollars in the construction of the canal. But this fact must not blind us to the importance of so exercising the authority given us under the treaty with Panama as to avoid creating any suspicion, however unfounded, of our intentions as to the future.
>
> *We have not the slightest intention of establishing an independent colony in the middle of the State of Panama,* or of exercising any greater governmental functions than are necessary to enable us, conveniently and safely, to construct, maintain and operate the canal under the rights given us by this treaty. Least of all do we desire to interfere with the

interest and prosperity of the people of Panama.[2]
(Emphasis added.)

Taft, a most genial emissary, spent 10 days on the Isthmus, discussing the problems with Panamanian officials and conveying Roosevelt's message to the Panamanian people. He smoothed a lot of ruffled feathers. Shortly after his return to the United States, an executive order was issued designed to ameliorate many of the troublesome situations. Free importations into the Canal Zone were to be limited to coal, fuel oil, construction materials, and merchandise in transit to points outside the Isthmus. No tariff duties were to apply to Panamanian goods entering the Zone. The two cent postage rate for letters to the United States was to be available in Panama as well as in the Zone. Touching on other matters, the order provided that patients from Panama were to be admitted to one of the Zone hospitals. The U.S. would construct a highway to run six miles out of Panama City. Arrangements were to be made for Panamanians residing in the Zone to vote conveniently in Panamanian elections. Certain currency problems were to be ironed out.

These matters are mentioned in this detail because they developed so early in the game and are so indicative of the types of problems that were to keep cropping up and causing irritation in the years ahead. As can be seen, they stemmed about equally from commercial interests and the exercise of governmental functions. However, since all commercial activities in the Zone were carried on by the United States government, not by private business interests, the element of sovereignty underlay almost every situation.

Taft's visit smoothed things over for only a brief period. Within a year another major problem developed, one that still disturbs the relationship between the two countries. It is particularly illustrative of the situation in the early days when the Panamanian economy was totally incapable of supplying the needs of the rapidly developing Zone community.

By 1905 it had become quite clear that Panama could not produce an adequate amount or variety of food for the workers on the Canal project. It became necessary to set up commissaries within the Zone, stocked with foodstuffs from the United States. These commissaries initially were made available to everyone, whether they lived in the Zone or outside, whether they worked for the United States or not. Once again the Panamanian mer-

78

chants and farmers became concerned. But in spite of their protests, the commissaries soon, of necessity, went even further and entered the general merchandising field, including the sale of luxuries.

The Panamanian government formally demanded of the U.S. that access to the commissaries be restricted to those living and working in the Zone, that the use of coupon books be discontinued, that the sale of European merchandise be prohibited. All of these demands were rejected.

In time, the United States government even went into the hotel business. It established dairies. It roasted coffee. It engaged in almost every type of enterprise. At least during the construction period, there was no other answer. The services and goods were needed not only to maintain the construction force; they had to be available to a degree beyond mere sustenance in order to attract and keep the white collar and skilled workers, mostly from the U.S., essential to the Canal project.

As a matter of hindsight and heeding the warnings of Roosevelt's "instructions" to Taft, it would perhaps have been a wise policy if the United States, from the very beginning, had affirmatively encouraged the investment of private U.S. capital in Panamanian business ventures designed to meet these needs. In this way, within a reasonable period of time, many of the wants of the Zone might have been met by Panamanian entrepreneurs encouraged by American capital. At the same time an independent Panamanian economy, developing markets outside the Zone as well as within, would have begun to evolve at an early stage.

When the Canal was completed and the situation began to settle down to the routine operation of the waterway and the long-haul relationship between the two nations, or, more accurately, between the two side-by-side communities, the problems, unfortunately, did not disappear. Many of the old ones continued to cause friction: the commissaries, postage, customs collections, business competition, contraband control, law enforcement, and hospital facilities, to name a few. Others were new. Among them were those relating to job opportunities for Panamanians, rates of pay, housing, and education, all within the Zone; acquisition by the United States of additional land and water areas needed outside the Zone in connection with Canal operations; and the establishment of military bases and installations both within and without the Zone for the defense of the

79

Canal. Here, again, there was a fairly even mixture of commercial and governmental underpinnings to each problem. But, because of the omnipresence of the U.S. government, the sovereignty question was an inescapable component of every situation.

The complaints against U.S. policies and practices increased in scope and intensity as Panama's national identity continued to emerge and her economy, however slowly, to expand. Proximity aggravated the slightest issue. At an early stage in Panama's national existence fanning the flames of dissatisfaction with the United States became a way of life for aspiring politicians. Anti-U.S. rhetoric became the coin of the political marketplace. United States officials in the Canal Zone, in the U.S. embassy in Panama City, even in Washington, have for almost 75 years been under the relentless pressure generated from this source. There have, of course, been respites, short periods between some Panamanian elections, brief aftermaths of major U.S. concessions. But, in the main, the pressure has always been there, nagging, annoying, frustrating, inducing weakness and compromise.

Panama's first successful run at the 1903 treaty occurred in 1926. Not only were formal negotiations undertaken, but a new treaty was arrived at, modifying some of the terms of the basic document.[3] But this first revision, though signed and sealed, came to naught. The Panamanian National Assembly, dissatisfied with the extent of the concessions made by the U.S., refused to ratify. No action was taken by the U.S. Senate.

The fact that the United States was willing to enter into treaty negotiations at all in 1926 was significant. It evidenced a new inclination to discard the "big stick" policy towards Latin America as a whole and to have more concern over relationships with individual nations. This had first manifested itself under President Woodrow Wilson when, in 1914, negotiations were undertaken to mollify the bitter feelings of Colombia against the United States for the loss of Panama in 1903. In 1922, these negotiations resulted in the $22 million indemnification treaty referred to earlier.

Naturally, the ultimate failure of the 1926 effort kept the pot boiling. In 1933 the Good Neighbor Policy of President Franklin D. Roosevelt came on the scene, the first official U.S. policy directed specifically at improving relations with Latin American nations. The Panamanians took immediate advantage of the opportunity afforded by this new U.S. approach. Negotiations requested by Panama in 1934 resulted two years later in the Hull-Alfaro Treaty. This was not to replace the 1903 treaty, but to change it in many respects and to cope with some of the situations not covered by it.[4]

The Hull-Alfaro Treaty of 1936 was a landmark in the realtionship between the two countries, and it made one thing quite clear: that the 1903 treaty was not immutable.

Foremost among the 1936 changes were those directly involving sovereignty. Three of them effected a modification in the basic relationship between the United States and Panama:

(1) Article I of the 1903 treaty was deleted. This was the article in which the United States undertook to guarantee the independence of Panama. Thenceforth, Panama was to be on her own, so to speak.

(2) The right of the United States under the 1903 treaty unilaterally to intervene in Panama to preserve order was abolished. Thenceforth, maintaining law and order outside the Canal Zone was to be the sole responsibility of Panama.

(3) The defense of the Canal was no longer to be the sole responsibility of the United States. Thenceforth, Panama was to share in this task.

These three changes represented a gigantic step forward in Panama's position, both domestically and internationally, even though the assumption by Panama of partial responsibility for the defense of the Canal was merely a gesture, a boost for Panamanian prestige. Panama was not at that time capable of making a significant military contribution towards the defense of the Canal.

Of the other two changes made in 1936 directly involving sovereignty, one was of particular significance. The United States relinquished its right under the 1903 treaty to take, entirely at its own discretion, any additional land or water outside the Canal Zone it might need for the effective operation, maintenance, or defense of the Canal. Thenceforth, Panama's consent would be a prerequisite. In the other sovereignty change, the U.S. gave up its right to acquire property in Panama City and Colon by eminent domain. Thenceforth, it would have to buy it.

An important provision of the 1936 treaty was one upping the annual payment to Panama from $250,000 to $430,000. This was not, however, an actual increase in compensation. It merely reflected the effect of the devaluation of the U.S. dollar in 1933.

81

In the area of commercial and community problems not covered by the 1903 treaty, there were several significant provisions in the new agreement. Residence in the Canal Zone and the privilege of patronizing the commissaries were to be restricted to certain categories of persons, primarily to employees of the United States and their families. The U.S. was not to establish any new business enterprises in the Zone unless directly related to the operation and protection of the Canal. Panamanian merchants were to be allowed to sell goods and supplies to ships arriving in the Canal Zone ports of Balboa and Cristobal or transiting the Canal. Up until then the United States had kept this lucrative trade to itself, mainly because at first there were no local firms that could be depended on to meet the needs of these vessels.

The 1936 treaty did not have easy sledding in either the United States or Panama. In the U.S. there was strong opposition to any dilution of the rights acquired under the original pact. In Panama there was, as in 1926, considerable dissatisfaction with the limited extent of U.S. concessions. Ratifications were not completed until mid-1939.

War clouds over Europe and growing concern over the activities of Nazi Germany in Latin America played a key role in bringing about ratification of the new treaty by the United States Senate.[5] They highlighted the importance of the Canal and the need for improved relations with Panama to meet the threat of another world war.

The war came. The defense of the Canal became a matter of the highest priority for the United States. At the same time Panama became the focal point for the defense of the entire southern portion of the Western Hemisphere. United States military bases and installations, with the consent of Panama, proliferated throughout the Isthmus. Tens of thousands of U.S. military and civilian personnel moved into the area.

Panama grew considerably during World War II, economically and nationalistically. The expenditure of large sums of money by the United States in the building of bases, fortifications, highways, communications systems, and all the other things that go into a massive defense effort were, of course, a tremendous stimulus to the economy. In addition, Panama had the opportunity to participate directly in meeting the needs for labor, goods, and services created by the U.S. effort and the large influx of people. The economic growth brought about by this situation was, of course, to a considerable extent abnormal and temporary. But the country's permanent economic base was inevitably broadened and strengthened to a measurable degree. The growth of nationalistic feeling during World War II was equally inevitable. Panama was given a taste of economic prosperity. The new structures, housing developments and airfields that sprang up outside the Canal Zone would someday belong to her. New roads and highways were built. New Panamanian communities developed. All these things tended to increase Panama's sense of nationhood, of being something more than just a jungle and farm area athwart the U.S. Canal Zone.

But part of this heightened nationalism stemmed from a negative source, from a natural resentment of the ever-increasing presence of a foreign power, particularly one in a military guise. The United States was everywhere, dominating, almost suffocating—a situation, from the Panamanian viewpoint, to be merely tolerated during the war emergency and affirmatively eliminated as soon as the justification for it was gone.

This gave rise to two confrontations, both related to the military bases, that were to have a profound psychological effect on the relationship between the United States and Panama. The first arose over the acquisition of the new bases. As has been noted, by the 1936 treaty the U.S. gave up its right to walk in as it pleased and take any area it needed outside the Canal Zone. Now Panama had to approve. In the initial phase of the military base build-up outside the Zone, roughly, from 1936 to 1940, there was no real problem. Cooperative Panamanian administrations were willing to authorize the acquisitions without much in the way of formalities. However, during Panama's 1940 presidential election this loose policy became a target. So much so that even before the election the incumbent administration reversed it and insisted that there could be no further acquisitions by the United States until the two countries had arrived at a basic agreement on two points: compensation to Panama and a fixed date for the return of the bases. Two years of intense and sometimes bitter negotiations ensued. During that period, the U.S. program for the expansion of defense facilities outside the Zone came to a complete halt. Panama took a firm stand: no agreement, no bases. She challenged the U.S. at a very critical time.

And she won. The Defense Sites Agreement was finally signed on 18 May 1942.[6] Panama got what she wanted in the way of compensation and the United States agreed to return the bases one year after the war ended. Panama had faced down the giant. Furthermore, Panama successfully used the military bases issue to wring from the United States several important concessions that were totally unrelated to the defense program.

Another showdown occurred after the war. The Panamanians took the not unreasonable position that under the Defense Site Agreement of 1942 the bases should be returned to Panama by September 1, 1946, one year after Japan's unconditional surrender. The United States stalled. The matter dragged along past September 1. Some of the bases were evacuated, many were not. This gave rise to a political furor in Panama. The matter became a major issue in the 1947 presidential campaign. Finally, in December, on the eve of the election, an agreement was arrived at that would have resolved the question of postwar U.S. bases outside the Canal Zone. But it was not to be.

A special session of the Panamanian National Assembly was called for the purpose of ratifying the agreement. The opposition mounted first a strike of university students, then a general strike. Riots developed. Just before the final vote on ratification, 10,000 Panamanian students descended on the legislature in a wild protest. The Assembly voted to reject the agreement.

On Christmas Day, without waiting for another demand to get out, the U.S. military forces began evacuating all the remaining bases, silently stealing away. Panama had again prevailed in a showdown. It was a dramatic diplomatic defeat for the United States.

If anyone is puzzled today over the brashness with which diminutive Panama stands up to one of the world's two superpowers and makes "or else" demands, a look back at these two military base confrontations will supply part of the answer. For it was then that Panama took on the "Jack the Giant Killer" role that has characterized her attitude towards the United States ever since.

In 1953 Panama launched another all-out effort to revise the 1903 treaty. Typical of the new confidence was the send-off given the Panamanian negotiating team as it left Panama City for Washington in August of that year. All Panamanians were urged to take part in this "appointment with the fatherland." Responding to the call, thousands of them, including the president and six ex-presidents, cabinet ministers, government officials, delegations from the provinces, and high school and university students, marched in a huge parade. One student group

carried a placard reading Negotiations Without Surrender.[7]
During the negotiations that followed, Panama presented 21 demands. Chief among them were these: (1) that the Panamanian flag be flown in the Zone wherever the United States flag was flown, (2) that Panama's sovereign control over the Zone be restored, (3) that the duration of the treaty be reduced from perpetuity to 99 years, and (4) that the United States turn over to Panama each year 20 percent of the gross revenue from Canal operations, with a minimum of $5 million.

None of these four demands was met by the United States during the two years of negotiations that followed. But another treaty was concluded in 1955, commonly known as the Chapin-Fabrega Treaty.[8] The annual payment was upped from $430,000 to $1,930,000, where it stands today. Panama was given the right to levy income taxes on Panamanians working in the Zone regardless of where they lived. Wages and benefits for Panamanians working in the Zone were improved. The United States gave up its right under the 1903 treaty to a monopoly over trans-Isthmian railroads and highways outside the Canal Zone. It also gave up its right under the 1903 treaty to regulate sanitary conditions in Panama City and Colon and transferred certain property in those cities to Panama. The United States agreed to deny commissary privileges to Panamanians working in the Zone but living outside. And it agreed to build a bridge across the Canal at Balboa.

In return for all these concessions, the U.S. got a 15-year lease on a military training area in the Rio Hato region outside the Canal Zone.

Both nations ratified the new treaty. For the next three years the pressure on the U.S. was relaxed a bit, although delay by the U.S. Congress in authorizing a new $22 million bridge across the Canal caused some agitation.

Then, in 1958, the high school and university students launched "Operation Sovereignty," the agitation over the flying of the Panamanian flag in the Canal Zone that was to go on intermittently for the next six years and culminate in the disastrous "Flag War" of 1964.

During 1958, riots and demonstrations involving the flag occurred on several occasions. Ten Panamanians died at the hands of the Panamanian police force, the Guardia Nacional. There was one "peaceful" invasion of the Zone.

The pressure continued in 1959. On one occasion U.S. troops

had to be called into action to repel the mobs invading the Zone. No deaths occurred, but there was considerable property damage.

In April 1960, apparently in a hasty attempt to calm things down, President Dwight D. Eisenhower announced a nine-point program of concessions to Panama, mostly having to do with employment and housing in the Zone.[9] That did not relieve the tension. In September of that same year, Eisenhower went even further, this time conceding on the flag issue itself. In defiance of an earlier admonition by the U.S. Congress, he directed that the Panamanian flag be flown each day alongside the Stars and Stripes at one place in the Zone, Shuler Triangle, "as visual evidence of Panama's titular sovereignty over the Panama Canal Zone."[10] This seemed to merely whet the appetites of the Panamanian activists.

The following year, President John F. Kennedy took office and unveiled his Alliance for Progress program, directed, like its forerunner, the Good Neighbor Policy, at improving relations throughout Latin America. When he got around to Panama in 1962, Kennedy met in Washington with President Roberto Chiari. They issued a joint statement covering many of the problems vexing the two countries and, with respect to the flag issue, reciting an agreement to arrange "for the flying of Panamanian *flags* in an appropriate way in the Canal Zone."[11] (Emphasis added.)

That this assurance accomplished little was demonstrated a few months later at the dedication of the new bridge across the Canal promised by the U.S. in the 1955 treaty. A grand ceremony was planned, participated in by high officials of both nations and the diplomatic representatives of many other countries. It ended up in shambles. While U.S. Under Secretary of State George Ball was delivering a major policy speech about U.S. relations with Panama, including an announcement that the Panamanian flag was to be flown at many places in the Zone, anti-U.S. demonstrators broke through police barriers, swarmed onto the bridge, and brought the proceedings to a halt in wild confusion.

From then on, until the final debacle in 1964, the flag issue held the spotlight. Demonstrations, "incidents," negotiations, agreements, disagreements, misunderstandings, all involving the flag question, passed across the stage. Nothing satisfied the instigators of the Panamanian mobs. In their vacillations between

86

firmness and weakness, U.S. officials did little more than aggravate the situation.

It appears now that no matter what concessions the United States made or might have made, the final bloodbath could not have been avoided. The Panamanian activists, particularly the students, organized and directed by Communists,[12] were going to use this issue, or some other one, as a pretext for a dramatic confrontation. Some say the initial concession by Eisenhower in 1960 was the fatal mistake from which all later events flowed. As a matter of hindsight, it appears just as likely that a firm refusal on his part would merely have hastened those events.

The Flag War started on January 9, 1964, and continued for a week. It began when some 200 Panamanians, mostly students, marched into the Zone and approached the flagpole at the Balboa High School. There, contrary to official orders, American students had flown a U.S. flag. It was the intent of the Panamanians to fly their flag beside it. A scuffle started when they were asked to leave. This touched things off. More demonstrators moved in from Panama.

From then on mobs numbering in the thousands began to run wild at various points in the Zone and throughout the cities of Panama and Colon, breaking street lights, overturning cars, smashing windows, setting fires. Many American residents of the Panamanian cities fled into the Zone for protection. The mobs were using Molotov cocktails, machetes, guns, stones, bricks, any lethal weapon that came to hand. Outside the Zone, in Panama City and Colon, the Guardia Nacional, at least for the first three or four days, made no effort to preserve order. Within the Zone, when the police became incapable of handling the situation, the U.S. military forces took over.

When the "war" ended, 20 Panamanian citizens and five American soldiers lay dead. Panama had suspended diplomatic relations with the United States and appealed to the United Nations and the Organization of American States against what was termed U.S. "aggression." The new president of the United States, Lyndon Johnson, had an international crisis on his hands.

At the instance of a peace committee of the Organization of American States, the U.S. and Panama agreed to undertake discussions of their mutual problems. These discussions got under way in May, after diplomatic relations between the two countries had been restored. Student riots and demonstrations resumed in Panama. The pressure was still on. It paid off.

In December 1964 President Johnson announced a startling reversal of U.S. policy, "the negotiation of an entirely new treaty on the Panama Canal."[13] Finally, in September 1965, came word of complete U.S. capitulation on the basic treaty issues. Johnson announced that the U.S. in preliminary negotiations had already agreed to abrogate the 1903 treaty, to substitute a fixed term of years for duration in perpetuity, to recognize Panama's sovereignty over the Canal Zone, to place the Zone under Panamanian jurisdiction, and to work out an arrangement whereby the Canal would be operated jointly by the two nations.[14] Negotiations in the future were to proceed from that new threshold.

The first 50 years of the relationship between the United States and Panama, were crucially determinative of the posture in which the two nations find themselves today, vis-à-vis one another and vis-à-vis the rest of the world. The clock cannot be turned back, but no one can fully understand the Panama Canal dilemma of today without an awareness of the conditions, the events, and the attitudes that developed during those formative years, the years of Panama's childhood, the years of her adolescence. What did this period produce?

Ever since World War II Panama has given the appearance of wearing her national pride on her sleeve. Baiting the United States has become a national pastime. Martyrdom and helplessness at the hands of U.S. "imperialism" have become a national pose. And out of this strange combination of national swagger and national impotence has apparently grown a confidence, ever more justified by succeeding events, that national tantrums will eventually gain for Panama everything she wants from the United States.

One might also conclude that the United States has failed dismally over the years to cope with these manifestations of Panamanian adolescence. With an attitude ranging from haughty indifference to placating indulgence, dictated at any particular moment by the degree and duration of pressure applied by Panama, the United States has appeared to act on a situation-by-situation basis, making no effort to search out root causes, to develop long-range, overall solutions. The policy, put in military terms, seems to have been one of steady retreat: no constructive moves forward, no leadership.

As a result, what was in its initial stages largely an economic problem and one which at least up until 1964 probably could have been solved by economic means, became one bound up in Panama's national pride. If, particularly during the period after World War II, the United States had made an all-out effort to develop the Panamanian economy in the areas of international trade, small manufacturing, and agriculture, it seems likely that that economy, located so strategically along the lanes of world commerce, could have reached a point where the Canal and the U.S. presence because of it became only an important component, not the dominant one. At some stage of the game young Panama might have stopped pressing her nose against the window and peering, forlornly and enviously, into the Canal Zone. She might have had something to turn her attention away, things of her own to take care of and gaze on with pride. National pride might have been nourished by something more than an insatiable lust for the Canal Zone.

That this was not done, that the Panamanian economy is still almost wholly tied to the Canal, that national pride has become exclusively centered on sovereignty over the Canal Zone, are the tragedies of those first 50 years. Panama had seemingly only one road to travel: that of satisfying her pride.

As for the United States, the policy of constantly giving ground on the basis of expediency seemed to have brought her back to the wall, with no more room for maneuver and seemingly nothing more to give up but the Canal itself.

It is within this dismal framework that the treaty negotiations concluded in 1977 must be assessed.

8

Stacked Deck: The U.S. Negotiating Phenomenon

The negotiations between the United States and Panama that started in 1964 and were concluded, for a second time, in August 1977, have been unique in the history of international treaty-making.

In the first place, it is highly unusual for one of the two nations in bilateral treaty negotiations to throw away its major trading positions before the negotiations commence. Yet the United States did just that in these negotiations, all the way through. President Johnson announced in 1965 that the U.S. was pre-committed to giving up the perpetual treaty duration, the rights of sovereignty, and the right of unilateral Canal operation that it acquired under the 1903 treaty. This precommitment was reaffirmed nine years later by the Nixon Administration in the Kissinger-Tack Statement of Principles. It was later adhered to by the Ford and Carter administrations. The relinquishment of these positions of strength before the negotiations even started obviously rendered them valueless as future trading points. This was an unusual gambit, to say the least.

In addition, there are two basic characteristics of normal bilateral negotiations that were missing here. In the usual situation both parties to the negotiations have things they want to gain and things they are willing to give up in exchange. The trading of advantages and disadvantages thus becomes the order of business. This was not the case here.

The other basic characteristic in the normal situation is that the attitudes of the negotiating representatives on the two sides are, in the main, adverse. These attitudes stem from firm beliefs in the correctness of the opposing positions of their respective principals. This, in turn, causes them to deal with each other on a partisan, adversary, albeit polite, basis. That was not the situation in these negotiations.

First, the absence of normal give and take. Bargaining was all one way. In a general sense, at least, Panama had nothing to give, nothing the United States wanted, other than such intangible, nonnegotiable items as good will, stability, and cooperation. By virtue of the 1903 treaty the United States has everything she wants. On the other hand, Panama wants everything the United States has.

This is a totally unorthodox foundation for negotiations. The negotiating has to be all one way. U.S. rights under the 1903 treaty are so extensive and complete that almost any modification, whether major or minor, must involve a relinquishment of something on the part of the United States, with nothing given in exchange by Panama. This situation has given rise to the term *giveaway* used constantly as a slogan by U.S. opponents of the new-treaty policy.

Giveaway is perhaps a literally and practically accurate term from the standpoint of those who believe there was nothing to be gained by negotiating. On the other hand, from the standpoint of those who believe, as apparently have the four most recent presidential administrations, that a new treaty based on the Kissinger-Tack principles is essential both to U.S.-Latin American relations and to the continuing viability of the Panama Canal as a world waterway, it is a totally inaccurate term. To those people, the concessions made by the United States to Panama will be paid for, not in the normal coin of treaty negotiations, but in kind, so to speak—in nonnegotiable intangibles such as good will, stability, and cooperation, and in improved relations throughout Latin America.

From the standpoint of the American people and the members of Congress who must now decide what, in all good conscience

91

and in keeping with the hard realities of the Panama Canal situation, is in the best interests of the United States, *giveaway* is nothing but a misleading, rhetorical gimmick. It is a term that would probably best be ignored. Slogans incite; they seldom enlighten.

What does enlighten in this situation is the realization that because of the peculiar circumstances created by the 1903 treaty, circumstances totally favorable to the United States, any change in the relationship created by that document necessarily results in the United States' "giving up" something. But it does not necessarily result in the United States' "giving away" something.

As to the lack of the other basic characteristic, the usual adverse attitudes of the negotiating representatives, the evidence is interesting. One spring 1976 morning in Washington in the waiting room of the State Department offices of the U.S. Panama Canal negotiating team, there was an astonishing thing to behold. The waiting room was just outside the office of S. Morey Bell, director of the Panama Division of the State Department and State's top representative on the negotiating team under Ambassador-at-Large Ellsworth Bunker.

In the dimly lighted room on a wall table there was a white cardboard sign perched behind a dark wooden pedestal. On the pedestal rested a small piece of what appeared to be bone or gristle. The sign bore this legend, crudely handprinted in ink:

THIS IS THE BRAIN OF
P. BUNAU-VARILLA—
A CONSTANT INSPIRATION
TO THE U.S. NEGOTIATORS

There, in the historic lair of U.S. international statesmanship, the home of U.S. diplomacy, the very workshop of the U.S.-Panama treaty negotiations, was a surprisingly childish indication of the oft-reported attitude of the State Department negotiators. There in a nutshell was an expression of the *mea culpa* complex, the "we-are-on-the-wrong-side" approach that has characterized the State Department's negotiating effort and related activities with regard to Panama for the past 25 years.

History shows that Bunau-Varilla was wily, even Machiavellian. His motives were often questionable, his interests conflicting. But small-brained? Gristle-brained? Hardly. He was a well-

92

educated, able engineer. Though untrained in the art of diplomacy, his draftsmanship of the 1903 treaty was a thorough and intelligent piece of work. But for him there probably would have been no treaty at all, no Panama Canal, certainly no Panama.

This evidence of puerile pique against Bunau-Varilla is highly significant as regards the posture of the United States in negotiations with Panama. For the 1903 treaty drafted by Bunau-Varilla is the source of all U.S. rights in Panama. It is the essence of the negotiations. Whatever we "give away," as the slogan goes, whatever we keep, in these negotiations, must stem from Bunau-Varilla's handiwork—handiwork concurred in by then U.S. Secretary of State John Hay, ratified shortly afterward by the United States Senate, and apparently approved of ever since by a majority of the American people.

What an individual employee of the State Department thinks of the 1903 treaty privately is his own business. What he says about it publicly is an entirely different matter. And yet the U.S. negotiating team, at least on March 18, 1976, was telling everyone who happened to come its way, including any Panamanians, that the 1903 treaty, the Magna Carta of the U.S. presence in Panama, was the product of an infinitesimal brain, and therefore, by implication, wrong, or as they would probably say, "evil."

The display in the waiting room is only one of frequent manifestations of the feelings of many State Department employees. For example, in a recent symposium on the Panama Canal issue at an American university, Assistant Secretary of State Hewson Ryan, speaking for the department, referred to the Canal Zone as "the last remnant of imperialism."[1] This is a rather strange way for a government official to characterize the United States involvement in Panama, to say nothing of the use of the word *imperialism,* the standard epithet of the Communists regarding U.S. foreign policy.

Coupled with this State Department *mea culpa* complex over the 1903 treaty is a defensive, almost paternalistic, attitude towards Panama and all things Panamanian. In State Department circles, for example, one hears little criticism of the Panamanian government, though its military leaders are notoriously corrupt, scarcely any adverse comment on the incessant attacks against the U.S. by the government-controlled Panamanian news media, no mention of the increasing number of Communist ideologues being placed in key government positions, no expressions of resentment over the wanton misconduct of Panamanian mobs during anti-U.S. demonstrations. On the contrary, inquiries concerning such matters are met with an instantaneous defense. Seemingly to many in the State Department the Panamanians can do no wrong, or if they do wrong, it is with ample provocation or justification.

This is a charitable way to view the people of another nation. But in this case it is so overdone as to become a ridiculous form of servility. The Panamanians are, as a whole, fine people. They are, in the main, friendly towards the United States. But they are human. Their interests do not always coincide with the best interests of the United States. It is the responsibility of the State Department to protect the latter, not to defend the former.

With the strongest negotiating positions precommitted, with bargaining, of necessity, a one-way proposition, and with this extremely pro-Panamanian, almost anti-U.S., attitude of many State Department employees, it is not surprising that the negotiations were often characterized as a "stacked deck" against the United States.

That this lopsided situation did not, early in the game, result in total capitulation to Panamanian "aspirations," regardless of cost, was due mainly to two countervailing factors. One was the independence of the leadership of the U.S. negotiating team, the other the wariness of the U.S. military with regard to concessions to Panama that affect national security. Unfortunately these factors have diminished in recent years, and their braking effect on State Department zeal has been lessened appreciably.

First, the leadership. In 1964 when President Johnson launched the United States on a revolutionary policy of abrogating the 1903 treaty and negotiating an entirely new one, he picked as head of the negotiating team fellow Texan and personal friend Robert B. Anderson, a man with no State Department background. Anderson was a successful lawyer and businessman. He accepted the position on the condition that he would be directly responsible to the president, not to the secretary of state. This freed him from the internal pressures of the State Department. In addition, Anderson sought and obtained from the White House written guidelines setting the limits beyond which the negotiating team could not go in making concessions to Panama. Because of these safeguards, any tendency on the part of the State Department to run away with the negotiations was significantly curbed while Anderson was in charge.

Anderson was succeeded in 1973 by Ellsworth Bunker, then 79 years of age. Bunker's appointment by President Richard M. Nixon was made under circumstances rather different from those that prevailed when Johnson named Anderson. In the case of Anderson, President Johnson was reacting to the crisis created by the Flag War. At that moment Panama was front stage center to Johnson. At the time of the Bunker appointment, President Nixon was deeply immersed in the Watergate scandal that led to his resignation. Secretary of State Kissinger was tending the international store, and although there was something to react to—the UN Security Council's vote in support of Panama's "aspirations"—it was Kissinger who was reacting. The appointment of Bunker emanated from Kissinger, although Bunker was well known to Nixon.

Like Anderson, Bunker had been a successful businessman. But unlike Anderson, Bunker had been retired from the business world for 22 years. And during those 22 years he had held a series of important posts in the Foreign Service of the State Department, including that of U.S. representative to the Council of the OAS at the time of the Panamanian Flag War. His most recent assignment had been a six-year tour of duty as ambassador to South Vietnam. Compared with Anderson, he was thoroughly State Department oriented. In his capacity as chief of the U.S. negotiating team he was responsible directly to the secretary of state. Obviously the restraint imposed on the State Department by the independence of the negotiating team's leadership was not the same under Bunker as it was under Anderson. In 1977 President Jimmy Carter named Sol Linowitz as temporary cochief of the team. Because of Linowitz' background and predilections it is doubtful that this appointment constituted any restraint.

In fact, speculation to the contrary, and even beyond, is unavoidable. Linowitz, a lawyer and businessman, served as U.S. ambassador to the OAS during the last three years of the Johnson Administration. For three years prior to that he had been the chairman of the State Department's Advisory Committee on International Organizations. During the past several years he has been the chairman of a private group known as the Commission on United States–Latin American Relations. Two reports by that group, one issued in October 1974,[2] the other in December 1976,[3] have strongly endorsed and advocated the State Department's objectives in Panama.

Beyond this, Linowitz, at the time of his appointment as co-chief of the U.S. team negotiating with Panama, was extensively involved in Latin American business affairs. With particular reference to Panama, he was, and is, a member of the board of directors and the executive committee of the Marine-Midland Bank of New York, which is a participant in a $115 million loan to the Torrijos government—a loan that is shaky, to say the least, in the light of Panama's current economic plight.[4]

In addition, Linowitz has been registered with the Department of Justice under the Foreign Agents Registration Act as the agent of two foreign countries: Colombia and Chile. His representation of the latter country was during the time the Communist government of Salvador Allende was in power.[5]

Linowitz' appointment as an ambassador for the purpose of the Panama treaty negotiations was made for a term of sufficiently short duration to obviate the necessity for Senate confirmation. Had it been otherwise, some of the activities and affiliations just mentioned might have made his confirmation a rather difficult accomplishment. At any rate, he was hardly the man to curb the State Department zealots.

The other important factor in thwarting a possible State Department runaway in the Panamanian negotiations—in fact, until 1975 probably the more important of the two factors—had been the previously mentioned concern of the U.S. military over the Panama Canal. During the period 1964–75, because of the watchdog vigilance of the military in this regard, every position taken by the United States in the negotiations was tested in the crucible of national security. Equating the bureaucratic fixations of the Defense Department with those of the State Department, it is probable that this testing was often either misapplied or overdone. It generated constant friction between the two departments. But, given the intrinsic attitude of the State Department towards the negotiations, it did tend to enhance the protection of U.S. interests by creating a balance of viewpoints.

On the other hand, this rivalry between the two departments made the task of the chief negotiator a particularly difficult one. He had not only to direct the negotiations with Panama, but to supervise, or at least encourage, negotiation and compromise between State and Defense. From the very beginning, Bunker apparently found this to be an intolerable situation. He brought it to a head shortly after he took over. The end result was the muzzling of the military.

Defense Department personnel became particularly active and recalcitrant with regard to the negotiations after the Kissinger-Tack Statement of Principles galvanized congressional opponents of a new treaty into action in 1974. Members of Congress turned to the Pentagon for assistance. At the same time they took the opportunity of reminding the military who held the purse strings and to encourage resistance to what appeared to be a rush towards an agreement with Panama. The military responded energetically.

In the summer of 1975, exasperated by this extreme disunity in his negotiating constituency, Bunker, the architect of the Kissinger-Tack pact, made the unification of the positions of State and Defense a condition of his returning to Panama and resuming negotiations.

Kissinger, already embroiled with Secretary of Defense James R. Schlesinger over the more pressing problem of the U.S. position in Angola, took up the cudgels again over Panama. President Gerald R. Ford, who had succeeded Nixon, apparently agreed with him. As a result, word went out from the White House to the top officials in the Defense Department and in the office of the Joint Chiefs of Staff that they should go along with the State Department and stop rocking the boat in Panama, or face the consequences.

Not long after this White House ukase, Schlesinger resigned as head of Defense. The part that the Panamanian situation played in that development is a matter for conjecture. Possibly it was only an additional irritant in his more important difficulties with Kissinger. In any event, everyone else in the Pentagon played ball according to the new rules. To dramatize the new "unity" with the State Department, Deputy Secretary of Defense William P. Clements and Gen. George Brown, chairman of the Joint Chiefs, flew to Panama with Assistant Secretary of State William Rogers, met with General Torrijos, and publicly announced their support of Bunker's negotiating effort.

Having won his point, Bunker returned to Panama. Negotiations were resumed. Not long afterward, Lt. Gen. W. G. Dolvin, a distinguished, recently retired Army officer, was named to the position of chief deputy for defense on the negotiating team, a new position created to pacify and reassure the military. Significantly, Dolvin's career had never included duty in Latin America. Asked by a newsman why, with this background, or lack of it, he had been picked for the job, Dolvin is reported to have replied: "I think they wanted someone who might be part of the solution rather than part of the problem."[6] One can assume that the primary responsibility for briefing and indoctrinating Gen. Dolvin for his march into virgin territory was assumed enthusiastically by the State Department.

Through these various developments, military vigilance over the Panama treaty negotiations was disarmed. "Unification" of the positions of the State Department and the Defense Department was, apparently, mostly on State's terms. The military brake on the State Department's zeal for U.S. atonement in Panama was almost completely released.

Now all that remained was the final drive to the finish line. But another obstacle, a quadrennial one, cropped up. The 1976 U.S. presidential election year was at hand. Another ukase issued from the White House: the less said and done about the Panama Canal for the time being, the better. Thus 1976 became another hiatus in the negotiating effort. But the U.S. negotiating team was ready—and "unified." In 1977, President Carter gave it the order to plunge ahead and to reach an agreement with Panama as quickly as possible. Linowitz was the new quarterback. The military was still muzzled.

9

Playing the Hand: The Treaty Negotiations

The treaty negotiations between the United States and Panama that were completed in the summer of 1977 had been going on, or more correctly, had been going on and off, since 1964. During that period, they ran, for no apparent reason, in three-year cycles.

At the beginning there was a three-year spurt, a real drive towards an entirely new treaty arrangement. The outcome was the initialling of the three abortive and hushed-up draft treaties of 1967.

This was followed by a three-year hiatus in negotiations, the early period of the Torrijos military regime in Panama. Token negotiations began again in 1970. They rocked along with little progress until 1973 when Torrijos was successful in forcing the United States into that embarrassing veto during the UN Security Council meeting in Panama.

On orders of President Nixon a step-up in the negotiating tempo began immediately. In February 1974 came the ceremonial signing in Panama City of the Kissinger-Tack Statement of Principles. This marked the beginning of another seemingly de-

99

termined effort to arrive at a final settlement. This renewed spurt, which soon produced three "conceptual agreements," ran its course to a conclusion in three years. Torrijos himself had marked 1977 as the "or else" year. Most experts had picked it as the year of final agreement or major crisis, or both.

Before looking more closely at the negotiations, mention should be made of one item, that of a new, sea-level canal. The possibility of such a canal, for several years after 1964 a definite U.S. objective, now for ecological and financial reasons reverted to a remote possibility, has played some part in the negotiations all along and could surface again in connection with the ratification proceedings.

Although talk of another trans-isthmian canal and of routes other than the one established across Panama has never died down completely, it was not until the late 1950s and the early 1960s, when the questions of the Panama Canal's vulnerability to military attack and its capability of handling the traffic of the future assumed seemingly urgent proportions, that a new sea-level canal received serious consideration. This consideration was enhanced by the purported availability of nuclear excavation techniques that would speed up such a project and reduce its cost.

In 1964 the United States, as part of the reaction to the Flag War crisis, took the first official step in the direction of a sea-level canal. Congress enacted legislation establishing the Atlantic-Pacific Interoceanic Study Commission, giving it a mandate to make a study and to recommend a suitable site for such a canal. In December 1964, when President Johnson announced the policy of negotiating an entirely new treaty with Panama, he coupled it with the announcement of his decision to go forward with "plans and preparations for a sea-level canal."[1] He named Robert Anderson as chairman of the new study commission, as well as chief of the new treaty negotiations.

Ever since that time the negotiations have included the possibility of a new canal in Panama. Naturally, if such a canal were to be built in some other country, the effect on Panama would be disastrous. However, as far as can be determined, the threat of that eventuality has never been used by the United States as a trading position in the treaty negotiations. Its potential for that purpose was diminished considerably in 1970 when the final report of the study commission was made public. The commission recommended that a new, sea-level canal be built in Pan-

100

ama, not far from the present Canal, but to the east of the Canal Zone.[2]

The commission concluded that "the technical feasibility of the use of nuclear explosives for sea-level canal excavation has not been established."[3] Thus the possibility of great cost savings went out the window. The subject of a new sea-level canal lay relatively dormant from that time until late in July 1977. Out of the blue, President Carter stated in a press conference that the prospects for such a canal were again under consideration.[4] This statement was made in the context of a need to transport Alaskan oil from the west coast to eastern ports, but it may also have been a ploy by the president to nudge Panama toward the final agreement on the new treaties that was reached a few weeks later.

Obviously a new canal would involve a whole new ball game either with Panama or some other isthmian nation or nations— new treaty, or treaties, new duration, all of the old problems in a new setting, and presumably a host of additional ones. Nevertheless, the possibility cannot be ignored.

The threshold of the last two phases of the negotiations was, of course, the Kissinger-Tack Statement of Principles of February 1974. In the light of that agreement it became certain that if the negotiations were to run their course successfully, there would be a new treaty with the following major features: (1) a fixed termination date, instead of duration in perpetuity, (2) recognition of Panama's sovereignty over the Canal Zone, (3) the prompt transfer to Panama of jurisdiction and control over the Zone, (4) joint operation of the Canal geared to Panama's assuming total operational responsibility at the end of the treaty, (5) an increase in the "economic benefits" to be derived by Panama from the operation of the Canal, (6) joint defense of the Canal, and (7) provisions "for new projects which will enlarge canal capacity."[5] (This last may mean that as of February 7, 1974, the U.S. had abandoned any idea of a new canal.)

Whether or not such a treaty would ultimately be ratified by the United States and Panama (under the present Panamanian constitution a national plebiscite is required for ratification) is beside the point at the moment. The point then was that by virtue of the Kissinger-Tack pronouncement the way had been clearly marked for the negotiating teams of the two countries to arrive at a new treaty, if that was what both countries wanted.

The negotiations proceeded on the basis of a well-defined

procedural technique. Its principal feature is the negotiation of a series of preliminary conceptual agreements, which then become the framework for the ultimate treaty. There are four steps in the overall process:

(1) Identifying the major issues to be resolved by the treaty.

(2) Negotiating an agreement on the "concepts," or basic principles, to be applied in resolving each of those issues. (These agreements are the so-called conceptual agreements. The reaching of a conceptual agreement with regard to a particular issue does not mean that the issue itself has been finally resolved. It means only that the ground rules for its resolution have been at least tentatively settled.)

(3) Negotiating, on the basis of the conceptual agreement for each issue, the treaty language covering the resolution of that issue.

(4) Integrating into a final treaty the sets of language negotiated under (3).

The conceptual agreements arrived at in the second step of this procedure obviously become the building blocks with which the final treaty structure will be fashioned. Each of them is, therefore, highly significant in regard to what the final terms on the particular issue it covers will be.

The conceptual agreement technique of negotiating is orderly and, in theory at least, thorough. It also is conducive to a leisurely negotiating pace and to stalling. With the number and complexity of issues and subissues involved in the Panamanian treaty negotiations, the final result could be conscientiously delayed indefinitely by either side.

The negotiations were carried on in secret. Until the spring of 1977 the negotiating sessions were usually held on the charming island of Contadora, 30 miles off the Pacific coast of Panama. Contadora is not readily accessible to either news media representatives or to demonstrators. But, as in all secret proceedings, leaks occurred. In fact, leaking negotiation secrets back on the mainland became a tactic commonly used by the Panamanians whenever it served their political purposes. By the same token, "signalling," both ashore and on Contadora, became a common tool in the hands of the United States—signalling to the appropriate Panamanian officials what concessions from the United States they might expect even though official indications were otherwise, a method of placating a negotiating adversary that tends to develop public tantrums. The State Department dislikes these tantrums exceedingly. Signalling is a handy pacifier. And the information signalled, as might be expected, was often leaked by the Panamanians, if to do so was helpful to whatever public posture Panama was assuming at the moment.

This leaking-signalling by-play was another unique feature, in addition to those discussed in the preceding chapter, of the U.S.-Panama negotiations. Unique because, while only one side did the leaking, both sides were the instigators.

Because the negotiations were conducted in secret, it might be supposed that it would be impossible to determine where the negotiations stood at the beginning of 1977. However, that is not completely the case. Not because of leaks or signals, but because of an angry Panamanian foreign minister, the world learned in the fall of 1975 that as of that time three conceptual agreements had already been reached and that the negotiations were moving along favorably from Panama's standpoint, notwithstanding presidential campaign rhetoric to the contrary in the United States. Foreign Minister Tack's angry announcement was precipitated by Kissinger's statement in Florida that the U.S. would retain its right to defend the Canal indefinitely. The existence of the three agreements was subsequently confirmed in the United States, and their texts became available.

The three conceptual agreements that are known to have been reached covered (1) Panamanian jurisdiction and control over the Canal Zone, (2) joint operation of the Canal, and (3) joint defense of the Canal.

There was no secret, of course, about the major issues remaining to be covered by agreements of the same type, since the list of all of the issues stemmed directly from the Kissinger-Tack Statement of Principles of 1974. They were, to complete the numerical sequence: (4) increased "economic benefits" to be derived by Panama from Canal operations, (5) designation of the land and water areas that would be needed by the United States to carry out operational and defense responsibilities during the new treaty period, (6) arrangements for expanding the capacity of the present Canal (and, perhaps, for constructing a new one), and (7) duration of the new treaty.[6]

A large order? Yes, and particularly when one considers the innumerable subissues that are included within each of these major ones. But not an impossible one, given the unusual characteristics of these negotiations and the fact that three of the "Big Four" (sovereignty, operations, defense, and duration) had already been disposed of.

As a means of seeing how far things had gone when the U.S. presidential election year caused a long pause, and, at the same time, of seeing where they seemed to be headed, a look at the principal features of the three conceptual agreements that had been reached at that time is illuminating.

First, the one dealing with Panamanian jurisdiction over the Canal Zone.[7] The issue this conceptual agreement covered was seemingly, at least at that time, *the* issue so far as Panama was concerned, and probably *the* issue so far as most Americans are concerned, the issue of *sovereignty*. And by this conceptual agreement that issue was resolved, at least tentatively, in no uncertain terms.

The agreement provided that the moment the new treaty became effective "U.S. jurisdiction over the Panamanian territory known as the Canal Zone shall cease." It provided that the moment the new treaty became effective "the U.S. entity known as the Canal Zone Government shall immediately terminate." And it provided that the moment the new treaty became effective "the Republic of Panama, in the exercise of its sovereignty, shall reassume general police authority in that part of its territory known as the Canal Zone."

To this last-quoted provision there was an exception. There would be specified in the new treaty the areas needed by the U.S. to carry out continuing operational and defense responsibilities. In those areas, the agreement provided that "the Republic of Panama will *grant* the United States police authority *up to a period of three years.*" (Emphasis added.) But even during that short period, in those same areas a system of joint police patrols would be set up so that the Panamanian police could arrest "Panamanian and third country nationals." And after the three-year period the United States would have no further police or civil authority whatsoever over either its own citizens or members of its armed forces, and "U.S. courts of law in the old Canal Zone shall cease operations."

What about schools, public utilities, hospitals, and fire protection currently furnished by the United States in the old Canal Zone? Who was going to provide those services and foot the bill for them? Panama? Not at all. The agreement spelled out the "concept" that the United States would be given by Panama "the operational rights" to render those services. Apparently, lest this provision might seem to denigrate Panamanian sovereignty, it was further provided that these activities should be carried out by the United States "in line with the exercise of jurisdiction by the Republic of Panama over its territory."

In other words, the United States government in exercising its "operational rights" to furnish these essential services would be subject to regulation by the Panamanian government. As to performance standards, school curricula, and textbooks? As to the chemical content of domestic water? As to rates for electricity? As to hospital procedures? As to fire prevention safety requirements? Presumably. The agreement did not say.

There were many more provisions in this conceptual agreement on jurisdiction over the Canal Zone, but these were the major features. What has been described is probably sufficient to indicate the overall concept that would govern the final treaty provisions in this regard. It is difficult to see how the United States could function as a government under such a "concept." As an agent of Panama, yes. As a government, no.

The conceptual agreement covering joint operation of the Canal, entitled simply "Increased Panamanian Participation,"[8] was far more vague than the one on jurisdiction over the Canal Zone. However, the preamble did recite the clear objective of the new treaty in this regard: "The primary objective of Panamanian participation is to guarantee that Panama is prepared to assume the complete responsibility for the efficient operation of the interoceanic waterway when the treaty expires."

The preamble went on to state that this objective was to be attained by making sure that there would be a sufficient number of qualified Panamanians on hand when the time came for Panama to operate the Canal on her own. That, too, seemed clear enough.

Then the fog rolled in. The agreement assigned to the United States the "primary responsibility for canal operations and the transit of ships" during the life of the treaty. But in the same breath it called for the immediate elimination of the Panama Canal Company, the present U.S. operating agency. In its place there was to be "a new administrative body, government or otherwise." But it did not say how this "body" would be constituted, or by whom. Since the United States would still have "primary responsibility" for the operation of the Canal, presumably it would be given control. On the other hand, maybe not.

105

Perhaps the negotiators were unable at that time to reach agreement on this crucial point.

As to the building up of a sufficient number of Panamanian personnel qualified to take over the entire operation of the Canal, there were references to employment and promotional preferences for Panamanian citizens and to "a growing participation on the part of Panamanian nationals at all levels and fields of employment in the canal operation, including participation in the drafting of overall policies as well as in daily operations." All this, in principle at least, seemed clear enough.

But it seems logical that this conceptual agreement, dealing as it did, among other things, with employment rights and practices, would have contained some concepts about the rights and interests of the key U.S. employees, such as Canal pilots and engineers, whose willingness to remain at their posts would be essential to the success of any transitional program. There is not a word on this, perhaps because it would not sit well in Panamanian labor circles. Failure to provide firm assurances from both governments to this group of key U.S. personnel could lead to the paralyzing result of a mass exodus. Maybe this is another vital area in which the negotiators either ducked the issue or had been unable to agree.

The third known conceptual agreement was the one covering the joint defense of the Canal.[9] And here the fog was dense, so dense that it is difficult to achieve any reasonable grasp of the concepts that had been arrived at on this issue.

One exception to that generality was the concept of what would happen when the treaty expired. On this the language was quite clear: "Upon the expiration of the treaty, Panama shall take over total responsibility for the protection and defense of the waterway." But this clarity was in itself confusing, because such unequivocal language seemed to fly right in the face of repeated assertion by highly placed U.S. officials that under any new treaty arrangements U.S. defense rights would continue indefinitely.

As to the defense situation during the life of the new treaty, the conceptual agreement recited that the "United States shall have the main responsibility." Not the *primary* responsibility, as in the case of joint Canal operations, but the *main* responsibility. What was the significance of this selection of words? *Main* seems to connote a lesser degree of ultimate responsibility than *primary*. If that is so, then the negotiators seemed to be saying that as far as Canal defense was concerned, as distinguished from Canal operations, although the United States would carry the heavier, the "main" burden, ultimate responsibility would be shared equally by both governments, one not being "primary" in relation to the other.

Then how were these relative responsibilities, whatever their relationship, to be carried out? Who was to be in command? Who was to make the decisions on military countermeasures in the event of an attack? Let the conceptual agreement itself answer these questions:

Answer No. 1: "Both parties shall establish a Joint Board, composed of high level Panamanian and U.S. military representatives, *in equal number*, whose respective governments shall entrust them with consulting and cooperating in all matters relative to the defense of the Canal, and planning the measures which shall be taken jointly to ensure the security or neutrality of the Canal." (Emphasis added.)

Answer No. 2: "Each of the parties, in accordance with its constitutional procedures, shall act to face the common danger arising out of an armed attack or other action which might threaten the security of the waterway and the transit of ships."

Answer No. 1 seems to say there would be a single, two-headed command. Answer No. 2 seems to say there would be two independent commands, each going its own way. The mind boggles at the thought of what would happen under either concept in the event of attack: under Answer No. 1, paralysis, under Answer No. 2, chaos.

It is hard to believe that any military man in his right mind, U.S. or Panamanian, participated in arriving at this conceptual agreement. Apparently the U.S. military was not just muzzled at the time. It must have been hog-tied as well. (In fairness to Gen. Dolvin, it should be pointed out that this agreement had been completed before he joined the U.S. negotiating team.)

Considering all three of these agreements, and particularly in the face of the musical comedy absurdity of the one on defense, it was difficult to guess what might transpire with regard to the four remaining major issues. Two of them, "economic benefits" and duration, were hardly susceptible to either vague or Alice-in-Wonderland concepts. But as to the other two, land and water areas the U.S. would need and the treatment of the question of either enlarged Canal capacity or a new canal, it was conceivable, given the negotiating performances demonstrated by the

107

joint operation and joint defense conceptual agreements, that more fuzziness, even madness, could emanate.

While the conceptual agreement on defense of the Canal was beyond all understanding, except perhaps as an out-and-out Panamanian propaganda gimmick, one measurement seemed to emerge from the other two. If the issue covered were one of paramount importance to Panama, involving both rights *and* *responsibilities* willingly assumed, as was the case with the issue of sovereignty, the concepts developed would be clear and direct. But where, as in the issue of joint operation of the Canal, Panama's objectives were certain up to a point, but beyond that subject to reservations, the clarity and directness of the concepts would vary accordingly. Thus in the case of joint Canal operations, the concept of more jobs for Panamanians is expressed clearly; the concept of more responsibility for Panama is clouded over.

Applying this yardstick to the remaining issues, it was reasonable to conclude that where Panama knew what she wanted she would get it and the concepts would be expressed clearly. Otherwise they would be couched in vague, even inconsistent, terms. This would mean that in the case of the economic benefits issue, the concepts would probably be clear up to the point of assuring a minimum guaranteed amount of money to Panama and vague as to additional possibilities. As to the land and water areas needed by the U.S., the concepts would probably be clear as to the maximum limit, but hazy up to that point, assuming one can be hazy in describing geographical areas. On Canal capacity and a possible new canal, they would be clear as to the former, vague as to the latter.

On the final issue, the duration of the new treaty, it was fairly well known that Panama would accept the end of the century as the termination date. One could expect, therefore, a clear concept fixing that date. However, if Panama had reservations about her ability to go it alone after that date, it would not have been surprising to find in this conceptual agreement some vague concept giving Panama the right to extend the treaty duration unilaterally to keep U.S. operating ability, financial assistance, and military support as long as she wanted them.

Since final agreement has been reached on the proposed new treaties, it may seem odd to have dwelt at such length on the three known conceptual agreements. They were merely a part of the process that produced the end result. Now, of course, they are water over the dam, absorbed in the final arrangement. Nevertheless, they provide the only real insight available into the negotiations themselves, and although they cover only a part, they are quite revealing of what must have been the attitudes and trends throughout.

When the negotiations resumed in the fall of 1976, after the election of Jimmy Carter to the presidency but before his inauguration, they were probably rather meaningless, maybe just congenial reunions on Contadora Island, time killers. There was to be a new U.S. administration, a new secretary of state, perhaps a new policy, maybe new negotiators.

However, the veil of secrecy was restored and remained in place from then on. There were, of course, the usual leaks and signals, but no petulant Panamanian official again gave the show away, at least textually. So the revelations contained in the three known conceptual agreements, three of the important cornerstones of the final structure, have much to contribute towards an understanding of how one-sided negotiations, a "stacked deck," are carried on. They also afford a background helpful in evaluating the final outcome.

It is not publicly known whether the conceptual agreement technique was used in completing the negotiations under President Carter. Probably not, because of the pressure imposed on the negotiators for a speedy wind-up.

According to news reports, June 1, 1977, was picked by the Carter Administration as the target date for a new treaty. After a few more sessions in Panama, the negotiations were moved from peaceful Contadora to bustling, bureaucratic Washington, D.C. The sessions were long and frequent. Speed was the controlling factor. It is hard to visualize the brick-by-brick procedures of the conceptual agreement technique functioning under such extreme circumstances. In fact, it is not unlikely that the remaining major matters in dispute were resolved by an auction technique with a strange twist: the United States acting as both auctioneer and high bidder.

June 1 went by with no final agreement. Money was apparently the stumbling block. It was rumored in the press that the Torrijos government was demanding a billion dollars down and $300 million a year during the life of the new treaty, a package of close to $7 billion. This was a big jump from the $20–$25 million figure with no down payment that had long been considered to be mutually acceptable before Linowitz began calling the U.S. signals.

On July 29 President Carter intervened personally in the negotiations for the first time, meeting with the negotiating teams of both countries, praising their work, expressing optimism over the ultimate outcome, and urging them to reach an early agreement. The same day he sent a letter to Gen. Torrijos, flattering him for his major role in the successful progress of the negotiations, but politely warning him that if he did not keep his money demands within reason, his, Carter's, difficulties in getting U.S. Senate approval of the new treaty would be insurmountable.[10]

This apparently did the trick. On August 10, back in Panama City for dramatic effect, the chief negotiators for the United States and Panama appeared at a crowded news conference and announced that they had reached "agreement in principle" on "the basic elements" of a new treaty.[11] Only the drafting of final language remained.

The 13 years of negotiations had come to an end. The strange card game was over.

10

Will the Real Panama Please Stand Up: Panama Today and Tomorrow[1]

On November 4, 1978, the Republic of Panama will be 75 years old. Not very old by normal standards, a mere fledgling. But compared to some of the younger nations of the Third World, quite hoary.

In the preceding chapters something has been seen of Panama in the process of being born. Something has been seen of her growing up, economically and nationalistically, during and after World War II. But nothing definitive, no real measure of her national stature.

Now Panama is seeking to assume vast responsibilities, in fact to take the place of the United States in a unique enterprise that is of great importance to the entire world, and of particular importance to the United States, to Panama, and to many Latin American nations.

Is Panama capable of fulfilling these responsibilities? This is the $64,000 question, and it must be answered correctly if the issue of the Panama Canal is to be resolved in fairness to all concerned. People will differ in the way they answer it, depending on their sympathies, their emotions, and their prejudices.

111

But those factors should play no part. Glib references to "banana republics" and "tinhorn dictators" will contribute nothing. Nor will pious deprecations of the United States.

Only the realities count, the realities of Panama today and Panama tomorrow. Panama has a right, as well as a reason, to aspire as she does. She also has the obligation to be judged, and judged objectively.

How does one judge the capabilities of a nation to perform a task of the magnitude of governing the Panama Canal Zone and operating, maintaining, and defending the Panama Canal? Panama has no experience or background, governmentally, economically, or militarily, by which such performance can be gauged.

The only way to answer the question is to look at Panama as she is today and may be tomorrow, to look at her in the light of the three basic elements of any nation: her people, her economy, and her government. Having done that, the task of determining Panama's capabilities becomes one of measuring the duties and responsibilities she seeks against the revealed strengths and weaknesses of her national makeup.

This is easy to say, not easy to do. The people, the economy, the government. These three elements may be of equal importance in the evaluation of a nation for some purposes. But for the purpose of sizing up Panama with regard to the Canal, they obviously are not equal. Particular weight must be given to the last two, the economy and the government. For people can be the finest in the world, but without an adequate economy and able leadership they do not make an effective nation. By the same token, even if the people are good and the economy is sound, poor leadership can disqualify a nation for international responsibilities.

Nevertheless, the people are important. They give character to a nation. The will of the people, or the lack of it, has a bearing on a nation's capability.

Who are the people of Panama? What are they like? First a few statistics. There are about 1.7 million Panamanians. They live in an area half the size of Florida. Much of it is impenetrable jungle. But there are parts of it that are habitable and cultivable, a varied terrain of fertile valleys, mountainous plateaus, and alluvial plains. It is hot and humid, with an average annual rainfall of 105 inches.

Seventy-one percent of the people are *mestizo*, part Spanish, part Indian; 13 percent are black, 10 percent white, 6 percent pure Indian. Spanish is the official and native tongue, but English is widely spoken. Roman Catholicism is the dominant religion.

The black population stems mostly from the West Indies, from the workers who came to Panama to build the Canal. They speak English more often than Spanish, clipped British English. This language preference, probably more than color, tended to create the relatively few racial problems there were in Panama until recently. Now those problems arise from the usual source, demographic and economic pressures.

Many of the people, almost half of them, are crowded into the sprawling metropolitan area of Panama City and into the other two cities of any size, Colon and David. David is the capital of the large western province of Chiriqui, where much of the nation's agricultural activity takes place.

As in the rest of Latin America, there is a wide disparity between the incomes of the small wealthy class and the major portion of the population. Since World War II, however, a middle class of some size and substance has been developing, particularly in metropolitan Panama City. Mass movement to the cities has produced the usual quotas of slums and ghettos. But in both the urban and rural areas extreme poverty is less prevalent than in most other parts of Latin America. In fact, the Panamanian per capita income, around $1000, is the third highest in Latin America. The literacy rate, close to 80 percent, is the fourth highest.

The "oligarchy" that traditionally, until 1968, ruled Panama through a facade of parliamentary government (but at that a system far more democratic than the present regime) is a small group of wealthy families that at one time owned much of the productive land and most of the successful business enterprises of Panama. Most of them have been educated in the United States, or elsewhere outside Panama. They are, in the main, a highly intelligent, cosmopolitan, and energetic group, seemingly capable of able national leadership if they were sincerely and demonstratively concerned with improving the lot of their fellow Panamanians.

The oligarchists are not typical. The average Panamanian is inclined to be lazy and indifferent. After all, it is hot and humid in Panama, and tomorrow is another day.

The Panamanians are likeable, friendly people. As a rule they

113

appear to be fond of Americans and to recognize instinctively and favorably the close ties, the traditional bond, between the two countries.

This is not true, however, in the Panama City and Colon areas, close to the Canal. Here Panamanians are inclined to make a distinction based upon their antipathy towards the Americans who live in the Canal Zone. This feeling of dislike for the so-called Zonians has increased greatly in recent years as a result of the steady barrage of propoganda against the "imperialists" and the "colonialists" laid down by the government-owned news media, and the constant exploitation of the Canal issue by Panamanian politicians. And it has been considerably exacerbated over the years by the arrogant and condescending attitude of many of the Zonians towards Panama and Panamanians. Unfortunately, because of this irritant, there is a tendency on the part of the urban Panamanians to lump all Zonians together as being undesirables. *Yanqui* go home!

Still, the distinction remains clear. If an American identifies himself as not living in the Zone, he is immediately treated in a friendly way. But until that identification has been established, he is almost certain to be persona non grata.

The Panamanian activists on the Canal issue—the demonstrators, the rioters, the graffiti artists—are to be found mostly in Panama City and Colon. They consist of various left-wing groups, particularly those within the high schools and the university. The student groups seem susceptible of being turned on or off at will by those who wish to use them for their purposes.

The further one gets away from the Canal Zone, the less one finds in the way of strong feeling, or even an interest or concern, about the Canal. Seemingly some Panamanians in the rural areas are completely unaware of the existence of the Canal, much less of any problem between the United States and Panama with regard to it. The story is told that on one of his recent surprise visits to the remote areas General Torrijos asked a local agricultural worker, a *campesino*, "What do you think about the Canal?" It happens that in Spanish *canal* also means "channel." Panama has two television outlets, Channel 2 and Channel 4. The *campesino* is said to have replied to Torrijos, "Qual canal, numero dos o numero quatro?" Hardly the basis for a national crusade.

These, then, are the people of Panama. To say that they dislike Americans and want the United States to disappear from their

114

lives would be an untruth. The opposite seems to be the case. To say that they dislike the Americans living in the Canal Zone would be true. And to say that most Panamanians, particularly those living in the neighborhood of the Canal Zone but also a great many living elsewhere, resent intensely the denial of Panama's sovereignty over the Zone would be stating the situation correctly, even mildly.

The people of Panama want desperately to control the Canal Zone area. It is a national "thing" with them, a matter of pride, of identity. But to conclude from this that the people of Panama have either the will to operate and defend the Canal, or the desire to oust the United States from that responsibility, would be a mistake.

At the beginning of this book it was observed that perhaps the only thing Panama really has going for it is the Canal. An analysis of the nation's economy bears this out.

True, there are a lot of other things happening in Panama from an economic standpoint, and the principal ones should be accounted for. But if the Canal were taken out of the picture, the basic economy of Panama would be extremely shaky and the outlook for the future quite dismal.

Panama's annual gross national product (GNP) is about $1.2 billion. Almost a fourth of that is derived directly from the Canal, from within the Canal Zone: the annual payments from the U.S., the wages paid by the U.S. to Panamanians working in the Zone, and the goods and services purchased by the U.S. in the Republic of Panama for Canal purposes. All in all, these items total about $300 million. If you add to this figure the portion of GNP attributable to the commercial activity generated in the Republic of Panama by the Canal, it is fair to say that nearly half of Panama's economy has its roots in the Canal.

How to characterize the other half is a problem. Certainly it is not industrial. Manufacturing accounts for less than 15 percent of GNP. What there is of it is small manufacturing. Mostly for local consumption, it consists primarily of construction materials and consumer goods such as processed foods, beverages, clothing, leather goods, and furniture.

How about agriculture? Here, again, the figures are surprising. Bananas and sugar are the major products. They also are Panama's principal exports. Other items produced in significant quantities, some sufficient for export, are rice, corn, coffee, beans, and tobacco. Then, stretching the term agriculture a bit,

115

there are the fish and shrimp that are caught, the cattle that are raised, the trees that are felled. But when it is all added up, agriculture accounts for only 16 percent of Panama's GNP. And what comes as quite a shocker is the fact that almost 50 percent of the foodstuff consumed in Panama is imported!

What about the service industries? They, of course, exist, particularly in the metropolitan areas. But the principal servicing activities are related to the commercial needs generated by the Canal, right back where we started. They constitute a third of the GNP. And they represent the element of the Panamanian economy that appears to have the greatest potential for growth. For the future of Panama's economy seems to lie primarily in the advantages of her geographical location and configuration, the fact that she is ideally suited from a physical standpoint to be a crossroads of trade, a hub of international commerce. That is where her future began. That is apparently where her future lies.

Thus far the basic ingredients of the Panamanian economy have been reviewed. But the picture is incomplete if its other important features, and its anomalies, are not brought into focus as well.

For example, the high per capita income figure for Panama, fourth highest in Latin America, seems somewhat out of proportion in the light of the basic factors just considered. It *is* out of proportion, except for the portion of it represented by the income attributable to the Canal and Canal-related activities. The remaining portion is distorted by the fact that the United States lavishes financial assistance on Panama. On a per capita basis, Panama receives more financial aid from the U.S. than any other nation in the world: $200 million in grants and loans from the U.S. Agency for International Development (AID) during the last 15 years. In 1976 alone the AID program amounted to $22 million. Most of this assistance is directed towards the rural areas of Panama, where the poverty is greatest.

The banking business is an important but misleading feature of the present economy. Banking activity has a very high profile in Panama. Much of it has developed in recent years.

There are now nearly 80 separate banking institutions operating in economically diminutive Panama, almost all of them foreign, many of them U.S. owned. These banks were lured into Panama by the Torrijos government through laws highly favorable to "offshore" transactions: no tax on incomes from loans

116

and investments made *outside* Panama, no restrictions on taking money out of the country, no exchange controls (the Panamanian currency, the balboa, is tied to and used interchangeably with the U.S. dollar), no impediments to Swiss-type numbered accounts. As a result of these enticements, many Latin American individuals and businesses in countries with softer currencies and stricter regulations have been pouring money into the Panama-based banks. The deposits now total about $9 billion.

This has made Panama an important center for financial activity throughout Latin America, but aside from the prestige factor, it has so far benefited Panama only marginally. The banks do furnish employment to some 17,000 people. And some of them in the early 1970s made rather substantial loans to the construction industry, setting off a boom in that industry and an attendant proliferation of high-rise buildings in Panama City, a bonanza while it lasted, now a headache of unfinished structures and unoccupied office and apartment space.

Still, the international banking activity in Panama should not be downgraded. It is only that up until now it has tended to distort the true picture of Panama's economy. It is not, fundamentally, a local enterprise or a contributor to the local economy. But the development of it was probably a wise move. For if in the future it can be successfully integrated into an economic structure increasingly oriented towards commercial servicing, it can make a tremendous contribution. It is there, established, and available to make such a contribution when, and if, conditions warrant.

There are two components of Panama's economy that bear special watching. One is the Colon Free Zone. Panamanian officials claim this free zone to be "the world's largest after Hong Kong," housing over 300 companies representing more than 800 firms. In 1975 the Free Zone's gross volume of business (both exports and imports) was about $950 million, twice what it was five years before. Many financial experts share the view that this is a natural business activity for Panama, one that fits well into a commerce-servicing economy and one that probably should have been initiated long ago.

The other economic component to keep an eye on is the presence in Panama of rather large mineral deposits. One ore body currently being developed by a U.S. company in conjunction with the Panamanian government, the Cerro Colorado Project, contains reserves estimated at over a billion tons of ore with a 0.6 percent copper content. Because of the deposit's isolated location and the complete absence in Panama of any infrastructure, the commercial feasibility of this development is still in doubt. But inevitably the day will come. And there are indications of other mineral resource potentialities, quite substantial for a country of Panama's size.

This, then, is a birdseye view of the economy of Panama, or, rather, of the bits and pieces that go into it. For the economy is a melange that eludes characterization in usual terms.

What does it all add up to? Its one dominant feature is obviously the Canal. The rest is a conglomerate of activities, many of them relatively unproductive, some of them with considerable potential, others, for example, agriculture, seemingly unable to surmount heavy odds.

The basic economy of Panama, at least *ex* the Canal, would probably be best classified as insubstantial and vulnerable. In the light of its present condition the latter term is particularly apt. For Panama's economy appears to be badly wounded.

Here the statistics are far from dry. The Torrijos government seized power in 1968 when the Panamanian economy was riding the crest of a wave that began in the early 1960s. The rate of growth was an astounding 8 percent. Then, in 1974, the wave began to recede. According to the experts, this was partly because of a late catch-up with a worldwide economic recession, partly because of the cumulative effect of government profligacy, government interference, and government corruption.

By 1975 the excuse of outside economic conditions was gone. Things were picking up everywhere in Latin America. Everywhere, that is, except Panama. By 1977 Panama's economy was a shambles.

The economic growth rate had sunk from 8 percent to less than one percent. Unemployment had risen to 20 percent. Deficit spending by the government had reached the point where it exceeded 50 percent of the annual budget.

The national debt had risen from $167 million in 1968 to an estimated $1.5 billion in 1977, almost a 1000 percent increase in eight years. The per capita debt had become the largest in all of Latin America. The annual interest payment on the national debt alone had reached $150 million, almost half of the current revenue taken in by the government.

118

The balance of payments, that is, the annual measurement of exports against imports, stood at a staggering minus $500 million, almost half of GNP.

There is no need to go on. Suffice it to say that Panama, financed for the past several years by loans from abroad, most of them short-term and derived principally from the Eurocurrency market (there is no central bank in Panama), has just about run out of credit. Three-fourths of the current debt will come due within the next 10 years.

Up until 1968, Panama's governments changed quite often. In 1968 Arnulfo Arias, Panama's perennial populist, twice elected, twice ousted (1941, 1951), was for the third time elected president of Panama, this time by the largest popular majority in Panamanian history. But 11 days after he took office he was out again.

Arias had made the mistake during his election campaign and afterward of indicating an intention to shake up the Guardia Nacional, the national police force–army, when he took office. He never got the chance. The Guardia, or, more correctly, a lower echelon segment of it, in a carefully executed move, beat him to the punch and seized the government.

This happened on October 11, 1968. The event has ever since been called by those who engineered it the "People's Revolution." It was hardly that. The people had just expressed their will, overwhelmingly, in favor of Arias. It was just another Latin American–style coup d'etat by what passes in Panama for the military.

But the man who rose immediately to the top of the heap, Omar Torrijos Herrera, quickly captured the imagination of the people of Panama. Born and raised in the impoverished sugar-and-rice-growing province of Veraguas, the seventh of twelve children in a poor family, Torrijos soon demonstrated a knack for populism that put Arias to shame. He also demonstrated a knack for seizing and holding power, total power.

He immediately banished the National Assembly, declared political parties "extinct," and took over the news media. He sent into "exile" any ambitious politicians who threatened his leadership. One of the first to go was his fellow conspirator and Guardia officer, Boris Martinez, reputed to have been the "brains" of the revolt (Torrijos being the "guts"). Panamanians do not ordinarily shoot their "undesirables"; they deport them. Martinez was whisked off by plane to Miami, Florida, often referred to in Panama as the *Valle de los Caidos* ("Valley of the Fallen").

In 1972 carefully controlled elections were held for a new Assembly of Community Representatives decreed by Torrijos. This body, consisting of 505 members, heavily weighted in favor of the rural areas, adopted a new constitution presented to it by Torrijos. The constitution contained a provision designating Torrijos, by name, to be "the maximum leader of the Peoples Revolution" with complete and exclusive power to govern Panama for the following six years.

Including the period before the adoption of the new constitution, Torrijos has now ruled for almost 10 years, the longest continuous single government in Panama's 74 years. Under the constitution, his "term" expires in 1978. Then there are supposed to be elections. *Vamos a ver.*

Until recently, Torrijos' rule was not considered unduly oppressive as military dictatorships go. And he has done a great many things to improve the lot of his fellow *campesinos.* He has launched an extensive land reform program. With massive help from the U.S. AID program, he has opened more than 350 health centers in the remote villages. With that same help he has been promoting modern farming methods among the peasants and encouraging family planning. New schools and low-cost housing developments have proliferated. So have new water systems for villages that never had them before, new roads, and new buildings—all things that can be readily seen and pointed out as government good works. Never before have the rural people of Panama seen so much evidence of their government's concern for them. They have benefited considerably.

Governing in Latin America has always involved some degree of graft and corruption. Panama, during its short history, has been no exception. Traditionally the political leaders supported by the oligarchy have feathered their nests while in office and then moved on to give their successors a chance. Nor has the top echelon of the Guardia Nacional missed out on a share of the loot.

But the new leader of Panama and his henchmen came from the lower echelons of the guard. They were not versed in the big-time art of making money out of political leadership. As a result, for the first few years of the Torrijos regime there was, from all accounts, a rather unique absence of dishonesty in high places. This did not last long; Torrijos and his "five colonels" (the governing phalanx just below him) caught on quickly, and soon they were involved in the orthodox "protection" rackets—prostitution, dope, and contraband.

That was just the beginning. Torrijos is a socialist. He calls his brand of socialism the "Scandinavian type." At any rate, it was not long before the Torrijos government began to move aggressively into the private enterprise sectors of the economy. All Panamanian utilities were taken over—power, water, and communication systems—and their services greatly expanded geographically. In the manufacturing field, the government went into the cement business, as a "service" to the construction industry. In agriculture, the government went into the sugar business, building sugar mills, again as a "service." The government went into the banana business whole hog, expropriating all of the plantations of the United Brands Company, successor to United Fruit, the colossus of the Latin American banana industry. Where the government is not directly involved in agriculture, it spends lavishly on subsidies and price supports.

The justification for all this government activity has been, of course, stimulation of the economy. But there are many indications that the motives have not been all that lofty and selfless, that Torrijos and his five colonels have successfully skimmed the cream off the top of every business enterprise the government has undertaken. Torrijos himself is reputed to have become a millionaire many times over, one of the richest men in all Latin America.

The government's stance toward the areas of private enterprise that it has not chosen to enter or usurp is one common to states that espouse labor-socialism. Legislation, or, more correctly, government fiat, with the exception of that applied to the international banking business, tends to be highly restrictive. There is a close interrelationship between the government and the trade unions.

One law that has caused particular havoc in the private sector is a prohibition against the discharge of a worker, regardless of cause. Another is one forbidding a landlord from ousting a tenant for failure to pay rent.

The relatively high wages paid by the U.S. to Panamanians working in the Canal Zone and the high minimum wage rates established by the Torrijos government for work outside the Zone have caused the Panamanian wage structure to be higher than it is in most parts of Latin America. This makes it difficult for Panamanian products to compete in world markets.

Politicians are not the only people "exiled" by the government. Businessmen who speak out against government policies and practices often share the same fate. Not very long ago 12 of them were shipped out at the same time when they protested a large government sale of rice to Cuba at a price well below the market.

Torrijos is often labeled a Communist. This probably is not literally true, although many of his relatives and close associates are apparently staunch Marxist-Leninists. He is a professed admirer of Fidel Castro. And the military fatigue uniform he wears constantly and the Havana cigars he smokes incessantly (supplied by Castro) indicate, if not hero worship, at least a strong tendency to emulate.

One of the first moves made by Torrijos when he seized power was to declare all political parties "extinct." But this declaration was never enforced against what is commonly referred to as the Communist party of Panama, officially known as the People's Party. Although it may not be an integral part of the international Communist network, this organization is sufficiently Marxist-Leninist oriented to be labeled at least communist with a small *c*. It has been permitted to function openly, the only political faction so privileged.

In running the government Torrijos has zigzagged from left to right, depending on the politico-economic pressures of the moment. However, a fairly clear reading of his basic inclinations can be obtained from looking at the makeup of his official civilian family. These are the civilians he has named to be the titular officials of the government, that is, the president and the vice-president of Panama and the heads of the various ministries. Each of these officials is closely directed from behind the scenes by Torrijos and his five colonels. They have virtually no independence of action or decision.

For example, in the spring of 1977 the president of Panama was a retired businessman, presumably a conservative. The vice-president was a communist, active and influential. The foreign minister was an ambitious politician and seasoned diplomat, a firebrand but reputedly not a communist. The treasury minister was a communist. The minister of economic planning was a noncommunist, a University of Chicago–trained economist, young, wealthy. Minister of labor: communist. Minister of housing: young, wealthy businessman. Minister of education: communist. Zig. Zag. Personal advisor to Torrijos: former chancellor of the University of Panama, highly active and outspoken communist. This man, Dr. Romulo Escobar Bethancourt, was chief of Panama's treaty negotiating team when agreement with the U.S. was reached.

It should be noted that the term *communist* used in the above description of the official civilian family is predicated upon the individual's having been widely and reliably reported to have been at least at some time in recent years active in the People's Party.

At the top levels of both the U.S. State Department and the Department of Defense it is asserted that there is no hard evidence linking Torrijos and his government either with Moscow or with the Soviet's surrogate in Cuba, Fidel Castro.

Recently an organization called the Panamanian Committee for Human Rights, has been active in Panama, apparently operating underground. During the fall of 1976 three reports reached the United States from this organization. They document charges of extensive violations of human rights by the Torrijos government—murder, torture, expatriation—giving names and dates.

Predicting the future of the present government of Panama is not an easy task. True, it has been in office longer than any previous government. But under the old constitution a president's term was limited to four years and he could not succeed himself. There was no "maximum leader" around.

The basic fact to be kept in mind is that the Guardia Nacional has the guns and apparently intends to use them to stay in power. It has never pretended to be functioning as an interim or caretaker government. Given this intention of permanency and the absence of any military strength outside the Guardia, it is difficult to see how it might be ousted.

Torrijos is not yet 50 years old. He could go on for a long time. But the present state of the economy of Panama has cost him much of his popularity and aura of infallibility. In the fall of 1976 an unheard of situation developed in Panama City. For a week the students at the university demonstrated and rioted in protest *against the government*—not against the usual target, the *"Yanqui* imperialists and colonialists," but *against the government.* And the government had to use considerable force against the students to restore order.

This was a unique and significant development. Food prices

and government economy measures were at the bottom of the disturbance. The problems still exist, as does the unrest. And they are not confined to Panama City.

Recently there have been reports of a struggle for power going on within the Guardia Nacional, as Torrijos' star seems to be waning. This could ultimately be the source of a change in individual leadership. But it is likely that the Guardia will continue to be the government for some time, with or without Torrijos at its head—as long as the guns hold out.

Here, then, is the government of Panama, the third element in the composition of the nation: totalitarian for certain, but in many respects less so than many of its counterparts in Latin America; socialist for certain, but, again, not surprisingly so for Latin America. Communist-oriented? Apparently, and unusually so for Latin America. Long-lived? *Quien sabe?*

Has Panama the capability of fulfilling the tremendous responsibilities she seeks with regard to the Canal? This can only be answered by measuring her strengths and weaknesses, her stature and character as a nation, against those responsibilities. This has been an attempt to provide the yardstick for such a measurement. What follows will include a look at the responsibilities.

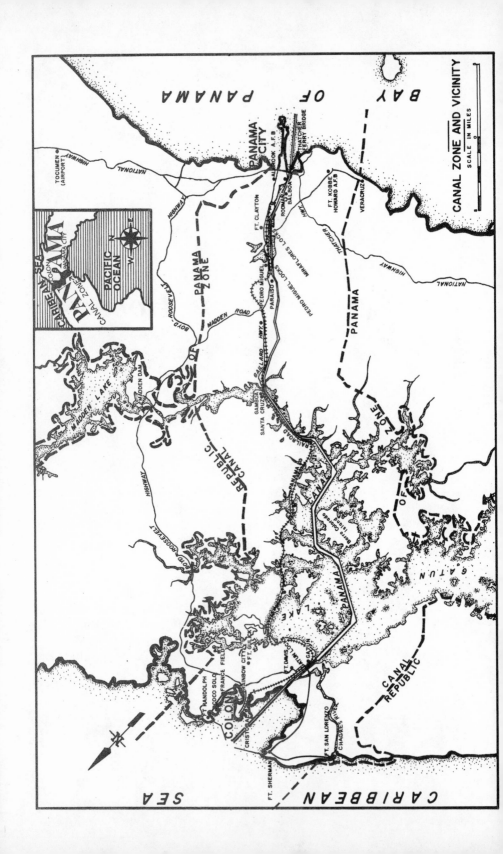

CANAL ZONE AND VICINITY
SCALE IN MILES

11

A Home
Away from Home:
The Canal Zone [1]

The heart of the Panama Canal issue, at least emotionally, is the Canal Zone. If there were no such slice of territory through the heart of the Republic of Panama, it is unlikely that the problems generated by U.S. operation and defense of the Canal would have attained their present magnitude and complexity.

Some people would, of course, reply immediately to that observation by asserting that without the U.S.-controlled Zone there could not have been, nor can there be, a Panama Canal effectively meeting the commercial needs of the world. And in part this is so. The existence of the Zone has played a major role in the creation, development, and operation of the Canal. But whether its continuance under exclusive U.S. control is indispensable to the Canal's future is the very essence of the current controversy.

To gain an understanding of this critical aspect of the Panama Canal issue, at least a general, overall picture of the Canal Zone is needed—what it is geographically and physically, both in and of itself and in relation to the Republic of Panama, who the people are who live in it and under what circumstances, what goes on in the Zone, and how it is governed.

Such a picture can serve many purposes, but two in particular. First, it affords a clear insight into the subjective attitude of the Panamanians, and, for that matter, of most Latin Americans, toward the Zone. Second, it highlights the nature and magnitude of the many problems involved in attempting to change to any appreciable extent the Zone's fundamental characteristic, that of a unique U.S. military reservation designed for one purpose, the effective operation and defense of the Panama Canal.

The Canal Zone comprises a land and water area of something over 500 square miles, an area about half the size of the state of Rhode Island. A great deal of it is unreclaimed jungle and swampland. Canal and military installations are spotted throughout, but, in the main, along the course and at the ends of the famous waterway. The major concentrations are at the ends of the Canal, particularly at the Pacific end, in the Ancon-Balboa area.

Where the land is occupied or used, the general appearance is one of neatness and order. Where there is grass, it is usually cut. The palm trees are trimmed, the roadways and streets kept in good condition. Rules against littering seem to be well observed.

This neatness and orderliness apparently annoys many people, particularly visiting American journalists. They constantly refer to the Zone's "manicured lawns," to its "suburban-type atmosphere," in tear-jerking contrast to the adjacent tenements and unkempt areas of Panama City and Colon. The United States, they intimate, is at fault for permitting this shocking comparison to exist. Presumably they would feel better if the premises of the Zone were ramshackle and filth-ridden. It is never suggested by them that Panamanians might follow the example set by their neighbors. Nor is it remarked that the worst Panamanian slum areas seem to be those adjacent to the Canal Zone, almost as if they were kept that way in order to maintain the contrast.

Use of the phrase "manicured lawns" is usually an indication of the speaker's or writer's approach to the Canal issue: contemptuous of the United States, apologetic towards Panama. Lawns are cut in the United States, "manicured" in the Canal Zone. As for the suburbia these critics deplore, it is a far cry from the suburban elegance of, say, Connecticut or California— a far cry even from the better areas of Panama City itself.

The Zone is perhaps best described as a typical 1920-vintage tropical U.S. military post: many houses raised above the ground, mostly frame, some stuccoed, almost all old and old-fashioned. The grass and jungle vegetation are kept down primarily to discourage mosquitoes. An up-and-coming suburban realtor from the United States would not give the Canal Zone a second look.

It is true that the golf courses in the Zone look nice. Most golf courses do. But these are not like the Masters in Atlanta, Georgia, or the Winged Foot in Larchmont, New York. They are more like the country club courses outside Salina and Butte.

No. Americans who have not visited the Zone and seen for themselves should not be made to feel guilty over the "manicured lawns" and the "suburban atmosphere" of the Canal Zone. These are snide travesties. The average American would probably consider the Zone and its facilities drab and outmoded. But he can take some pride in the fact that our government keeps property as old as that in the Canal Zone looking neat and orderly, and does so in a distant tropical land not noted for those characteristics.

And if anyone has the idea that going from Panama City, for example, into the Zone is like going through Checkpoint Charlie between East and West Berlin, they are quite mistaken. In effect, the boundary line is nonexistent, or, at least, fluid. The stranger is hardly aware of crossing from the Republic of Panama into the Zone. Anyone may walk or ride freely from one area to the other. There are no guards or sentry boxes, although, of course, inside the Zone there are sentries at the entrances to some strictly military installations. Away from the two Panamanian cities that adjoin the Zone, the boundary is, in the main, jungle to jungle, with a fence marking the dividing line.

On the other hand, the boundary line between Panama City and the Zone has its ridiculous aspects. For example, a main thoroughfare, called the Avenue of the Martyrs by the Panamanians in memory of those who died in the Flag War of 1964, runs along the southern boundary between the Zone and Panama City. The avenue itself is inside the Zone, but the sidewalk along its southern edge is in Panama City, the actual boundary line being the south curb of the avenue. If a miscreant snatches a purse from a lady walking along the sidewalk, he has violated the Panama law against theft. But if he steps onto the avenue, his crime is reduced to possession of stolen goods in violation of U.S. law. This is the kind of petty jurisdictional

129

problem that exasperates both the Panamanians and the U.S. police forces, in hot pursuit or otherwise.

And it cannot be denied that particularly where Panama City abuts the Zone there is an appearance of cramping and pressing. For the city is constantly growing and its development in the direction of the Zone, a natural one, is obviously thwarted. Furthermore, the city of Colon cannot grow in any direction. It is completely surrounded by the Zone. As its population increases, it just becomes more and more crowded.

Another annoyance is that, because of the Canal itself, those wishing to go from one half of Panama to the other can only do so where crossing facilities are available—and there are only three along a 50-mile stretch, two bridges and one ferry. Of these the only really satisfactory one is the Thatcher Ferry Bridge on the international highway at the Pacific end of the Zone. This situation obviously creates many inconveniences.

Finally, so far as geographical and physical characteristics are concerned, it should be noted again that the only deepwater ports on the Isthmus of Panama, those at Balboa and Cristobal, are both located within the Zone. Most shipping to and from the Republic of Panama must pass through these U.S. ports.

The population of the Zone is sparse. In 1976 there were about 40,000 people living in the 500 square mile area. Another 9000 persons come in each day to work in the Zone. The residents are made up of 25,000 U.S. military personnel and their dependents (the actual military force is about 9000), 10,000 U.S. citizens employed by either the Panama Canal Company or the Canal Zone Government, and their dependents, and 5000 Panamanians similarly employed, and their dependents. Those who come into the Zone each day to work are mostly Panamanians.

There are 11 residential communities within the Zone for employees of the Canal company and the Zone government. Generally speaking, these communities are divided between U.S. citizens and Latin Americans, since the government assigns housing on that basis. This, of course, brings charges of racial segregation because a majority of the Panamanians living in the Zone are blacks of West Indian ancestry. Ever since 1954, however, black and white U.S. citizens have been living in the same communities.

Of the seven communities for U.S. citizens, most, including Ancon-Balboa, the largest with over a thousand dwelling units, are on the Pacific Ocean side of the Zone. Others are located along the Canal in the vicinity of the two larger locks and on the Atlantic side. Of the four Latin American communities, there is one at each of the three locks areas and a fourth at the Atlantic end of the Canal, near Colon. There are no Latin American communities at the Pacific end of the Canal. There are, however, a few Latin Americans, particularly doctors, who are assigned houses in the U.S. communities near the hospitals. And some of the Zone's non-U.S. policemen also live in U.S. communities so they can be close to their assigned beats.

There are no military personnel or their dependents living in these civilian residential communities. They live in separate military communities that are part of the defense organization.

The people in the Zone live and work on a U.S. military reservation. The Zone is often referred to, derogatorily, as a colony or an enclave. But essentially it is a military reservation. It is owned by the U.S. government and run by the U.S. Army. There is no privately owned real estate in the Zone. There are no privately owned houses, no private businesses. Everything is government—stores, motion picture theatres, restaurants, dry cleaners, laundries, bowling alleys, marinas, gas stations, clubs, churches, golf courses, tennis courts, schools, hospitals—everything that goes to make up a community.

And the person in charge of all this is a U.S. Army general. Appointed by the president of the United States, traditionally from the Army Corps of Engineers, he holds two positions simultaneously, wearing two hats, so to speak. He is president of the Panama Canal Company. He is also governor of the Panama Canal Zone. He thus heads up and directs all the activities in the Zone except those related to Canal defense. The latter are the province of a separate and distinct military organization, the United States Southern Command.

The responsibility for operating and maintaining the Canal and related facilities is in the hands of the Panama Canal Company, a U.S. government corporation. The members of the board of directors of the company, mostly residents of the United States rewarded for party political support, are appointed by the secretary of the army who, as the representative of the president of the United States, is the "nominal" stockholder of the corporation.

The major activities of the company are the all-important Canal transit operations and the necessary supporting services. The transit operations consist of functions directly related to the

Canal itself and the movement of ships through it, including service to shipping and maintenance of the channel, locks, dams, and bridges. The supporting services are many and varied. They include vessel repairs, harbor terminal operations, operating and maintaining the Panama Railroad, and the operation of a supply ship that plies regularly between New Orleans and Cristobal. The Canal company also maintains motor transportation facilities throughout the Zone, storehouses, an electric power system, and communications and water systems. One of its major responsibilities is, of course, housing and, through a multitude of service activities, meeting the various needs of the people living and working in the Zone.

The Canal company has approximately 11,000 employees. 82 percent (9000) of them are Panamanians, 18 percent (2000) U.S. citizens.

The Canal company operates, or, more correctly, until recently did operate, on a self-supporting basis, its revenue being derived almost entirely from Canal tolls. Its financial responsibilities are extensive, and come to a total of about a quarter of a billion dollars a year. The company is required by law to recover all the costs of operating and maintaining its own facilities, including depreciation; to pay interest to the U.S. Treasury on the government's investment in the company; and to reimburse the Treasury for the portion of the annuity paid to Panama that was prescribed by the 1936 treaty ($493,000) and the cost of operating the Canal Zone Government.

The toll rates charged by the company for transiting the Canal remained the same for the first 60 years of the Canal's operation. In 1974 they were increased by about 20 percent. They were increased another 20 percent in the fall of 1976.

The Canal company met all of its financial obligations each year until 1973. In that year it had a deficit of $1.3 million. In 1974 the deficit was $11.9 million; in 1975, $8.2 million, in 1976, $7.4 million.

The Canal Zone Government is not a government corporation like the Canal company. It is an integral part of the federal government, an operating governmental unit, functioning, except for its court system, under the direction of the United States Army. There are no elective offices, and the residents of the Zone have no vote, though some do serve on "civic councils" that function as instruments for airing grievances and making suggestions.

The Zone's legislative body is the Congress of the United States. The Zone is governed by laws passed by Congress and by regulations issued by the Zone government (the governor). The court system, consisting of a federal district court and several lesser magistrate courts and the U.S. attorney's office, is under the jurisdiction of the Department of Justice. Congress has enacted a Bill of Rights for the Zone, but the provisions of the U.S. Constitution are applicable in the Zone only to the extent that Congress, by legislation, makes them so. The laws of the Republic of Panama have no application.

The Canal Zone Government issues its own postage stamps, but mail addressed to the United States is classified as domestic for rate purposes. Both U.S. and Panamanian currencies are legal tender in the Zone.

The Zone government provides most of the usual government services. These include education, health, sanitation, police and fire protection, postal service, and vehicle licensing and registration. They also include customs and immigration, enforcement of narcotics laws, and the guarding of all nonmilitary property in the Zone.

In the field of health services, the Zone government operates two major hospitals: Gorgas Hospital on the Pacific side and Coco Solo Hospital on the Atlantic. It also has minor hospital and clinic facilities elsewhere in the Zone.

There are two separate education systems, giving rise, again, to charges of racial segregation: the English language schools for U.S. citizens (black and white) and the Spanish language schools for Panamanians. The latter, the so-called Latin American schools, are now being phased out as, for reasons of economy, the number of non-U.S. citizens permitted to live in the Zone is being steadily reduced. In 1974 there were about 10,400 pupils in the English language schools and 1400 in the Latin American. The former figure includes children of military personnel as well as over 600 tuition-paying students of parents who live in the Republic of Panama.

The education function of the Zone government includes a junior college, special education, summer and recreational programs, the operation of library and museum facilities, a botanical garden, and a zoo.

The Zone government's police department operates several jails, a penitentiary (for convicted Panamanian felons only; their U.S. counterparts are shipped to penal institutions in the United

States), and detention facilities for women and juveniles. The police force numbers about 260, 85 percent of them U.S. citizens. The number of Panamanians on the force is limited to 40. These Panamanian policemen cannot rise above the rank of private and serve only in Canal Zone border areas and areas heavily traveled by their fellow Panamanians.

On the other hand, of the 132 members of the Zone's fire department less than 30 percent are U.S., and all of the 96 firefighters are Panamanians.

The expenses of the Canal Zone Government are met by the Canal company. The Zone government has about 3000 employees, 53 percent (1600) of them Panamanians, 47 percent (1400) U.S. These figures are comparable to those for the nonmilitary population of the Zone (including the 9000 who come in each day to work): 24,000 persons total, 57 percent (14,000) Panamanian, 43 percent (10,000) U.S.

The third major activity of the United States in the Canal Zone, in fact, by far the largest from the standpoint of the number of U.S. citizens involved, is that of the military. There have, of course, been defense facilities and installations in the Zone from the very beginning. But since World War I, aside from containing the Canal which the military is charged with defending, the Zone has become a vital part of the overall U.S. military system, an important center for its radio, telephone, and teletype communications and for its air and sea traffic.

The United States Southern Command, Southcom, is one of five regional, unified commands of the U.S. military establishment. Headquartered on Quarry Heights on the Pacific side of the Zone, Southcom has responsibilities that extend far beyond just the defense of the Canal. (Panamanian legal experts have long claimed with some merit that this is a violation of the 1903 treaty.) These responsibilities encompass geographically the land masses of Central and South America (excluding Mexico but including the Dominican Republic). Southcom thus serves as the organizational arm of the Department of Defense in Latin America. Its two major responsibilities, other than that of defending the Canal, are supervising U.S. military aid programs and providing U.S. military representation throughout Latin America. The command is made up of Army, Navy, and Air Force components.

U.S. military installations are located, in the main, at each end of the Canal. Surface-to-air missiles guard the approaches. The subordinate headquarters for the three components are in the vicinity of Southcom on the Pacific side. Also in this area is Howard Air Force Base, on which transport and tactical aircraft and a commando squadron are stationed. An Army mechanized battalion, an airborne battalion, and a logistical support complex are on the Pacific side; a Special Forces group, on the Atlantic side.

The Navy component, which has no ships other than a training vessel assigned to it, maintains and operates a complex of petroleum pipelines and storage facilities across the Isthmus. By means of the pipelines, petroleum products can be pumped directly from a tanker berthed at one end of the Zone into one berthed at the other. (The nonavailability to Panama of certain unused U.S. trans-Zone pipelines has long been a bone of contention between the United States and Panama.)

There are a number of residential communities for military personnel and their dependents, as well as training areas and gunnery ranges, throughout the Zone. In fact, about 70 percent of the total area of the Zone is assigned to Southcom. Of that assigned area, as much as 25 percent is not used at all (another Panamanian grievance).

Southcom has become well known throughout the military world for its schools and training centers, all operated for the benefit of Latin American countries as part of the U.S. military assistance program. The Latin American alumni of the schools now number well over 50,000. Graduates are to be found in high governmental places throughout Latin America. This is particularly so because government and the military have become virtually synonymous in all but three Latin American countries. General Omar Torrijos, the "maximum leader" of Panama, is a graduate of the U.S. Army's School of the Americas.

The Army has the Jungle Warfare Training Center on the Atlantic side of the Zone; the Air Force, the Tropical Survival School on the Pacific side. At Rodman, in the Pacific area, the Navy has special schools and training classes for Latin American naval officers and ratings. But the principal schools are the Army's School of the Americas, Torrijos' alma mater, and the Air Force's Inter-American Air Forces Academy, the former at Fort Gulick on the Atlantic side, the latter at Albrook Air Force Base on the Pacific side. Both of these schools provide a full field of military education, ranging from command and staff courses for officers to specialized training courses for enlisted men. In addition to the U.S. teaching personnel, each has on its staff a substantial number of Latin American guest instructors, all of them honor graduates of the schools.

Particular mention should be made of one course given at the Army's School of the Americas, because, for no immediately apparent reason, it has long been the subject of controversy. This is a course in the techniques of counterinsurgency warfare. A unique, carefully planned and executed curriculum, developed in the 1960s in response to the Communist Latin American insurgency program launched by Fidel Castro from Cuba, its benefits have disseminated throughout the armed forces of Latin America. Now it is a prime target of the "antiimperialists." The reaction to it and the sources of that reaction seem to prove its effectiveness.

Other activities of Southcom centered in the Canal Zone are search and rescue, disaster relief, and mapping and charting operations, each of them encompassing most of Central and South America. The disaster relief efforts have been singularly helpful in recent years in the aftermaths of the great earthquakes in Nicaragua and Guatemala.

To complete the picture of what goes on in the Canal Zone and who is involved, mention should be made of the operations of three federal agencies that are separate and distinct from the Canal company, the Zone government, and Southcom.

Under an agreement with Panama, the United States provides air traffic control services throughout the airspace over Panama, including the Zone. This is the responsibility of the Federal Aviation Administration.

In 1972 the regional office of the Federal Highway Administration was moved from San Jose, Costa Rica, to the Zone to direct the completion of the Pan-American Highway through eastern Panama to Colombia, known as the Darien Gap Highway Project. Here again the activity is carried on pursuant to agreements between the U.S. and Panama.

And on Barro Colorado Island in Gatun Lake, the Smithsonian Institution, through its Tropical Research Institute, maintains a 3600-acre tropical forest research preserve. The Smithsonian also has other facilities in the Zone, all related to research in the areas of tropical biology, education, and conservation.

All told these three agencies employ about 180 persons, 75 percent of them U.S. citizens. By far the largest of the three is the FAA's air traffic control operation.

This is the Panama Canal Zone. This is the strip of land in the middle of the Republic of Panama, paralleling both sides of the great Canal, that is exclusively controlled and governed by the United States—a key ingredient of the controversy over the Panama Canal.

No one should misunderstand this piece of real estate as presently structured, populated, and functioning. It means many things to many people.

The Panamanians, supported by most Latin Americans at least emotionally, view it as a national affront, as stolen property, as a flagrant impediment to Panamanian development and identification—so much so politically and sensitively as to obscure its present economic and security value to Panama and to make the issue of its control, that is to say, jurisdiction over the geographical area of the Zone, a smoldering potential for bloodshed.

On the other hand, to many Americans, perhaps to a majority, it is an integral part of the United States, sacrosanct, untouchable, a piece of American soil to be clung to forever—a symbol of national honor.

Setting to one side these completely opposite points of view, both tinged quite naturally with national pride and prejudice, what, from a truly objective standpoint, is the Canal Zone?

Is it part of an "imperial" scheme? Perhaps it was to some Americans at the turn of the century when the United States was flexing its muscles internationally for the first time. But today such a charge is wholly without foundation. The United States has neither aspirations nor delusions in imperial directions. It is no more engaged in maintaining or establishing an empire in Central or South America than are Panama's other immediate neighbors, Costa Rica and Colombia.

Is it a United States "colony"? Obviously not. The United States is no more engaged in colonizing Panama than it is engaged in colonizing the Moon or Mars.

The Canal Zone is nothing more nor less than the long-established, traditional governmental and geographical structure through which the United States maintains, operates, and defends the Panama Canal for the benefit of itself, for the benefit of Panama, and for the benefit of the entire world. It is the United States government in place and in action abroad, for that sole purpose, under valid, long-standing treaty arrangements with the Republic of Panama.

The real question, therefore, that the Panama Canal Zone presents for decision, as part of the overall Panama Canal issue, is not one involving semantics, not one concerned with resolving charges of "imperialism," "colonialism," "giveaways," and the like. Rather, it is a practical question of foreign relations, intertwined with matters of foreign commerce and national security, a question involving realities, basically, a question of feasibility.

Can the United States' sole legitimate purpose in Panama, the maintenance, operation, and defense of the Panama Canal, be accomplished under a new arrangement that would substantially modify the present status of the Canal Zone? Or, more specifically, can the United States relinquish all or any amount of control of the Zone to Panama and still effectively operate and defend the Canal?

This is the basic question. For there can be little doubt that the long-established, traditional structure, the Canal Zone as presently constituted, is unique in modern international society. No parallel to the Canal Zone can be found in the U.S. military bases established at strategic points throughout the free world or in the international arrangements under which those bases are maintained. There are parallels to Southcom, but not to the Canal Zone. For the Canal Zone is, and always has been, one of a kind.

Nor can there be much doubt that many of the situations created by the Zone that frustrate Panamanians—particularly the partition of their country, the obstructions to the orderly development of their major cities, the denial of much unused, valuable land to their economy, the lack of deepwater ports in a vital shipping area, and the complete negation of sovereign rights—can, and should, be remedied.

Looking carefully at the Canal Zone of today, there appear to be no unanswerable reasons why the transfer to Panama of substantial geographical areas and many civil government functions in the Canal Zone cannot be effectively and safely accomplished. Nor are there valid reasons why this cannot be done while simultaneously preserving the United States' capability to maintain, operate, and defend the Canal for whatever periods of time may be necessary.

The Canal Zone problem is not an insoluble element of the Panama Canal issue. But it requires delicate handling.

12

No Job for Amateurs: Operating the Canal[1]

Night and day, rain or shine, ships pass through the Canal, 30 to 35 of them every 24 hours—freighters of varying size, huge containerships, large and small tankers, cruise ships, an occasional naval vessel, sometimes a small pleasure craft. Unless they are so large or so underpowered as to need tug support in critical areas, they go through under their own power, except in the locks. There they are towed by locomotives running along both sides of the lock compartments.

Travelling at reduced speed, they seem to glide along the 50-mile waterway, quietly, smoothly, almost relentlessly, with no noticeable degree of human activity involved, save at the locks. The average time in the Canal proper is about 8 hours, the entire passage, from deep water to deep water, about 15.

It is a leisurely journey, with only occasional delays. The traffic is two-way, even in the locks, although in the nine-mile-long, 500-foot-wide Gaillard Cut, traffic is one-way on occasions when a ship of unusual size or one carrying a hazardous cargo happens to be going through. Otherwise, along the route ships bound in opposite directions for ports all over the world slip quietly by one another, sometimes but a few yards apart. Although risk is ever present, accidents are infrequent.

It all seems so simple. Obviously someone has to schedule the traffic. Obviously someone has to throw the switches that open and close the lock gates and raise and lower the water level. Obviously someone has to operate the tow locomotives at the locks. Obviously the occasional tug has to be manned. But that is about it. Or so it seems.

It is not that simple. Far from it. There are a thousand and one things that go on behind the scenes, day and night, to produce this appearance of simplicity. Things that require special skills, special know-how, special equipment, special effort—even special loyalty and special dedication.

The Canal is not just a complex of engineering and machinery. The Canal does not run by itself. It is run by conscientious, experienced human beings, and the role these people play in its operation becomes increasingly greater as the Canal grows older and as more and more ships that nudge the maximum dimensions for Canal transit are designed and built. These two factors, Canal age and ship size, combine to place an ever higher premium on skillful, experienced management, maintenance, traffic control, and ship handling.

Some of the statistics about the Canal are startling enough to be interesting—and significant. It takes 52 million gallons of fresh water—the water used to change the level in the locks—to put one ship through the Canal. The total amount of water consumed in the operation of the Canal during a 24-hour period is enough to keep Boston supplied for two weeks.

No pumps are used in filling and emptying the lock chambers. It is all done by gravity flow, from lake to sea, the water entering the locks through a system of main culverts the size of the Hudson River tubes of the Penn Central Railroad.

The water pressures developed are enormous. Coping with them are the gates at each end of the lock compartments, massive steel structures 65 feet wide and 7 feet thick, varying in height from 47 to 82 feet and weighing from 390 to 730 tons each. Heavy and cumbersome, they nevertheless open and close with the application of a mere 40 pounds of force.

All lock gates now in use are those installed during the initial construction of the Canal, more than 60 years ago.

To keep the Canal open, about 3 million cubic yards of earth and rock, the product of constant erosion, silting and slides, must be dredged from the waterway each year—enough to fill a train of railroad cars 60 miles long.

These few facts alone serve to highlight perhaps the most important point about the operation of the Panama Canal: at least 75 percent of the work effort required to keep the Canal operating effectively goes into maintenance. Maintenance is the touchstone of the enterprise.

And it is not just garden variety maintenance, repairing things that have already fallen into disrepair or ceased to function. That kind of maintenance comes too late in the Panama Canal. Such occurrences must be anticipated and prevented at all costs. The Canal is like the theater—the show must go on.

The Panama Canal is old. There have been few major structural replacements in her lifetime. She creaks in spots. She tends to fall apart in places. It takes a sizeable team of "doctors," a team of experienced, imaginative, and devoted managers, engineers, and mechanics, to keep her in operating fettle.

Her vital organs—her locks, her dams, her power plants—and her nervous system—her power and communication networks—must be constantly checked and fine-tuned. Her arteries—her channels, her lakes, her Gaillard Cut—must not be allowed to harden. They must be kept unclogged, not only by dredging, but by anticipating and forestalling the calamitous slides and rockfalls that are a chronic threat. The doctors must know the patient thoroughly—and be devoted to her.

Preventive maintenance is the key to the Canal's viability. It takes constant vigilance, anticipation, and ingenuity. A classic example of the latter is the recent development of complicated engineering techniques by which lock machinery and valves can be overhauled without draining the locks and taking them out of service.

But the Canal does not run by preventive maintenance alone. Highly refined operating skills are required as well. Because of the many twists and bends in the Canal's course, the tricky currents and winds, the fogs, the close draft tolerances, the narrow passing areas with attendant interplay of ships' washes, and the difficulty of the lock entry maneuvers, it takes a force of some 200 skilled and experienced canal pilots to take the ships through—always one, sometimes as many as four, for each ship, depending on size. And they do, literally, take them through. The

Panama Canal is the only waterway in the world where the boarding pilot takes complete charge of the vessel, replacing the ship's captain during the entire passage.

Then there are the marine traffic controllers, the people that schedule the transits and keep the traffic moving in a safe, orderly, and efficient manner. Although in recent years the system has become extensively computerized and now includes a data network of 23 remote communication stations located at key points along the Canal, decision-making is still in the hands of these carefully trained individuals. They, too, like the "doctors," must know the great lady well, anticipate her idiosyncracies, her contrariness. Errors in judgment can be very costly.

These are just some of the principal assignments where skill, experience, and dedication are so vitally important. There are, of course, many others.

In considering the Panama Canal of today and tomorrow, particularly the latter, its age has to be constantly stressed. The day is coming, soon and inevitably, when substantial capital expenditures will have to be made to replace many of its basic structures and major items of equipment. Requirements of large amounts for these purposes, sums that cannot be developed through increased revenue from Canal tolls, clearly lie ahead. Nor, in this same connection, can the desirability and feasibility of augmenting the Canal's present facilities, in order to handle the ever-increasing number of large ships, be ignored. The answer is not a new sea-level canal. That, at least for the foreseeable future, is not in the picture; the amount of money required would be prohibitive. But the same is not necessarily true of long-standing plans for expansion of the present facilities, plans such as the Terminal Lake–Third Locks project, which at one time was actually commenced. But here, too, large capital expenditures would be required, several billion dollars at current costs.

All of this—the Canal's age and fragility, the high degree of skill and experience required to maintain and operate it, the prospect of large capital expenditures to keep it going effectively —leads into another very basic element of the Panama Canal issue, the question of operational control and responsibility. Panama wants at some definite future date to take over the Canal, to run it by herself. The proposed new treaties meet Panama's aspirations in this regard. Is this realistic? Is it wise?

Leaving aside for the moment the economic, foreign relations, and security aspects of such a prospect, the question becomes a simple, practical one, a matter of present and future capability. Is Panama capable of running the Canal? Can she become so?

Most responsible Panamanians would be the first to admit that Panama does not have the capability of doing so, at least not with her own people, at the present time. They would quickly add, however, that, in their opinion, this incapability stems not from a lack of inherent capacity, but from lack of opportunity to develop that capacity. And this, of course, has been a subject of controversy between the United States and Panama for a long time: the matter of job opportunities for Panamanians in the higher paid, more skilled, and more responsible positions in the Canal enterprise.

There is considerable background to this controversy. No purpose would be served by detailing it here. Suffice it to say that up until about 20 years ago little effort was made by Canal management to afford job opportunities to Panamanians above the unskilled, manual labor categories. But in the 1955 treaty the United States agreed to change that situation. The principle agreed to was set forth in a "Memorandum of Understandings Reached" in these words:

> The United States will afford equality of opportunity to citizens of Panama for employment in all United States Government positions in the Canal Zone for which they are qualified and in which employment of United States citizens is not required, in the judgment of the United States, for security reasons.

This agreement has been gradually implemented over the years by acts of Congress, presidential orders, and regulations of the Canal Zone Government. A Canal Zone merit system, an apprentice program, and various worker-trainee and learner programs have been established.

It should be borne in mind, however, that this commitment to increase job opportunities for Panamanians was made in the context of an existing treaty that contemplated retention by the United States in perpetuity of the right and responsibility of operating the Canal. Nevertheless, in recent years, and particularly during the just completed negotiations, which envisioned an interim joint operation and finally one exclusively

143

Panamanian, the Canal management has been under ever-increasing pressure from Washington, emanating primarily from the State Department, to move faster, to put more and more Panamanians into higher positions, to build a statistical record of pro-Panamanian accomplishment, to do everything possible to please Panama. It is not unlikely that this constant pressure has caused the Canal management to do things that, in the interest of efficiency, would not otherwise have been done and to lean over backwards in favor of Panamanian employees. A typical example of the latter was the establishment several years ago of a dual register for entry into the apprenticeship program, a system in which lower standards were set for Panamanians than those set for U.S. citizens, a built-in reverse discrimination that has since been abandoned.

The end-result of the job opportunities program has been less than satisfactory. Seemingly no one is happy. True, more Panamanians have moved into higher paid jobs. But there has been no diminution in the number of Panamanian complaints, and on the other side of the coin, there has been a constant increase in the number of charges by U.S. citizen-employees, the "Zonians," that they, not the Panamanians, are now the victims of discrimination.

The obstacle to equal opportunity that galls the Panamanians the most is the security position system authorized in the 1955 memorandum. Under the system, Canal management restricts certain key jobs to U.S. citizens only for "security reasons." As a result of constant hammering by Panama and the U.S. State Department, this system is disintegrating rapidly. In 1965 there were almost 2000 jobs designated as security positions, most of those involving the higher technical skills and managerial functions. By 1974 that figure had been reduced to about 1000. By 1976 it was down to 500.

The security position system was developed to insure that, notwithstanding the increased job opportunities and advancements to be afforded to Panamanians, the United States would retain the capability of operating the Canal and governing the Zone even under the most aggravated circumstances of Panamanian "noncooperation." It was also designed to insure U.S. retention of control of operational and governmental policies and decisions.

Nothing could be more logical and reasonable as long as the United States is running the show and has sole responsibility for doing so. And that still is the situation. But for the past 12 years both the United States and Panama have proceeded as if a new treaty calling for interim joint control and ultimate Panamanian control had already been signed and ratified.

Perhaps this is a natural consequence of the United States committing itself in advance of negotiations to the ultimate outcome of those negotiations. At any rate, it has put the U.S. officials responsible for running what is still a U.S. operation in a most difficult position. To carry on such an operation on the basis of personnel policies imposed by the State Department has to be one of the most frustrating, impractical, and nerve-wracking assignments ever conceived. Canal operations are bound to suffer. In fact, they are suffering from rather large-scale resignations by key U.S.-citizen employees; in 1976 those resignations numbered 290, 25 of them canal pilots.

The Panamanians have been clamoring for years to have the category of canal pilot, the aristocrat of the Canal, opened to non-U.S. citizens. In 1973 the citizenship requirement was eliminated, but the job category still would not have opened up to Panamanians if the license requirements for qualifying had not been simultaneously reduced. Prior to October 1973, in order to become a canal pilot, the entrant had to have a master's (ship captain's) license issued by the U.S. Coast Guard. There just are not many, if any, Panamanian sea captains who could meet that requirement. But in 1973 Canal management also reduced the entering license requirement to that of a U.S. Coast Guard *second mate's* license *or* a master's license issued, not by the U.S. Coast Guard, but by the Canal Zone Board of Local Inspectors. Thus the Canal management changed the rules, presumably under pressure, so that it could qualify canal pilots on the basis of its own judgment and standards, not those of the U.S. Coast Guard. The Panamanian foot was at last in the door.

The controversy over that change has been raging ever since between the Canal Pilots Association and Canal management. The association claims that the lowered standards will create an unjustifiable safety hazard on the waterway. Management replies that it had to lower the standards because of a shortage of pilots, but that the requirements still assure safety in Canal operations. Only an expert could decide which side is right. But it takes no expertise to deduce that pressure from Washington caused Canal management to stretch a point, however reluctantly.

One point should be noted in particular with regard to further development of a Panamanian takeover plan, either unilateral or as the outcome of a new treaty. Unless ironclad guarantees of some sort can be devised for protection of the remaining key U.S.-citizen employees, the chances of a mass exodus on their part are far from remote. And if such an exodus should occur, it will not make any difference who has the responsibility of operating the Canal. The Canal will have to be shut down. And it will have to stay shut down for a long time. No on-the-job training can take place when there are no jobs.

Back again to the basic question of Panama's capability of operating the Canal on her own: In 1956 when the Egyptians took over the Suez Canal there were dire predictions about the canal's future. But the Egyptians had the good sense to retain or go out and hire people who could get the job done. Just because the Suez Canal was nationalized did not mean that the canal was thereafter to be managed and operated exclusively by Egyptians. Not at all. Egyptian citizenship was not a requirement for employment. Skill and experience were, particularly in the key positions. Qualified people were available, many of them the very foreigners who were on the job before the takeover. They were hired, and the Suez Canal operated successfully.

Although the Panama Canal and the Suez Canal are not comparable because of the vast differences in their characteristics, fundamentally and operationally, nevertheless, on the basis of the Suez experience, it would be ridiculous to say that Panama could not, technically at least, operate the Canal if she had to. In fact, eventually she could achieve the *technical* capability of operating the Canal with nothing but Panamanian employees, though that would be a long way down the road even under the most favorable circumstances.

But technical capability is only a part of what it takes when one is dealing with an elderly, fragile, and unpredictable prima donna like the Panama Canal. Remember, she needs constant, skillful, devoted care. And she is getting to the point where transfusions of capital will be obligatory. Accordingly, motivation and financial capacity become just as important as technical capability. All three are needed if the Panama Canal is to continue to provide to the nations of the world the impartial, uninterrupted, efficient, and reasonably priced transit service that has been the hallmark of the operation under the United States for more than 60 years.

146

Can the Panama described in chapter 10 fill the bill? Many knowledgeable people have grave doubts.

First, the matter of motivation. We have seen that maintenance, preventive maintenance, is the major feature of the Canal operation. It can scarcely be said that maintenance-mindedness, much less preventive maintenance-mindedness, is an inherent characteristic of Latin Americans. The *mañana* approach to life, one of the charms of Latin America and its people, is hardly conducive to an activity calling for such immediacy.

And that is only one element of the motivation required in the case of the Canal. Another is pride, the kind of pride that induces loyalty and dedication. The people of the United States look on the Panama Canal as one of their nation's greatest achievements, the moonshot of its day, an accomplishment that took endless courage and sacrifice and produced great heroes. That feeling of pride has always been particularly reflected in the attitude of the U.S. citizens working in the Canal Zone. Most of them care immensely about the Canal's performance, the implementation of their heritage. This has produced a unique personal touch, a job thoughtfulness and loyalty, that means a great deal in an operation such as that of the Panama Canal. It is not reasonable to expect that non-U.S. citizens would have the same feeling. How successfully can the Canal be operated without that ingredient?

Another element of motivation with regard to the effective and efficient operation of the Canal is impartiality. Could the Panamanian government as we know it today, or as it might exist in the foreseeable future, refrain from using the Canal for purposes of domestic politics, or, and perhaps more disturbing, as an instrument of foreign policy? For example, would the ships and cargoes of the United States really be given the same treatment with regard to transit scheduling and servicing as the ships and cargoes of every other nation using the Canal? Or would the United States be harassed at every turn either in subtle retaliation for alleged historic grievances or at the behest of a foreign power hostile to the U.S.? Would small ships receive the same treatment as larger ones? Would small nations receive the same treatment as larger ones? Another lurking question: would *mordida*, the Latin American bribe bite, become an element of Canal transit? And would Panama exercise restraint in setting Canal tolls so as to insure the continuance of the Canal operation as a service to the world and as an instrument for the diversified, long-range economic growth of Panama? Or would Panamanian political leaders tend to use the Canal as the source of a quick bonanza and thus kill the goose that lays the golden eggs? These are not easy questions to answer, to say the least.

As to the third essential part of the capability to operate the Canal, the necessary financial capacity to meet the demands for new capital, Panama's situation seems to be self-evident. For her to meet those demands on her own is out of the question. Panama is bankrupt. By the same token, it would seem to be impossible for her to raise the needed money through international lending agencies, if the normal financial criteria were applied to her situation. This leaves but one answer: the footing of the bill by some nation that has both the capacity and the incentive to do so. And in that case it would be only logical to expect such a nation to insist on management and control until its investment was recouped. That brings one back full circle to the continuation of U.S. operation of the Canal, albeit Panama might participate to a far greater extent than she does now, both operationally and financially.

The point of all this is that the United States has the technical ability, the motivation and the financial capacity to operate the Canal efficiently and impartially for the benefit of all the nations of the world. It has demonstrated this over a period of almost three-quarters of a century. That Panama has or can achieve the technical capability cannot reasonably be denied. But whether she can generate the motivation and the financial capacity to produce a comparable performance is a matter fraught with extreme doubt.

Therefore, leaving aside considerations of foreign policy, economics, and national security, from an operating standpoint it would seem to be both unrealistic and unwise for the United States to relinquish control of the Canal to Panama. Whether the answer is the same in light of those other considerations remains to be considered and determined.

13

Forgotten Man: The "Zonian"

What? The Panama Canal shut down for a week by a work stoppage of U.S.-citizen employees? Impossible. Nothing like that had occurred in the 62 years of Canal operations. Pride and loyalty would never permit it.

And yet it did happen in March 1976—a "sick-out" by canal pilots that brought Canal operations to a complete halt. Ostensibly, the sick-out was a protest against economy measures that were being proposed by Canal management in an effort to stem the tide of mounting deficits, measures that would curtail many job-related benefits and would freeze salaries for a long period of time. As the week progressed, the pilots were joined by the Zone teachers. They, too, became "sick," and the schools had to close down. By week's end some 700 U.S.-citizen employees were directly involved in the work stoppage.

The sick-outs were instituted not so much to protest the economy measures as to bring the plight of the "Zonians" to the attention of the American people in general and the United States Congress in particular. It was undertaken with great reluctance. One can easily imagine how truly sick at heart the perpetrators must have been when they saw the fruit of their handiwork: the ships of the world piling up at the entrances to the Canal because there were no pilots to take them through. Nor is it hard to picture how heartsick the Canal management was to see how far the morale and loyalty of the Zonians had sunk as a result of the treaty negotiations. For to the Zonians the negotiations were a sword of Damocles hanging over their jobs, their lives, their futures.

The term *Zonian* is applied to the U.S. citizens employed by the Panama Canal Company and the Canal Zone Government. There are only about 3000 of them left. Together with their dependents they number in the neighborhood of 10,000 persons. Most of them occupy managerial or technical jobs, but their group includes such categories as canal pilots, teachers, doctors, engineers, accountants, maritime traffic controllers, shopkeepers, firemen, and policemen. Many were born and raised in the Canal Zone. Some are second and third generation Canal employees.

Perhaps because they live far from their native land, they cling desparately to the Zone as a symbol of their country. Perhaps because they live in a close-knit, insular community, they are inclined to take a rather narrow view of things, particularly things that threaten to disrupt their well-ordered way of life. Many of them are criticized for their aloofness towards Panama and the Panamanian people, for their failure to reach out and become a part of a broader, more diversified culture.

They are fervently patriotic. They led the resistance in the 1950s and 1960s to the flying of the Panamanian flag in the Zone. They oppose a new treaty because they view Torrijos and his government as instruments of communism and the treaty negotiations as a conspiracy to sell the United States down the river. If possible, they distrust the U.S. State Department more than they do the Panamanians.

The Zonians are often referred to derisively as superpatriots, "150 percent Americans." They do not deserve such derision. In the main, they are loyal, hardworking U.S. citizens who have an overwhelming problem. Their problem is the future, the future of their jobs and their lives. They see the handwriting on the wall, and they are frightened.

Some Zonians express fear over the prospect of living under the jurisdiction of Panama, of being governed by Panamanian laws, courts, and police. They say their families would not be

150

safe under such circumstances. It is difficult to sympathize with this position. All over the world American citizens engaged in activities of their own or of the U.S. government live under the jurisdiction of the host countries. That is a normal element of living and working abroad. And in Panama, thousands of U.S. citizens live outside the Canal Zone, under the protection of Panamanian laws and Panamanian police, without unusual qualms or problems. The Zonians' fear in this regard is symptomatic of their introverted, almost paranoic, feeling that they are the targets of conspirators who want to get rid of them.

Their fear over job security is more realistic. They are employees of the U.S. government, but their civil service status in the Canal Zone does not give them job rights back in the States. If they are forced out of their jobs in the Zone, they will lose out completely. So the constant talk of a new treaty under which they would be replaced by Panamanians, even though the transition might be a gradual one, has been enough to make them wake up at night in a cold sweat wondering what would become of themselves and their families.

During the past few years it has often been suggested that the Zonians should be given full status under the U.S. Civil Service System so they would know that if they gave up or lost their jobs in the Zone they would be entitled to comparable jobs "back home." But Canal management has not favored such an extension of civil service rights for the Zonians, at least for the time being, for fear that given such assurance of other jobs in the States they would tend to move out immediately and take advantage of their newly acquired rights. The services of these people are so essential to Canal operations that perhaps management's reasoning has been something like this: better a scared, disgruntled employee with no place to go than a scared, disgruntled employee who can pull up stakes at will. Such reasoning, though perhaps natural under the circumstances, is both unfair and unsound. The services of scared, disgruntled employees can become counterproductive. Witness, for example, the 1976 sickout.

There is a possible way out of this dilemma. What the Zonians are afraid of is a new treaty and its effect on their jobs. They tend to foresee and anticipate the worst. This is why so many of them have left during the past few years. On the other hand, many of them, with deep roots in the Canal Zone, have indicated that they would be willing to take their chances under a new treaty, or at

151

least give it a try, if they had binding assurances of a job elsewhere if things did not work out. It has been suggested that, catering to that attitude, such assurances could be made contingent upon a new treaty's going into effect.

To have any real impact on the Zonians' situation, the job assurances should come from Congress in the form of legislation. For example, it could be provided by legislation that if at any time after a new treaty went into effect a U.S.-citizen employee in the Canal Zone were displaced from his job by the operation of the treaty, he would immediately acquire civil service rights in the United States. And those rights could be spelled out so as to assure him that he would be entitled to a comparable job with comparable economic benefits, that his time in service in the Zone would count toward his retirement, and that to the extent possible his geographic preference would be accommodated.

Something of this sort has been needed badly for a long time. It is needed even more now that the proposed new treaties are a reality. The mere introduction in Congress of a bill that would lead to such legislation would go a long way toward reassuring the Zonians, just by letting them know that they are being thought of and that their interests will be protected. They deserve at least that.

The Zonians are a very real element of the Panama Canal issue. Numerically they are a small group, but in terms of the critical value of their services to the Canal operation and the political clout they have in the United States, they are a very potent factor in the current situation. Their value is self-evident. Without them the Canal could not operate.

Their political influence in the United States is perhaps not so apparent. But it is there. They have the active support of all the patriotic organizations, the American Legion, the Veterans of Foreign Wars, the Daughters of the American Revolution, to name the more prominent ones. Their "alumni" body in the United States is sizeable, widespread, active, and vocal. The members of Congress are well aware of the Zonians, and to a considerable extent it is a sympathetic awareness.

When all of these components of influence are put together—and that seems to happen almost automatically whenever the American people's Panama Canal nerve is touched—the political potential of the Zonians becomes enormous. They may be the forgotten men of the Panama Canal issue, but they are forgotten men with sharp fangs. Any U.S. presidential administration that either ignores or underrates them in trying to solve the Panama Canal dilemma does so at its peril.

14

Looking into the Crystal Ball: The Economic Future of the Canal[1]

A major reason for building the Panama Canal was to promote the ocean commerce of the United States. Since its inception, it has clearly served that purpose, as well as benefiting the entire world.

By the same token, a major consideration involved in resolving the longstanding controversy over the Canal has to be the future economic importance of the Canal to the United States—and to the world.

If that importance is going to continue to be substantial, then, from an economic standpoint, much is at stake in the present discussions regarding the proposed new treaties, particularly in relation to the Canal's future operational control. On the other hand, if in the near future the Canal is going to mean less and less to the United States, to the point of nonimportance, then the matter of who will eventually operate it and in what fashion has less economic significance.

In attempting to gaze into the future in this regard it is fortunately not necessary to enter unexplored territory. Much attention has been given, particularly during the past 15 to 20 years, to analyzing the Canal's economic prospects. These studies have been prompted, in the main, by growing concerns over the capacity of the Canal to meet the future needs of world seaborne trade and, more recently, over the development of a toll policy to meet the ever-increasing costs of operating the Canal. In these studies can be found a myriad of statistics, analyses, and projections by specialists with years of experience in the economics and logistics of the Canal.

The nonspecialized crystal ball gazer has, therefore, a seemingly reliable platform on which to stand while peering into the future. But it is helpful to look back as well, in order to determine trends and directions.

The Canal's true economic significance has always been in the distance and time savings it affords to interocean shipping. In their school days most Americans were exposed to the dramatic figures that portray those savings. Nevertheless, it is interesting to review a few of them.

The Canal cuts 7873 miles off the distance between New York and San Francisco, 6250 between New York and Callao, Peru, 5705 between New York and Yokohama, Japan. The distance between New Orleans and San Francisco is reduced by 8868 miles, between Liverpool, England, and San Francisco by 5666.

The days saved mount up impressively. For example, a ship traveling at a speed of 15 knots can reach Los Angeles from New York in 13 days by way of the Canal; it takes more than a month through the Straits of Magellan. A vessel moving at 25 knots can make the journey from Yokohama to New York in 17 days via the Canal, as against 25 days around the Cape of Good Hope. A ship bound from Seattle to Europe at a speed of 20 knots can reach Bishop's Rock Light off of southwestern England by way of the Canal in 17.5 days; it takes 31 days going around.

Savings in miles and days mean fewer ships required for the movement of the same amount of cargo and speedier cargo deliveries. Savings in miles and days also mean reduced fuel consumption and lowered crewing costs. The seafaring nations of the world were quick to take advantage of these highly significant economies. As world seaborne trade grew by leaps and bounds, so did the use of the Panama Canal.

Commercial ocean traffic through the Canal during three benchmark years—the first uninterrupted year of operations, a post–World War II year, and the peak year to date—reflect that growth:

155

Year	Commercial Transits	Cargo Tonnage
1917	1738	7,054,720
1947	4260	21,670,518
1974	14,033	147,096,914

Thus over a period of 57 years there was an eightfold increase in the number of commercial ships passing through the Canal each year and a twentyfold increase in annual cargo tonnage. Of additional significance in these figures is the startling disproportion between the rates of growth in the two categories, ship transits and cargo tonnage, particularly after World War II. Over the 57-year span the average cargo load per ship transiting the Canal more than doubled. This is a striking indication of the trend in the size of vessels engaged in international trade, a fact that, as will be discussed later on, has considerable bearing on the economic future of the Panama Canal.

What does the Canal mean to the United States from an economic viewpoint today? The volume of U.S. foreign trade going through the Canal has, until very recently, grown steadily since World War II. During the 14-year period 1958–71, the fraction of total U.S. oceanborne foreign commerce going through the Canal increased from 10.7 percent to 17 percent. During the same period the dollar value of that U.S. traffic through the Canal increased even more than the tonnage volume. Both increases were due in considerable measure to the expanding trade between the East Coast of the United States and Asia, particularly between the Atlantic ports and Japan.

About 66 percent of all the cargo that moves through the Canal comes from or goes to United States ports: 34 percent exports from the U.S., 23 percent imports into the U.S., and about 9 percent U.S. intercoastal trade.

But these figures can be somewhat misleading. It should be pointed out that during 1972, for example, *by value* only 13 percent of U.S. exports and 5.3 percent of U.S. imports went through the Canal. The reason for these relatively low value figures lies in the large volume–low-unit-value categories of commodities that make up the major portion of Canal-transiting cargo: raw materials, agricultural items, petroleum products, and semi-manufactureds. Manufactured goods such as motor vehicles, machinery, electrical and electronic equipment, and the like, contribute much less to overall Canal tonnage.

It should also be pointed out that less than 3 percent of U.S.

intercoastal trade now passes through the Canal, as compared with 50 percent 35 years ago.

But these qualifying factors do not detract appreciably from the fact that the Canal has and continues to be an important factor in United States foreign trade.

The Canal is of much greater relative importance to many of the Latin American nations than it is to the United States. The countries most dependent on the Canal send these percentages of their oceanborne commerce through the waterway:

Nicaragua	76.8%
El Salvador	66.4
Ecuador	51.4
Peru	41.3
Chile	34.3
Colombia	32.5
Guatemala	30.9

Nor can one overlook the importance of the Canal to the countries of the Far East. Up until recently not less than 50 percent of all westbound cargo going through the Canal was headed for Japan. Twenty-three percent of the eastbound shipments originated in that country. And the Canal has become an essential commercial lifeline between countries like Australia and New Zealand and their traditional European and U.S. East Coast markets.

Before peering into the future, attention should be given to what has been going on at the Canal during the past three or four years, developments that are highly retrogressive from both a traffic and an economic standpoint. They probably can be attributed in the main to special conditions. Yet they may provide some signals for the future.

Generally speaking, the number of ships transiting the Canal has increased steadily over the years. The annual transits by commercial, ocean-going vessels reached a peak of 14,000 in 1971. They dropped off a bit the next two years, but went back up to over 14,000 in 1974. Since then, however, the decline has been marked: 13,609 in 1975, 12,157 in 1976. During the period 1973–76 the number of ships transiting the Canal each day dropped from 39 to 33. Meantime, operating costs, particularly wages, have continued to rise. In 1973, the Canal company sustained a loss for the first time in Canal history. It has lost money

157

every year since then, despite a hike in toll rates in 1974, the first one since the tolls were originally set in 1914, and another in the fall of 1976.

Those who wish to denigrate the economic importance of the Canal seize on these recent statistics as marking the beginning of the end. But the downward trend in transits can be explained by temporary world economic conditions and the reopening, in 1975, of the Suez Canal. And the recent annual deficits can be attributed primarily to ever-rising operating costs.

One big factor in the present situation is Japan's temporary but drastic curtailment of steel manufacturing. The coal and coke shipped from Atlantic ports to meet Japan's steel mill requirements represented a sizeable portion of Japanese traffic through the Canal.

There is no reason to believe that the current slump is anything but temporary. But this is not the case with the increasing costs of operating the Canal; they probably will continue to rise.

What, then, is the economic future of the Canal? It is probable that for the foreseeable future foreign trade in bulk commodities, such as coal, oil, ore, agricultural products, and large manufactured goods, will continue to be transported primarily by ship. But there is no escaping the fact that a revolution has been going on for some time in the technology of transportation.

One manifestation of this is the constantly increasing volume of air transportation. As far as transoceanic passenger service is concerned, we have already seen the end of express passenger ships; they have been replaced by the airplane. With the advent of the jumbo jets, air freight has grown at a rapid rate. Although in total volume it is still relatively insignificant—less than 3 percent of U.S. foreign trade moves by air—there can be little doubt that advancing technology in air freight transportation will continue to produce growth in the amount of air traffic in goods, particularly those in the small bulk–high value categories. It is unlikely, however, that this will become a significant rival to oceanborne trade of the kind usually passing through the Canal.

A development that could, in time, have a substantial effect on Canal traffic is that of the "mini-bridge" system being advanced by the U.S. railroads. This involves the movement of goods in containers across the United States on fast, unitized trains operating on schedules synchronized with ship arrivals and departures at the East and West Coast ports. The mini-bridge system has particular usefulness in the case of goods headed to high-intensity markets, as, for example, electronic equipment and motor vehicles. Even though the trend in marine transportation is moving steadily in the direction of high-speed containerships, the mini-bridge system has already become competitive and is beginning to offer a real alternative to the Canal for some shippers. If the nation's railroads should be rejuvenated, the effect of the mini-bridge concept on the Canal's economic value to U.S. foreign trade could be substantial.

The element of the technology revolution in transportation that is most frequently mentioned in connection with the economic future of the Canal is that which is occurring within marine transportation itself, the Canal's lifeblood. First of all, ship sizes are increasing progressively. Already there are over 1000 vessels in the world's mercantile fleet that cannot go through the Canal because of their size. There are nearly double that number that can make it only if they are carrying loads below their full capacities. And there are more of these giants on the drawing boards.

The maximum dimensions of a ship for Canal transit, known as "Panamax," are:

Length	975 ft.
Width	106 ft.
Draft	40 ft.
Tonnage	65,000 DWT

The most prevalent type of oversize ship unable to transit the Canal at present is the huge oil tanker. Many of these now have load capacities in excess of 300,000 tons. They exceed all the Panamax limits and were designed specifically for all-ocean routes such as those from the Persian Gulf to European and North American ports. Their speeds and carrying capacities are such as to make it cheaper for them to travel the longer distances than to take canal shortcuts and pay tolls. The closing of the Suez Canal in 1967 was a great incentive to their development.

There are other oversize superships that cannot go through the Canal. Some carry large quantities of dry bulk commodities such as ore, coal, and grain. Others are giant containerships. In total, these oversize vessels do, of course, have some economic effect on the Canal. And this will continue to be so.

159

But three things, in particular, should be kept in mind in evaluating the impact of these large vessels. First, they constitute fewer than 10 percent of the ships in the world's mercantile fleet. Second, they were specifically designed to circumnavigate *all* interoceanic canals. And, third, although the Panama Canal is an important element of the worldwide ocean shipping system, the traffic passing through the Canal in any one year has never exceeded 10 percent of the total traffic in the system. Thus the above-Panamax ships are, primarily, nothing more than a relatively new high-speed, high-volume component of normal non-Canal shipping.

And there are realistic inhibitions to the extensive use of these supervessels, such as lack of deepwater ports (particularly in the U.S.) and scarcity of the highly specialized port equipment required for their effective operation. In the case of supertankers, environmental concerns are entering the picture more and more.

These giant ships are, of course, significant. But they have by no means taken the place of the cargoliners, tankers, containerships, ore ships, and bulk carriers that are the principal users of the Canal. In fact, there is another phase of the revolution in marine transportation technology, aside from the development of the specialized superships, that tends to enhance, rather than detract from, the future economic value of the Canal.

While the all-purpose, odd-lot-cargo, small freighter has been disappearing from the scene, new types of specialized vessels have been emerging—containerships, auto carriers, refrigerated cargo ships, specialized types of tankers, automated dry-bulk carriers, even barge-carrying vessels (LASH)—larger than the old freighters, but most still comfortably within Panamax limits. Energy costs, an ever-increasing premium on turnaround times, port facilities, and similar factors seem to be actually generating a limitation on ship size for general use. This, plus a constant increase in overall world seaborne cargo tonnage, commensurate with general economic growth, seems to assure a gradual continuation of the upward trend in Canal traffic.

There are, of course, limitations on the amount of traffic the Canal can handle. Many studies have been made over the years to determine what those limits are and when they might be reached.

Ship-size limitations have already been mentioned. Another limitation is that of the time involved in operating the locks. Since the average-size ship takes about two and a quarter hours to go through the six tiers of locks in the Canal, there are obviously limits to the number of ships that can transit the Canal in a day or year. The time limitations are increased by the additional maneuvering and handling times involved in transiting the larger ships.

A third form of Canal limitation is that imposed by the amount of fresh water available for lockage and navigation purposes. It takes about 52 million gallons of fresh water to put a single ship through the locks. If the water used for lockage operations is not replenished fast enough, restraints have to be placed on draft levels and on the number of lockage operations.

The consensus seems to be that something in the neighborhood of 25,000 transits a year will be the Canal's maximum capacity after all scheduled improvements in lockage operations have been completed. When will this limit be reached? The answer seems to change frequently.

In 1970, in its report to President Nixon, the Atlantic-Pacific Interoceanic Canal Study Commission estimated it would be reached in 1988. In 1970 there were 13,658 commercial transits of the Canal. Yet six years later, in 1976, there were only 12,157, and the high in between, in 1974, was only 14,037, still little over half of the commission's estimate of ultimate capacity.

More recent estimates put the date considerably beyond the year 2000. Since there are so many variables involved in any such prediction, particularly those concerned with the mixture of types and sizes of vessels that will make up future Canal traffic, no one can come up with a precise answer. But a minimum of 50 years from now, two generations, would not seem to be out of line.

And when capacity is reached, what then? Does the Canal automatically become valueless? Obviously not. The fact that it will have reached full operating capacity would seem to indicate that it will be playing an important role at least with regard to the types of shipping making use of it at that time. And even though operating at full capacity would require a far greater degree of advance scheduling of transits than is now required, there is no reason to believe that such operations would not continue indefinitely. The crystal ball is far from clear.

Another thing that blurs the vision of the future is the problem of rising costs. Unless the Canal is subsidized, tolls will have to be increased further to make ends meet. Two increases, totaling over 40 percent, one in 1974, the other in 1976, have not done the trick. Prior to the 1976 increase, the average toll paid was about $10,000, the highest just under $50,000. The lowest was 36 cents, paid by author-traveller-romanticist Richard Halliburton in 1928 for the privilege of swimming through the Canal.

How much in the way of increases will the traffic bear? At what point will efforts to obtain more revenue become counterproductive? Here, again, there are several studies by Canal experts—and many different answers.

Every product shipped through the Canal varies in its sensitivity to increases in tolls, depending on its per unit shipping cost. And the sensitivity rate of a particular commodity itself can be variously affected by such factors as increased availability of alternates to Canal transit, long-run inflation (including ship construction costs), ship operating costs (especially fuel prices), and the general price level of commodities.

The experts are all agreed on only one thing: of all the commodities ordinarily going through the Canal in significant quantities, bananas, representing only 2 percent of total Canal volume, are the most sensitive; they can stand a toll increase the least.

According to one private study, products only one-half as sensitive as bananas are, for example, sugar, iron ore, and coal. One-quarter as sensitive are petroleum products. One-sixth: wheat, lumber, fertilizers, and miscellaneous ores. It is estimated that some commodities could take an increase of up to 150 percent. Others begin to drop off, by groups, at 100 percent and 50 percent. In a 1972 study the maximum toll rate increase that could be tolerated by bananas was estimated to be 25 percent. Since then they have had two increases, totaling over 40 percent. Will there be no more Ecuadorian bananas in New York?

The most one can say with any assurance is that tolls can be raised to some extent above present levels without stifling traffic. How much seems to be pretty much anybody's guess. If tolls were increased on a selective basis, the rate on some commodities could perhaps be raised as much as 200 percent without wiping out the value of the Canal shortcut to those products. Other commodities are more sensitive, all the way down the scale.

One thing seems clear: The balance between Canal revenue and Canal traffic is a delicate one. Anyone attempting to make a quick profit out of Canal operations would be taking golden eggs from a highly vulnerable goose.

Importance cannot be measured mathematically. It is a relative term. Much of it is in the eye of the beholder.

How important will the Canal be to U.S. foreign commerce, to world commerce, in the years ahead? Twenty-five years from now? Fifty years from now? Seventy-five years from now?

These are difficult questions to answer. To say the Canal will be of vital economic importance at any time in the future would probably be absurd. It may have been vital at one time. But it is not now, and it is very unlikely to become so again.

The other extreme—to say that the Canal will soon become totally unimportant, or become so, say, in 75 years—seems equally unsupportable.

A look at the conclusions of some of the "experts" affords some guidance:

> . . . the long-run economic role of the Canal will continue to be important, but it cannot in any sense be regarded as either overwhelming or crucial.
> The Economic Value of the Panama Canal
> *by Howell and Solomon, International Research Associates, Palo Alto, Calif., December 1973*

> The Canal's role in United States foreign trade is growing and will continue to grow.
> Maritime Commerce and the Future of the Panama Canal *by Padelford and Gibbs, MIT Sea Grant Report No. 74-28 (1975)*

> [The Canal] . . . is no longer the commercial lifeline— at least not for the United States—that it once was. It remains important, but its importance to other countries is far greater and increasing.
> *"Panama Paralysis" by Franck and Weisband,* Foreign Policy, *Winter 1975*

. . . the Canal is no longer worth having a foreign policy crisis about.

> Monthly Economic Thought Letter *by Brandes, International Research Associates, May 1976*

An adequate Isthmian canal is of great economic value to many nations, but especially to the United States since approximately 70% of the tonnage through the canal in recent years has been to, from, or between United States ports. This relationship is expected to continue.

> Interoceanic Canal Studies 1970, *report to the president by the Atlantic-Pacific Interoceanic Canal Study Commission*

The nonspecialist crystal ball gazer can be forgiven some confusion. If he should conclude that the Panama Canal will be of substantial but diminishing economic importance to the United States and the rest of the world during the foreseeable future, he probably could not be adjudged myopic.

15

The Crux of
the Canal Issue:
U.S. National Security [1]

During the Spanish-American War, the necessity for a trans-isthmian canal as an instrument of national security was brought home dramatically to the people of the United States. There were encounters between U.S. and foreign naval vessels in distant waters. Commodore Dewey scored a thrilling U.S. victory in far-off Manila Bay. As a finale, came the "race" of the U.S.S. *Oregon* around the Horn, 68 tortoiselike days from San Francisco to Cuba to participate in the last skirmish.

The emergent world power obviously needed the flexibility of military maneuver that only a waterway between the Atlantic and Pacific oceans could supply. So the Canal came into being, partly as a highway for peaceful commerce, but no less as an integral link in the U.S. national defense system.

In this latter capacity, the Canal has played a key role almost since the day it opened in 1914. The First World War had already started. Within three years the United States became an active participant. And for the duration the Canal was a beehive of combat vessel and military cargo transits.

The Canal's defense value became even more apparent some

24 years later when the United States found its military and logistic sinews stretched to the limit in a grim, two-ocean global conflict: World War II. Even though U.S. naval forces for that involvement were organized into three fleets—Atlantic, Pacific, and Asian—there was a constant interchange of fighting ships from ocean to ocean through the Canal. During that war, there were more than 6400 warship transits of the waterway and an additional 10,300 by other military vessels.

During World War II military supplies moved through the Canal in vast quantities. It became a lifeline in the war against Japan, as munitions, food, fuel, and every other type of military necessity poured from Atlantic ports, through the Canal, and out to far-flung U.S. bastions in the Pacific and the Far East. There is no way of evaluating the total savings in time and distance involved, but transportation facilities were obviously a limiting factor in World War II, and the Canal played a major part in reducing the number of ships required and in speeding deliveries. Nor can the contribution of the Canal towards the saving of lives and the shortening of the war be calculated, but it clearly was of considerable significance. And the story was much the same, on a far smaller scale, in the Korean conflict of the early 1950s. In 1962, at the time of the confrontation between the United States and the USSR over the Soviet attempt to introduce missiles into Cuba, thousands of U.S. Marines were moved rapidly by ship through the Canal from California to the Caribbean, making the possibility of a swift U.S. invasion of Cuba a startling and deterring reality to Moscow.

During the long struggle in Vietnam, the Canal again played a major role, particularly in the movement of the instruments and supplies of war.

That the Canal has up until now well served the national security purpose for which it was built cannot be denied. That role has been variously characterized in informed and qualified circles as "vital," "major," "extremely important," and the like.

Now, rather suddenly and seemingly in relation to the recently concluded treaty negotiations, there appears to be a tendency to downgrade the Canal's value for defense purposes. Top Pentagon officials have, to a degree, joined the chorus. This probably stems from the "unification" of the Defense Department's and the State Department's respective positions on the military aspects of the proposed new treaties. As was pointed out earlier, this unification was imposed in 1975 by White House decree and has continued ever since.

For example, Gen. George Brown, chairman of the Joint Chiefs of Staff, was quoted in July 1976 as stating that the Canal was "not vital" to national security. What did General Brown mean when he made that statement?

That question brings this presentation of the Panama Canal issue to perhaps its most critical point, the point of placing national security considerations in their proper perspective. For almost everyone will agree that national security is the crux of the issue from the standpoint of the United States.

Foreign relations considerations may suggest, indeed, according to many people, compel, regardless of cost, a "happy" solution to our differences with Panama—"happy," that is, from Panama's viewpoint, no matter how unhappy from that of the United States. Likewise, commercial considerations concerning the solution of the Canal issue may indicate the waterway to be of such declining importance to the United States that there is no longer enough at stake economically to justify a refusal to turn it over to Panama, at least eventually. In making a new treaty, one could be wrong on both these counts and still probably not jeopardize drastically U.S. long-range interests. But national security considerations are a horse of a different color. A mistake in this area can be fatal.

There is no question that the relative strategic value of the Canal has changed considerably since World War II. It changed the instant the first atomic bomb was exploded in New Mexico in 1945. The advances in nuclear weaponry since then have made *every* fixed defense installation susceptible to quick destruction. But this is just as true of an aircraft factory in California, a munitions plant in New Jersey, a weapons arsenal in Texas, an Air Force base in Nebraska, even an aircraft carrier on the high seas, as it is of a canal in Panama. If the degree of that susceptibility is to be the standard for measuring a defense facility's value and thus for predicating the justification for its abandonment, then all of the types of installations just mentioned, including the Canal, can be written off. In that sense, the Canal is no longer vital to national security, and that, perhaps, is the sense in which Gen. Brown made his statement.

The strategic value of the Canal also changed with the advent, at least in theoretical effect, of a two-ocean navy. After World

War II, the Navy, quite properly, used the increased vulnerability of the Canal to nuclear attack to ask Congress for the additional ships and facilities necessary to make that two-ocean capability a reality. In fact, however, that capability has never been achieved. It could never be said, nor can it be said now, with any degree of assurance, that either the Atlantic or the Pacific fleet was adequate to cope, without reinforcement by the other, with whatever situation might develop on its side of the world.

One military expert, Lt. Gen. V. H. Krulak, USMC (Ret.), recently expressed the current situation in these words:

> In truth, the Panama Canal is an essential link between the naval forces of the United States deployed in the Atlantic and in the Pacific. It is only because of the waterway that we are able to risk having what amounts to a bare-bones one-ocean navy.

The situation was highlighted again by four former chiefs of naval operations, Admirals Robert B. Carney, Arleigh A. Burke, George W. Anderson, and Thomas H. Moorer, the last-named being also a former chairman of the Joint Chiefs of Staff. In a letter to the president of the United States dated June 8, 1977, they described it in these words:

> Contrary to what we read about the declining strategic and economic value of the Canal, the truth is that this inter-oceanic waterway is as important, if not more so, to the United States than ever. The Panama Canal enables the United States to transfer its naval forces and commercial units from ocean to ocean as the need arises. This capability is increasingly important now in view of the reduced size of the U.S. Atlantic and Pacific fleets.[2]

One of the nation's most distinguished writers on military affairs, Hanson W. Baldwin, recently put it this way:

> It is ironic, indeed, that in an era when the United States Navy needs the canal to a greater degree than at any time since World War II, Washington is considering its abandonment. The navy today is in the same strategic bind it was in prior to World War II: it is a

one-ocean navy (in size and power) with two-ocean responsibilities.

Now, with defense spending an ever-increasing political target and defense costs, particularly those for new construction and operating fuel, in an ever-mounting spiral, it is likely that a two-ocean navy will become less and less of a reality. In this sense, the Canal seems to be maintaining, rather than losing, the importance of its role in the U.S. national defense system.

Here, again, it is possible to say that even the U.S. Navy is no longer "vital." For with the almost limitless secret mobility of the modern nuclear submarine, naval surface vessels are perhaps becoming as susceptible to quick destruction as the fixed defense installations mentioned earlier. If, in that sense, the Navy's ships must be written off, along with all the rest of our defense apparatus, then clearly the Canal, too, is no longer vital. Nor is anything else.

Another change in the strategic value of the Canal was caused by its inability to handle the over-Panamax-size ships of the Navy, the supercarriers and supertankers. On the face of it, this does diminish, at least to some extent, the importance of the Canal to national security. In the main, this ship-size situation parallels the one discussed earlier regarding the oversize commercial vessels that cannot use the Canal.

It is true there are some 20 Navy ships, 13 of them aircraft carriers, that are too large for Canal transit. But these vessels are only a portion of the Navy's total striking force. Furthermore, except for the big aircraft carriers, warships are getting smaller, not larger. The day of the battleship is over; cruisers are stabilizing in size below World War II dimensions and, for some missions, giving way to the new class of frigates. The nuclear submarines and special purpose vessels of the Navy, with the exception of the supertankers, are all well within Panamax limitations and capable of transiting the Canal.

The basic fallacy of all of the factors and arguments advanced to downgrade the strategic importance of the Canal is that they are predicated on the existence of what is euphemistically called a general war, actually an all-out nuclear holocaust. This conveniently ignores the fact that "limited" wars, not general wars, have been the rule for the past 30 years and are likely to continue to be the rule in the years ahead without exception—that is, until the first exception, the world's "last hurrah."

Another misleading factor in the tendency to downgrade the Canal's importance militarily is the placing of almost entire emphasis on the Canal's role in relation to the movement of the Navy's combat vessels, while saying little or nothing about its role, equally important if not more so, in the movement of military supplies and equipment.

It should not be overlooked that about 90 percent of the bulk tonnage needed to support military forces abroad moves by ship and that the Canal has played, and will continue to play, in times of peace and in times of limited war, a key role in that logistic effort. For example, during 1968, a representative year of the Vietnam conflict, 33 percent of the dry military cargo shipped from the continental United States to South Vietnam, Thailand, the Philippines, and Guam went through the Canal. The proportion was 29 percent for petroleum, fuel oil, and lubricants.

A military force inadequately supplied is an ineffective one. The role of the Canal in maintaining military effectiveness abroad seems bound to be of continuing importance in any conflict short of a general war. The evolution of conventional war techniques is placing an ever-greater emphasis on mobility and logistics. While increasing numbers of troops and their basic equipment can be moved by air, their long-range effectiveness depends on sea transport.

What do some of the experts, pseudoexperts, and quoters of both have to say about the importance of the Canal to U.S. security? Here are some samples, with emphasis added to highlight the evaluation:

> The second principal reason the Pentagon is willing to go along with a new treaty is that the case claiming the Panama Canal is vital to the security of the U.S. no longer stands up under scrutiny. The canal is *useful but* it is *not vital.*
> "Storm over the Canal" by Hudson, New York Times Magazine, *May 16, 1976*

> Many military experts concede that the Canal is *no longer vital* to U.S. security. But most of them also insist that the waterway between the Pacific and At-

170

lantic Oceans continues to play a *substantial role in U.S. defense plans.*
U.S. News & World Report, *May 24, 1976*

Our national security interests in the Panama Canal and the Republic of Panama will continue to be of *utmost importance* to the United States.
Gen. Brown, chairman, Joint Chiefs of Staff, letter to Sen. Strom Thurmond, September 1975

Yesterday Brown said that the Canal is *'not vital'* to United States' security.
Minneapolis Star, *July 2, 1976*

As far as the waterway's strategic value to the United States, Gen. George S. Brown, Chairman of the Joint Chiefs of Staff, said in an interview . . . : "The Panama Canal is *of great military importance.*"
U.S. News & World Report, *May 24, 1976*

The Canal remains *a prime consideration* in the planning and accomplishment of the safe and timely movement of naval units between the Atlantic and Pacific Oceans.
"Choices for Partnership or Blood in Panama" by Cox, Congressional Record, *May 20, 1975 (inserted by Sen. Hubert Humphrey)*

. . . the Pentagon correctly declares that it is *a vital American interest* that [the Canal] be kept open.
"The Panama Negotiations—A Close-Run Thing" by Rosenfeld, Foreign Affairs, *October 1975*

171

But the canal has *considerable military impor-*
tance.
"Should We Give Up the Panama
Canal?" by Reed, Reader's Digest, *May*
1976

The national defense aspects of the Panama Canal
are . . . *a vital U.S. concern.*
Lt. Col. McDonald, Strategic Plans and
Policy Division, Joint Chiefs of Staff,
Military Review, *December 1975*

The Panama Canal is of *major importance* to the
defense of the United States.
Conclusions, Interoceanic Canal Studies
1970, *Atlantic-Pacific Interoceanic Canal*
Study Commission

The Panama Canal represents a *vital* portion of our
U.S. naval and maritime assets, all of which are abso-
lutely *essential* for free world security.
Admirals Carney, Burke, Anderson, and
Moorer, letter to President Carter, June
1977[3]

A weighted average derived from these quotations, taking
into consideration the source of each, would seem to put the
importance of the Canal to U.S. national security at a point just
short of "vital," say, at "utmost importance."

Some skeptics attempt to avoid the issue of importance entirely by asserting that, even in a limited war, the Canal would
be indefensible. To this assertion there is a recent specific answer by the Department of Defense.

In July 1976 the State Department released to the press a
response by it to a member of Congress who had posed a
number of questions regarding the force requirements for
the defense of the Canal in various hypothetical situations.
The information and estimates contained in that response
were furnished to the State Department by the Department
of Defense.

According to this document, the Canal Zone police and security forces (watchmen and guards) would be "the minimum de-

fense forces" required to defend against sporadic terrorist attacks aimed at the locks, dams, and other key positions in the Canal system. It was pointed out that these numerous defense forces could, if necessary, be "reinforced by elements of the 193rd Infantry Brigade which is stationed in the Zone and has the mission of Canal defense."

In the event of a concentrated and well-organized commando operation, several thousand strong, against the key points in the Canal system and against the American civilian population in the Zone, the document states that "there are plans for reinforcing existing defense forces in the Canal Zone. The size of such reinforcement would be determined by the actual magnitude of the threat to the Canal and/or American citizens and property in the Zone."

The final estimate has to do with force requirements in the event of an all-out attack on the Canal Zone "by Panama, with the aid of 10,000 Cuban and other Latin American irregular troops trained in guerilla and commando-type operations, using military equipment from Cuba." According to the document, the Defense Department estimates that "the *maximum* force requirement" (emphasis added) needed to defend the Canal against such an attack would be a corps of three divisions, a force totalling "approximately 100,000 men with supporting air and air and naval forces."

But suppose U.S. military forces had already been withdrawn from Panama and an attack on the Canal should occur. What then? This question highlights a point of both military and political significance with regard to any defense of the Canal, and particularly with regard to the proposed new treaty on U.S. defense rights.

The Defense estimates in the State Department document just discussed are all predicated on the presence in the Canal area, at the time of an attack, of U.S. military forces with a defense capability at least as great as that of the forces presently stationed there. These are the forces that, in the event of a substantial attack, would "hold the fort" until reinforcements could be brought in. In the absence of this preliminary holding capability, the attacking forces, unopposed, could become speedily entrenched in all strategic areas and the task of dislodging them could be a major and highly destructive one, a task far more difficult and costly than any of those envisioned in the State Department document.

And, from a political standpoint, there is a vast difference between, on the one hand, augmenting military forces already legitimately positioned in an area, and, on the other, introducing forces into an area where there have been none, no matter how clearly the right, even the obligation, to do the latter may have been spelled out beforehand in a treaty. In this day and age the cries of "imperialist aggression" and "imperialist intervention" seem to have far more acceptance and effect than actions in the rightful defense of lives and property.

These considerations seem to make it clear that if the defense of the Canal is to continue to have any real meaning, it must involve the continued presence in the area of the minimum military forces necessary to hold the fort until reinforcements arrive.

Summing up with regard to the charge that the Canal is indefensible, these observations seem pertinent. In the first place, both the State Department and the Defense Department, as indicated in the July 1976 release just referred to, are agreed that the Canal *is* defensible even in the most exaggerated sort of scenario: an all-out attack on a U.S.-defended Canal by Panama with the aid of 10,000 Cuban and other Latin American troops. That, in itself, would seem to be a complete answer to the charge of indefensibility. But, notwithstanding this fact, the claim is made that the Canal is indefensible in three senses of the word. All three are unrealistic.

It is said that the Canal is indefensible in the sense that it is vulnerable to sabotage. But that vulnerability has always existed, ever since the Canal was opened in 1914. It is a vulnerability shared by every defense installation, everywhere, in varying degrees.

It is said that the Canal is indefensible in the sense that it could be knocked out by a long-range nuclear missile. As already stated, this is true of every fixed defense installation.

It is said that the Canal is indefensible in the sense that the American people do not have the will to defend it. The unreality of that sense can be determined by asking almost any American what his reaction would be if American troops legally stationed in Panama were attacked by Panamanian, Cuban, or any other military forces.

There is, however, one situation in which a claim of indefensibility would be quite valid. That is one in which the U.S. military presence had been withdrawn from Panama prior to an attack or infiltration. Obviously, under those circumstances the Canal could be easily and quickly overrun by a hostile force. And that is the stark reality posed after the year 1999 by the proposed new treaties.

This brings our discussion of the United States national security concern over the Canal down to the crucial point. What is the threat to the Canal?

If one has no qualms about the Soviet Union's plan for world domination, there probably is no real threat. There are no indications that any other power with an *independent* capability covets the Canal. But to be unconcerned about the Soviets' intentions is to be isolated from reality, to be unaware of what has happened during the past 40 years in Eastern Europe, in the Middle East, in Africa, and in the Far East, to be oblivious to the relentless Soviet probings and infiltrations elsewhere, including Latin America, and, above all, to be blind to what has occurred in Cuba.

The Soviets have not been secretive about their overall plan. The blueprint is there for all to see, as revealed in Soviet activities around the world. And included in it is a program, long under way, to gain control of the world's strategic interoceanic passages: the Dardanelles, the Suez Canal, the Straits of Madagascar, the Straits of Gibraltar, the Malayan Straits, the Straits of Magellan, and the Panama Canal.

Over the years the Soviets' success in implementing this program has varied. But of particular significance has been the method consistently used to achieve the desired end: not the direct use of Soviet military forces, but efforts to control the governments and the military forces of the countries dominantly located in relation to these strategic passages. And by building the Red Navy to the point where it can patrol the entire world, including the approaches to the crucial waterways.

That Panama, not neighboring Colombia or Costa Rica, is the long range target as regards the Panama Canal, there can be little doubt. For Panama's importance to the USSR goes beyond the strategic value of just the Canal. Panama's geographical location and the U.S. military presence there, plus the Canal, make her the key to the achievement of Soviet aspirations in Latin America as a whole.

The Western Hemisphere has been a relatively tough nut for the Soviets to crack. This has been so for two reasons in particular. First of all, there is the fundamental opposition throughout

175

the Hemisphere to intrusion by any ex-Hemisphere power—in other words, because of general agreement with the principle of the Monroe Doctrine. And, secondly, there is the military presence of the United States *in* Panama. The nut, however—always afflicted with various soft spots—has now developed a wide crevice in its shell: Cuba.

The Cuban revolution of 1958 under Fidel Castro and its later unveiling as a Communist accomplishment gave the Soviets the entering wedge into Latin America they had long sought. The bold dimensions of Moscow's plans to exploit this strategic foothold in the Caribbean began to unfold with the Cuban missile crisis in 1962. By then the militarization of Cuba by the Soviets was well under way. It has gone forward steadily ever since. This, presumably, has not included large nuclear missiles—though without inspection this cannot be known for certain. But it has included training and equipping of Cuban troops and air units, and, during recent years, the development of a major facility in Cuba for servicing and otherwise implementing Soviet nuclear submarine operations in the Western Hemisphere.

The success of this program of Cuban militarization and its purpose were demonstrated to the world in a startling way in 1975–76. Fourteen thousand Cuban combat troops, equipped with the most modern Soviet weapons and vehicles, were airlifted in Russian planes to far-off Angola on the African continent. They went there to strengthen the wavering Communist forces in that country in the struggle for power that followed Angola's independence from Portugal.

If there ever was a signal of things to come in Latin America, Angola was it. President Kennedy seemed to have sensed the potentiality of such a development when, right after the Cuban missile crisis, he told the American people that there would be peace in the Caribbean only so long as "Cuba is not used for the export of aggressive Communist purposes." Fourteen years later in Havana, in the wake of Angola, Mikhail Suslov, a top Soviet strategist, confirmed Kennedy's suspicions and gave a clear indication of Soviet intentions:

> The revolution-liberation movement, now as never before, is linked into a unified global whole. The Cuban revolution has placed an indelible imprint on the development of the whole liberation process in

Latin America. Prospects for the second liberation of the continent are becoming increasingly real.

Suslov, it should be recalled, played an active role in the "liberation" of Hungary, Czechoslovakia, and South Vietnam. The Soviets have been attempting to prepare the way in Panama for many years, and Cuba has been the instrument. The Cuban embassy in Panama City is staffed by over 200 persons, making it the largest embassy of a foreign nation in Panama. Thousands of Cuban agents are reported to be active throughout Panama. There is ample evidence of the major role the Communists played in the tragic Flag War of 1964. The orientation of the present Panamanian government towards Havana and Moscow is quite clear.

What then is the threat to the Panama Canal? The answer is obvious: the Soviet Union. Not directly, but through Moscow-controlled forces, military and political, emanating from Cuba. All that is needed to put those forces in motion is for the United States to create a power vacuum in Panama by withdrawing its own military presence there. Time is not of the essence to Moscow; the Soviets have waited for a long time, and they will probably continue to wait until the time is right. After all, 22 years is but a fraction of a second in history.

There can be few situations of more vital concern than this to the national security of the United States.

16

Cards on the Table: The Proposed New Treaties

On September 7, 1977, one of the greatest diplomatic extravaganzas in U.S. history was staged by President Carter at the headquarters of the Organization of American States in Washington, D.C. There, in the presence of top officials of 26 Latin American nations and Canada, with pomp and circumstance befitting a royal coronation, Carter and Brig. Gen. Omar Torrijos, the Panamanian dictator, signed the proposed new treaties and then clutched each other in an awkward *embrazo*.

With this pageantry the cards of the negotiating game the United States and Panama had been playing for the past 13 years, cards referred to on occasions as the "stacked deck," were laid face up on the table. Now, for the first time, the American people and their elected representatives could step up to the table, peer over the shoulders of the players, and look at the score.

But the game did not end with the pageant. For unless these newly admitted kibitzers approve what they see, the score will not count. The game could be called off. Or it could continue under new rules.

The final settlement consists of two proposed new treaties: one called the Panama Canal Treaty, the other, the Treaty Concerning the Permanent Neutrality and Operation of the Panama Canal.[1] The first, the Canal Treaty, covers the period starting six months after the day ratifications are exchanged until December 31, 1999. During that time the United States' presence in Panama would continue, and the two nations would jointly operate, maintain, and defend the Canal. The second, the Neutrality Treaty, would cover the same period but also an additional one with no termination date, during which the United States would be completely out of Panama—lock, stock, and barrel, including gun barrels.

The Canal Treaty, with its attached Annex and Agreed Minute and its two separate Agreements in Implementation, is detailed and lengthy, 171 pages in all. The Neutrality Treaty, on the other hand, is very brief. Even with its Annex and Protocol it runs a scant 10 pages.

Long or short, neither treaty could be classified as light reading. Both demand the most painstaking scrutiny—in the case of the Canal Treaty, to absorb and evaluate a mass of detail, wide-ranging in scope; in the case of the Neutrality Treaty, primarily to read between the lines, or attempt to.

It is, of course, for the Congress to examine, to question, and to weigh every word in, or missing from, these highly important documents. But it is equally important that the American people have a clear, though general, picture of what they propose, of how they would work. It is to the presentation of such a picture that this chapter is directed.

Take the Canal Treaty first, the one that deals with the operation, maintenance, and defense of the Canal until the turn of the century when the United States would vanish from the scene.

The Canal Treaty not only implements to the letter the 1974 Kissinger-Tack Statement of Principles outlined in chapter 1. In several areas, one in particular, it goes far beyond the prenegotiation commitments made in that statement.

Abrogation of the 1903 Treaty. The first item in the Kissinger-Tack agreement was the commitment that the 1903 treaty would be abrogated and replaced by an entirely new treaty. This commitment is fulfilled to the hilt. The slate is wiped clean of the 1903 treaty and of every other subsequent treaty between the United States and Panama concerning the Canal, including the major ones of 1936 and 1955.[2] No ifs, no ands, no buts.

Duration. The second commitment was to do away with the concept of perpetuity and to negotiate a new treaty with a definite termination date. Here, again, there is no equivocation: "This Treaty shall terminate at noon, Panama time, December 31, 1999."[3]

Sovereignty and Jurisdiction. Next was the commitment that the treaty to be negotiated would specifically recognize Panama's sovereignty over the Canal Zone and provide for the prompt relinquishment by the United States of governmental jurisdiction over the area. These promises are kept in clear terms.[4]

Although the matter of flying national flags was not mentioned in Kissinger-Tack, it was, of course, inherent in the issue of sovereignty and emotionally of major consequence to the Panamanians. The Canal Treaty nails it down with certainty and in detail:

> The entire territory of the Republic of Panama, including the areas the use of which the Republic of Panama makes available to the United States of America pursuant to this Treaty and related agreements, shall be under the flag of the Republic of Panama, and consequently such flag always shall occupy the position of honor.[5]

The flag of the United States could only be flown at the headquarters of the proposed Panama Canal Commission, the site of the proposed Combined Board (the joint defense board), and the "defense sites" that would be authorized for use by U.S. military forces. And at each such place the Panamanian flag would have to be flown "in the position of honor" along with the American flag. Furthermore, at the entrance to, but just outside of each defense site, the Panamanian flag would have to be flown by itself.[6]

If the new treaty should leave any written doubt about sovereignty, it can be cleared up by merely stepping outside and looking at the flags.

The moment the new treaty went into effect, the Canal Zone, the Canal Zone Government, and the Panama Canal Company would cease to exist.[7] The laws of Panama, both civil and criminal, would immediately become applicable throughout the Canal Zone.[8] In this connection, however, during the first two and a

180

half years of the new treaty, during a so-called transition period, the criminal and civil laws of the United States would apply concurrently with Panamanian law in the "Canal operating areas," "housing areas," and "defense sites" specified in the treaty for the use of the United States, in the "areas of military coordination" (areas designated for joint U.S.-Panamanian military use), and in the ports of Balboa and Cristobal.[9] The new treaty provides that in the areas just mentioned and for the transition period the U.S. police, U.S. courts, and U.S. detention facilities would continue to function.[10] At the end of the transition period, however, they would cease operations.[11] From then on, U.S. policing activities in Panama would be limited to those of watchmen permitted to be employed in the Canal operating areas but not in the housing areas, and of U.S. military police at the defense sites.[12]

The Panamanian government would immediately assume the responsibility for providing throughout the former Canal Zone all services of a general jurisdictional nature, such as postal services, courts, licensing, and customs and immigration.[13] Within the Canal operating areas and the housing areas to be used by the United States, Panama would also provide immediately all such public services as police and fire protection, street maintenance, street lighting and cleaning, traffic control, and garbage collection. For these services the proposed Panama Canal Commission would have to pay Panama $10 million a year.[14] (Possibly because a quid pro quo on the part of Panama is involved here, this item has not been noticed or mentioned, so far as the author is aware, as one of the "economic benefits" to be derived by Panama under the proposed new Canal Treaty. But it is there—a flat $10 million annual fee.)

Because the utilities systems in the proposed housing areas are integrated with those of the Canal, the new Panama Canal Commission would provide utility services such as power, water, and sewers in those areas, as the Panama Canal Company does now. However, to the extent that such services were furnished to industrial and commercial enterprises and to persons other than U.S.-citizen employees in those areas, Panama would set the rates and bill the customers, turning the money received over to the Panama Canal Commission.[15]

Recalling the conceptual agreement arrived at by the negotiators during the course of the negotiations with regard to the assumption by Panama of jurisdiction and control over the Canal

181

Zone,[16] it is interesting to note that under the proposed treaty Panama would immediately take over the schools and hospitals. The negotiators obviously abandoned the earlier concept that the United States would be given the "operational rights" to provide these services. In fact, the proposed treaty would specifically prohibit the proposed Panama Canal Commission from providing "health and medical services . . . , including hospitals, leprosariums, veterinary, mortuary and cemetery services,"[17] and "educational services . . . , including schools and libraries."[18]

The Panama Canal Commission would be permitted, however, to send its U.S.-citizen employees and their dependents to the educational and medical facilities that the U.S. military would be permitted to maintain in the designated defense sites.[19]

In addition to the immediate loss of present sovereign rights in the Canal Zone and the relinquishment of governmental jurisdiction and control in that area in the manner just described, the United States would be required to turn over to Panama, immediately and without reimbursement, the Panama Railroad and the ports of Balboa and Cristobal. At the same time, it would have to transfer to Panama, also without reimbursement, title to all real estate and improvements in the Canal Zone, except in the areas specifically designated in the treaty for use by the United States.[20] It is estimated that under this arrangement about 50 percent of the Canal Zone area would be immediately turned over, *gratis*, to Panama.

The United States would only retain title to the property it would be permitted to use for Canal, housing, and military purposes. But, of course, when the treaty terminated on December 31, 1999, the title to everything, including the Canal and all the facilities, installations, and equipment pertaining to it, would pass to Panama, again *gratis*.[21]

United States' Rights. In the Kissinger-Tack agreement it was recited that, although the Canal Zone would be returned to the jurisdiction of Panama, the United States would *retain* specified rights of use for the duration of the new treaty. This recital is carried out in the proposed treaty not by the United States *retaining* any rights, but by Panama *granting* the United States new rights to manage, operate, and maintain the Canal,[22] and to share with Panama the defense of the Canal.[23] For the purpose of exercising those rights Panama would give the United States the right to use certain specified geographical areas, principally those designated "Canal operating areas," "housing areas," and "defense sites."[24]

Payments to Panama. Kissinger-Tack stated that under a new treaty Panama was to have a "just and equitable share" of the economic benefits derived from the operation of the Canal. That has been taken care of with a vengeance.

The current annual payments by the United States to Panama amount to $2.3 million. Under the proposed Canal Treaty these would be increased at least thirty-fold.

The new payments, described in the treaty as "a just and equitable return on the natural resources which [Panama] has dedicated to the efficient management, operation, maintenance, protection and defense of the Panama Canal," would be of three types:

(1) A fixed annuity of $10 million payable out of Canal revenues.

(2) A royalty of 30 cents a ton for each ship transiting the Canal under toll charge, also payable out of Canal revenues. It is estimated that, on the basis of current Canal transits, this royalty payment would produce at least $50 million a year for Panama.

(3) An additional annual payment of "up to" $10 million out of surplus Canal revenues, if earned.[25]

One observation about the source of these payments: Because all three would be payable out of Canal revenues, the proponents of the treaty claim that they would cost the U.S. taxpayer nothing. This is not true. The Canal has been losing money in substantial amounts for the past four years. It is expected to continue to do so for some time to come. Canal operating deficits are made up out of congressional appropriations—appropriations of U.S. taxpayers' money.

In addition to these annual "economic benefits," Panama has been assured by the United States, outside of the proposed treaty, that she will receive various types of loans, guarantees, and credits totalling $300 million—plus $50 million worth of military hardware.[26]

Canal Operation. It was stated in Kissinger-Tack that the new treaty would call for Panamanian participation in the administration of the Canal, the ultimate objective being a complete Panamanian takeover at the expiration of the treaty. It will be recalled that a conceptual agreement on this issue was reached by the negotiators sometime in 1974 or 1975.[27] Although it was contemplated in that agreement that a new U.S. agency would be created to take the place of the Panama Canal Company and that both nations would be involved, it was not decided what the agency would be, how it would be created, or who would control it. These and many other points have now been clarified.

A new U.S. government agency called the Panama Canal Commission would take over. It would "be constituted by and in conformity with the laws of the United States of America." It would have nine members, five of them U.S. citizens, four Panamanian. All would be officially appointed by the United States, but Panama would nominate the four Panamanians.[28] Up to January 1, 1999, the top administrative official would be an American, his deputy a Panamanian. During the last year of the treaty the nationalities would be reversed.[29]

Acting in an advisory capacity to the commission and as an inter-nation go-between on Canal operating and policy matters would be a Coordinating Committee consisting of one representative of each country, both "with equal authority."[30]

The commission would be given a wide range of power, including the power to set the toll charges for transiting vessels.[31] Of particular significance, however, is the listing in the treaty of the activities and operations currently carried on by the Panama Canal Company and the Canal Zone Government that the new commission would be prohibited from engaging in. Two of these, the operation of schools and hospital and medical facilities, have already been mentioned. A look at the rest of the list gives perhaps a clearer picture than anything else of how things would quickly change in the Canal Zone if the treaty were to go into effect.

No more U.S. wholesale or retail stores of any sort. No more U.S. production of food or drink. No more U.S. public restaurants. No more U.S. movie theaters. No more U.S. recreational and amusement facilities of any sort. No more U.S. laundries or dry-cleaning establishments. No more U.S. service stations or garages. No more U.S. cold-storage and freezer plants. No more U.S. commercial services or supplies to privately owned and operated boats. No more U.S. ferries. No more U.S. commercial pier and dock services for the handling of cargos and passengers.[32]

There is, however, a delay factor. If any of these activities or operations are "necessary to the efficient management, operation or maintenance of the Canal," the commission would be permitted to engage in them until other "arrangements can be made."[33] Who is to be the judge of the necessity is not stated.

Title to all the housing units in the Canal Zone would pass immediately to Panama. Nevertheless, the units needed by the commission to house U.S.-citizen employees and their dependents would continue to be made available for that purpose. Those units would be managed, assigned, and rented to tenants by the commission.[34] However, by the time the treaty had been in force 5 years, the number of such units would have to have been reduced by 20 percent; in 10 years, 30 percent; 15 years, 45 percent; 20 years, 60 percent.[35] This would mean, assuming the treaty were to go into effect in 1978, that by 1999, the last year of the treaty, only 40 percent of the present number of housing units for U.S.-citizen employees would continue to be available.

The provisions in the treaty dealing with employment by the Commission of non-U.S. citizens, that is, of Panamanians, are numerous and extensive in scope. They deal in considerable detail with such matters as notice of employment opportunities, preferential hiring treatment, training and apprentice programs, recognition of professional licenses issued by Panama (a new foot in the door for Panamanian ship pilots?), recognition of unions, collective bargaining rights, social security, early retirement options, health insurance, medical benefits, and so forth.[36]

Little of significance is said, however, about U.S.-citizen employees of the commission except (1) that by the end of five years 20 percent of those currently employed must have been laid off, (2) that those who lose their jobs as a result of the new treaty "will be placed by the United States of America, to the maximum extent feasible, in other appropriate jobs with the Government of the United States in accordance with United States Civil Service regulations," and (3) that all new hires will be rotated back to the U.S. on a five-year basis.[37]

For U.S.-citizen employees and their dependents running afoul of the Panamanian criminal law, Article XIX of the Agreement for Implementation of Article III of the treaty would constitute, in effect, a status of forces agreement almost identical to the one in another portion of the treaty for U.S. military personnel and their dependents. In both instances the agreements are similar to the agreements the United States has, for example, with the European nations in which U.S. troops are stationed.

Joint Defense. Some attention was given in chapter 9 to the conceptual agreement reached by the negotiators as a basis for implementing the joint defense assurance in the Kissinger-Tack Statement of Principles. Incredibly that musical comedy fantasy has been embodied in the new treaty almost word for word.[38] The only seemingly significant change is that instead of giving the United States the "main" responsibility for defense, as was the case in the conceptual agreement, that responsibility has been relabeled "primary." However, since the same two-headed command structure, coupled with complete independence of combat action for the two military forces, would continue, the change appears to be meaningless.

Much as one may deplore the idea of separate, secret agreements supplementing this or any other international treaty, it is devoutly to be hoped in this instance that assurances have been secretly given to the United States by Panama that Panama's rather small and ineffectual combat force would be kept confined to quarters in the event of an attack on the Canal. Otherwise, the confusion might be unmanageable.

The new material on the defense of the Canal is contained in the Agreement in Implementation of Article IV. Of particular importance are the provisions that designate the defense sites that the U.S. forces will be permitted to use and the conditions of their use. The effect, apparently, is to reduce substantially the number of U.S. bases and to diminish, again substantially, the geographical area of U.S. military activity. However, beyond the assurance given by the United States that it will try "in normal times" to maintain its armed forces in Panama at not more than present levels,[39] there appear to be no actual restrictions on the number of U.S. troops and no prohibitions against the continuation of the various military schools, training programs, and activities that are currently being carried on. Likewise, the authority to maintain schools, hospitals, commissaries, post offices, recreational facilities, and other service activities within the U.S. defense site areas is made quite clear.[40] The status of forces agreement with regard to violations of Panamanian criminal law seems to be more or less standard.[41]

What happens to the U.S. military in Panama when the treaty expires in 1999? For the clear answer to that, one needs merely to look at Article V of the other proposed new treaty, the Neutrality Treaty:

> After the termination of the Panama Canal Treaty, only the Republic of Panama shall . . . maintain military forces, defense sites, and military installations within its national territory.

Again, no ifs, ands, or buts.

A New Canal. Kissinger-Tack referred only to the possibility of enlarging the capacity of the present Canal. There was no mention of a new canal. Article XIII of the proposed new treaty, entitled "A Sea-Level Canal or a Third Lane of Locks," comes, therefore, as a surprise. It starts right out by breaking new ground with the recognition by both nations of a potential need for a sea-level canal, a commitment for a joint study, and a further commitment, if such a new canal in Panama turns out to be necessary, to negotiate the terms for its construction.[42]

Then come two peculiar pledges, one by Panama, the other by the United States, with regard to the construction of a new canal. In the first, Panama promises, in effect, that during the life of the treaty, that is, up until December 31, 1999, no nation other than the United States will be permitted to build a new canal in Panama.[43] As a practical matter, this provision seems to be rather meaningless, because while the United States is still present and operating the Panama Canal, it seems a remote possibility that any other nation would, even with Panamanian permission, start building another one.

The U.S. pledge that follows, however, is far from meaningless. The United States promises that during the term of the new treaty it will *not even negotiate* for the right to build a new canal *anywhere in the Western Hemisphere.*[44] This *is* a surprise provision.

Apparently Panama has struck a bargain whereby she can both eat her cake and keep it; there is not going to be any cake anywhere else, no canal to compete with the one she is going to take over. Given the lead time required for negotiating the right to build a canal and then to build it, this provision makes it quite clear there is no possibility of a U.S. sea-level canal in Nicaragua, Colombia, or Mexico for many years to come.

As far as enlarging the present Canal is concerned—which the United States would hardly be inclined to undertake for the few years of operational control that would be left if it were undertaken—the new treaty would allow the United States to go ahead with the Terminal Lake–Third Locks project mentioned in chapter 12 as long as copies of the construction plans were furnished to Panama and no nuclear excavation techniques were used without Panama's permission.[45]

The other proposed treaty, the Neutrality Treaty, is brief. Some may call it enigmatic.

It would go into effect at the same time as the new Canal Treaty.[46] Actually, it would only have real meaning and significance after that treaty expired, after the United States had pulled out of Panama. It purports to be an agreement—with no termination date (perpetuity?)—assuring the "permanent neutrality" of the Canal.[47]

The treaty starts out with a unilateral declaration by Panama "that the Canal, as an international transit waterway, shall be permanently neutral."[48] It then goes on to state that Panama makes this declaration of neutrality "in order that both in time of peace and in time of war it [the Canal] shall remain secure and open to peaceful transit by the vessels of all nations on terms of entire equality . . . so that the Canal, and therefore the Isthmus of Panama, shall not be the target of reprisals in any armed conflict between other nations of the world." However, in order to be entitled to such equality of treatment, every transiting vessel would have to pay the required toll and other charges, abide by the applicable rules and regulations, and refrain from any "acts of hostility while in the Canal."[49]

The tolls and other charges and the rules and regulations are to be "just, equitable and reasonable."[50] Panama, apparently, would be the sole judge of her own compliance with that commitment.

It is provided in one article that the warships "of all nations shall at all times be entitled to transit the Canal, irrespective of their internal operations, means of propulsion, origin, destination or armament, without being subjected, as a condition of transit, to inspection, search or surveillance." In fact, such warships "shall be entitled to refuse to disclose their internal operations, origin, armament, cargo or destination."[51] Then, in another article, identical assurances are given with regard to the warships of the United States and Panama,[52] but added to those assurances is one not specifically given to those of other nations:

188

an assurance that the warships of the U.S. and Panama "will be entitled to transit the Canal expeditiously."[53] The meaning of this provision has caused considerable argument, the U.S. State Department claiming that it would give a priority of transit to U.S. warships, the right to be moved to the head of the line, so to speak. Negotiators for Panama say that is not so, that during the negotiations the United States sought such a preference but Panama refused to agree. At any rate, without anything more specific than the word "expeditiously," there is plenty of room for argument over what the provision really does mean in this context—if anything.

The key provisions of this treaty so far as United States defense rights after December 31, 1999, are concerned, are Articles IV and V, for only out of them, or rather only out of Article IV and in spite of Article V, can any conjuring up of residual defense rights of the United States be predicated.

Article V has already been quoted in connection with the clear termination of U.S. defense rights in Panama under the proposed Canal Treaty, but because of the crucial nature of the issue of residual defense rights under the second treaty and because it is in effect, though not in numerical sequence, a preface to Article IV, its wording is worth repeating:

> After the termination of the Panama Canal Treaty, only the Republic of Panama shall . . . maintain military forces, defense sites and military establishments within its national territory.

Then look at the wording of Article IV:

> The United States and the Republic of Panama agree to maintain the regime of neutrality established in this Treaty, which shall be maintained in order that the Canal shall remain permanently neutral, notwithstanding the termination of any other treaties entered into by the two Contracting Parties.

Nowhere in the entire treaty are the rights and obligations of the United States with regard to the implementation of this article set forth. Nowhere in the entire treaty is it stated that if the neutrality of the Canal is threatened or breached the United States would have the right to violate Article V and send military

189

forces into Panama. Here, again, the spokesmen of the two nations are arguing over the meaning of the treaty—in this instance arguing over the meaning of its most important provision from the standpoint of the United States.

One more provision of the Neutrality Treaty should be mentioned. It is one in which the United States and Panama agree to sponsor a resolution in the Organization of American States giving all nations of the world the opportunity to signify their adherence "to the objectives" of the treaty. This they could do by signing a "Protocol" which would be deposited with the OAS.[54]

Here, then, are the principal features of the two proposed treaties, the cards finally laid face up on the table for all the world, and particularly the American people and the Congress, to see.

What happens next? So far as Panama is concerned, nothing further, at least for the time being. In accordance with the provisions of the Panamanian constitution, on October 23, 1977, the treaties were submitted to a vote of the people and were overwhelmingly approved. This was not surprising since only a yes or no vote was permitted, and only one point of view was expressed in the government-controlled news media. Dictators have a way of winning plebiscites.

In the United States the constitutional procedures for ratification are quite different. Much is happening and much remains to happen.

The treaty-making power resides jointly in the president of the United States and in the United States Senate. Article II, Section 2, of the Constitution provides that the president "shall have power, by and with the advice and consent of the Senate, to make treaties, provided two-thirds of the Senators present concur." In other words, a treaty negotiated and signed by the president, as is the case with these proposed Panamanian treaties, is of no force or effect whatsoever unless and until it is approved by the Senate. If all senators are present at the time the vote is taken, 67 votes will be needed to approve.

When the president submits a treaty to the Senate for consideration, it is assigned initially to the Senate Foreign Relations Committee. That committee holds hearings, takes testimony pro and con, and ultimately reports the treaty to the Senate as a whole with its recommendations as to what action should be taken: approve, approve with changes, known as amendments and reservations, or reject. Other Senate committees having a direct interest in the subject matter of a treaty can also get into the act and go through similar proceedings.

The important thing to be noted is that the final action taken by the Senate does *not* have to be a flat approval or rejection. The range of permissible action is unlimited. This fact is often overlooked in a heated controversy over a treaty. The proposed Panamanian treaties are a typical example of this. Listening to the president and his treaty supporters, one gets the impression there are only two alternatives: take the treaties as they are or reject them as they are—and God help you and the nation if you choose the latter course. Many of the ardent opponents of the treaties are guilty of creating the same false impression: yes or no, nothing else. This just is not so.

The Senate has the power to take any position it chooses. It can change a treaty, shape it in the manner it deems to be in the best interests of the nation, and then approve it, just as it can amend any proposed piece of legislation before it and then pass it. If it changes a treaty and approves it in its changed form, the ball goes back to the president. It is then up to him to explore with the other nation that is party to the negotiated treaty the possibilities of accepting the changes made by the U.S. Senate or of undertaking to resume negotiations on the basis of those changes. This is precisely the situation with regard to the Panamanian treaties.

What about the other half of Congress, the U.S. House of Representatives? Does it have nothing to say in treaty matters? Technically, the answer is that it does not—not in the actual approval or rejection of a treaty. But as a practical matter, in the case of certain types of treaties, of which the proposed Panama Canal Treaty is a prime example, it would appear to have a lot to say.

Article IV, Section 3, of the Constitution provides that the "Congress shall have power *to dispose* and make all needful rules and regulations respecting the *territory or other property belonging to the United States.*" (Emphasis added.) Not just the Senate, but the "Congress," and that means both houses. When a proposed treaty, such as the Panama Canal Treaty, calls for the disposition of territory or property of the United States, it would seem the House must get into the act. Such a treaty can, to be sure, be approved by the Senate without

House concurrence and become a valid obligation of the United States. But that obligation might remain meaningless and unperformable until the entire Congress, that is, both houses, has enacted legislation to implement the treaty's provisions regarding the transfer of U.S. territory and property to another nation.

This is particularly true in the case of the Panama Canal Treaty. A vital feature of that treaty is the transfer to Panama of ownership of the Canal Zone, to which the U.S. has complete title, and of the Panama Canal, every lock, every gate, every dam, every installation of which is U.S. property.

So both houses of Congress have a big job on their hands. It took 13 years to negotiate these treaties, and it is bound to—and should—take a considerable period of time for Congress to act on them. The responsibility is a great one—just as great as that of the presidency.

In the presentation of the proposed treaties in this chapter, an attempt has been made to avoid burdening the reader with too much detail. Congress, however, cannot avoid those details, not a single word or bit of punctuation.

There are a thousand and one questions to be asked by Congress. The views and advice of hundreds of experts must be sought and weighed. Take, for example, the situation that would be faced by the new, bi-national Panama Canal Commission in attempting to manage and operate the Canal under the conditions prescribed in the proposed Panama Canal Treaty. Can the Canal be effectively and efficiently operated and maintained under those conditions? Is the bi-national structure workable? Is there enough authority given? Enough control? Can key U.S. employees be persuaded to stay on? Is enough land and water area made available, compared with the present set-up? Is it certain that all the vital functions of the operation can be carried out?

The answer to these and similar questions must be elicited from the many dedicated, experienced people who have run the Canal in the past and those, similarly dedicated and experienced, who are running it now. Congress cannot guess at the answers. They have to be obtained from the right people—and particularly *not* from the treaty negotiators or aspiring politicians.

The same is true with regard to the situation that would be faced by the U. S. military under both proposed treaties. Can our forces continue to operate effectively in Panama while they remain there under the proposed Panama Canal Treaty, particularly in the event of an attack? Or would they be hamstrung? Are the areas of operation left to the military sufficient? Is the number of bases to be retained adequate?

And then, most crucial of all, what about the situation to be faced by the U.S. armed forces under the proposed Neutrality Treaty? Is it realistic to believe that the United States can defend the Canal after having pulled out of Panama completely? Even if the answer to that question should be yes, could the U.S. successfully go back into Panama and "defend" the Canal, that is, evict an occupying hostile force, in the absence of treaty provisions spelling out what could, or could not, be done?

Here, again, and maybe most particularly, the Congress cannot rely on guesses. The security of the United States and the entire Western Hemisphere is at stake. The advice of highly qualified, experienced military experts and personnel must be sought and weighed. The military views received must be uninhibited, unfettered. And in this latter connection both the Congress and the American people should keep in mind constantly the possible presence of what, for want of a better term, might be called the "Singlaub Syndrome."[55] It is this. Military officers still on active duty, particularly those in high places, have a natural nagging concern over the consequences of disagreeing with the commander-in-chief.

Only views expressed in the highest interest of the nation can serve the purposes of Congress and the American people.

17

In the Highest
National Interest

Of the two men at the *New Yorker* bar in the spring of 1976, the one who wondered what was wrong with himself and why, all of a sudden, he could not live without the Panama Canal, decided to find out. He made quite a project of it.

First, he went to the public library and read up on the history of Panama and the Canal. He read everything he could lay his hands on to bring himself up to date on the development of the current treaty negotiations and the problems involved.

Then he went to Washington. He talked with government officials—in the White House, in the Pentagon, and in the State Department, including members of the U.S. negotiating team. He talked with members of Congress. He talked with former government officials and with retired military personnel.

Finally he took his wife on a trip to Panama. There he saw the Canal, the Zone, Panama City, Colon, and some of the country-side and coastal area. He talked with Panama Canal Company and Canal Zone officials. He talked with the military at South-com. He talked with Zonians, with U.S. embassy officials and staff personnel, and with U.S. businessmen and bankers in Panama City.

To see Panama's side of the coin, he talked with Panamanian government officials, with members of the Panamanian negotiating team, with Panamanian businessmen, church leaders, and labor leaders. He talked with people outside Panama City, in the country—farmers, store owners, and the like.

Returned to the United States, he sought out his pal at the bar. After the usual greetings and the opening toast, his friend asked him whether, after all his efforts, he had found out what was wrong with him.

"Yes, I have," the traveler replied. "I've got Panama Canalitis. I'm really concerned about what's going on. I guess it was that Reagan fella who got me worrying about it, got me kind of upset—in the gut, that is. But I didn't know why I was upset. Now I do."

"Do you still feel you can't live without the Canal?" his friend asked with a smile.

"Yes," he said, very seriously. "At least I feel I *shouldn't* live without it for a long time to come." He paused. Then he added in a stubborn tone, "Furthermore, I don't think I have to, and I'm not going to."

In September 1977 he saw the proposed new treaties.

The Panama Canal problem is just as difficult today as it was yesterday, or a year or two ago. In fact, it is probably more difficult.

First of all, the executive branch of the government has crawled way out on a limb in its eagerness to get a new treaty with Panama and avoid trouble. Second, the government of Panama, once, in spite of obvious faults, at least thought to be stable, is now coming apart at the seams. So much so that entering into a new treaty with the present leadership might be a futile exercise.

And, third, nothing has transpired, either in the way of events or an effective educational program, to change the instinctive attitude of the American people toward giving up U.S. rights in Panama. A majority seemingly is opposed—still without really knowing why. And when, like the man from the *New Yorker* bar, the American people move from instinct to observation concerning the Panama Canal issue, as they have now that they are faced with the new treaties, there is little likelihood of a substantial change in that attitude. Some change, perhaps, but not much.

Thus it appears that U.S. government policy with regard to Panama and American public opinion are at loggerheads. This is the Panama Canal dilemma.

Under the circumstances it seems essential to determine where the best interests of the United States lie. For the dilemma must be resolved in the light of those interests.

There are three fundamental interests of the United States involved: foreign relations, foreign trade, and national security. They are, of course, inextricably bound up in one another, and considerations with regard to one may outweigh those with regard to another. Yet they should first be examined independently. Then the conclusions with regard to each should be reconciled, if possible, with those regarding the others.

Regardless of how it came about and whether or not there is justification for it, there can be little doubt that the Panama Canal, or, more correctly, the relationship between the United States and Panama with respect to the Canal, has for some time been a major stumbling block in U.S.–Latin America relations. The feeling seems to exist, officially at least, throughout Latin America that the provisions of the 1903 treaty between the United States and Panama demean Panama and that the failure of the United States to remedy the situation is the reflection of a similar, demeaning U.S. attitude toward all Latin American countries—in a word: an insult.

How deep this feeling goes, at least in many countries—indeed, whether it exists at all in some, except as an official expression—is debatable. But at any rate, it is there. And, because it is primarily an emotional matter, the voices raised in proclamation of it tend to be shrill and inflammatory. It has its consequences. It is a significant factor to be reckoned with. From a foreign relations standpoint it is something to be remedied if possible, something that cannot be brushed off.

At the same time the dimensions of this emotional feeling should not be exaggerated. What is it that is considered as demeaning Panama from a Latin American viewpoint?

Is it the fact that the United States owns and operates the Canal? No.

Is it the fact that the United States is the defender of the Canal? No.

196

Is it the relatively small amount of money paid by the United States to Panama? No.

Is it the fact that Panama's sovereignty is denigrated by the 1903 treaty? Yes, precisely that and nothing more.

It is true, of course, that Panama would like to play an increasing role in the operation of the Canal, particularly to have more Panamanians in the higher-paid Canal jobs, and someday, perhaps, to take it over. But this aspiration, rather than evoking sympathy and support in Latin America, creates concern, particularly in the countries that are the major users of the Canal.

It is also true that Panama would like to have the prestige of being considered a codefender of the Canal. But Panama and the rest of Latin America would be the first to admit that Panama is incapable of contributing more than a token on that score. And certainly Panama would like to have more money—as much as possible.

But none of these is an issue that would put Panama on the warpath, so to speak. Nor are these issues that would unite Latin American in support of such a course.

No. Sovereignty is the essence of the problem between the United States and Panama. It is also the essence of the problem between the United States and Latin America as regards Panama. What Panama is seeking and what the rest of Latin America is supporting was expressed in the resolution before the UN Security Council that the U.S. was jockeyed into vetoing in 1973. That resolution called for a new treaty between Panama and the United States that would "guarantee full respect for Panama's effective sovereignty over all its territory."[1]

These are high-sounding words, words ringing with nationalistic overtones. The most important thing about them, however, is the absence of any words about the ownership, operation, or defense of the Canal, or about money. The only thing mentioned is "respect for Panama's effective sovereignty."

This seems to indicate quite clearly that the U.S. foreign relations problem *as regards Latin America* in relation to the Panama Canal lies solely in the matter of Panama's sovereignty over the Canal Zone. From a foreign relations standpoint, therefore, it is in the interest of the United States to resolve that question in such a way as to eliminate the Latin American "feeling."

That, of course, would not necessarily resolve the U.S. foreign relations problem with Panama. But that is a nation-to-nation problem, not one encompassing as wide an area either geograph-

197

ically or substantively as the more general problem. Nevertheless, it would be wrong to think that our relations with Panama can be ignored, to believe that since Panama is a militarily powerless country we can treat her as we please, just as long as we keep the rest of Latin America happy.

That would be wrong on two counts. In the first place, Panama is the host country for the Canal operations that are of considerable importance to the United States. Propinquity between the citizens and officials of the two countries is close and constant. Over 70 percent of the Canal work force is Panamanian. Good relations are essential to carrying on Canal operations efficiently and effectively. Second, mollified as the rest of Latin America might be by a solution of the sovereignty problem, the Havana-Moscow axis is standing in the wings, waiting. Its cue to go on stage will come from a dissatisfied Panama, particularly one hostile to the United States.

What, then, are the dimensions of the foreign relations problem, the nation-to-nation problem, between the United States and Panama? What is the real "feeling" in Panama?

Recognizing that U.S. negotiating representatives have raised the hopes of Panamanians with regard to almost every possible issue and that political efforts will be made constantly to exploit those hopes, it is nevertheless the opinion of many people, Americans and Panamanians alike, that the problem can be measured solely in terms of three things: sovereignty, perpetuity (in reality, duration), and money.

The Panamanian feeling about sovereignty has been dealt with extensively in an earlier chapter. It is a strong feeling, widely held.

Perpetuity is a two-aspect element of the problem. In a practical sense, it involves only the question of duration—the logical insistence that a new but still delimiting treaty have some fixed termination date. In a psychological sense, however, it is broader; it involves the pride and hopes of Panama as regards ultimate ownership of the Canal. This, too, is logical, even though basically nationalistic.

The money dimension is also logical. The most important thing about the Panama Canal from the standpoint of the United States is its essentiality for national defense purposes. The Panamanians know this. The Panamanians know the United States pays Spain $20 million a year for military bases in that country. They know the United States is spending almost that much for bases in Turkey. They know that the most recent arrangement for remaining on Clark Field in the Philippines runs close to a billion dollars. They are fully aware that these are all payments for limited periods of occupancy, not for permanent tenure. They know that the U.S. defense budget is over $100 billion annually. And they know that in 1967 U.S. and Panamanian negotiators agreed to a provision in one of the abortive new treaties that would have today been the equivalent of an annual payment to Panama in excess of $20 million. All this as against the $2.3 million they now receive.

Sovereignty, duration, and money. These are the true dimensions of our *foreign relations* problem with Panama. It may seem strange not to include in that list control and defense of the Canal, the other major areas in which Panama has repeatedly expressed aspirations. But it only seems strange because U.S. precommitments with regard to those matters have always been included in the negotiation picture. That does not mean that they had to be there. Nor does it mean that they have to remain there. And certainly it does not mean that if a satisfactory settlement were reached with Panama on the basis of the three other, seemingly more urgent, matters, and the control and defense provisions remained unchanged, the U.S. foreign relations problem with Panama would not be resolved, at least with regard to the Canal. The realities appear to be otherwise.

To treat such an observation as being absurd and to maintain that commitments on control and defense of the Canal are indispensable to a resolution of the problem is to bind oneself blindly to negotiating errors of the past and to perpetuate as elements of the dispute matters on which Panama, or rather Panamanians, do not, in fact, feel strongly, regardless of the fact that *official* expressions may indicate to the contrary. After all, what must be done at this juncture in the situation is to assess the true dimensions of the foreign relations problem as regards Panama, that is, the scope and depth of *Panamanian* feeling—not to assess what it would take to assuage an ingrained, traditional feeling in the U.S. State Department that there are certain things that the U. S. *should* do, certain things that the U. S. *should* give up, in order to clean the slate of alleged past misdeeds.

As a matter of foreign relations, negotiations with Panama should be, and could be, a sincere effort, from a position of strength, to strike a bargain designed to rectify genuine grievances, not a vehicle for some sort of U.S. atonement. Such a stance could regain for the United States much of the respect it has lost as a result of its servile approach in the negotiations over the past 13 years.

Summing up with regard to the United States' foreign relations interest in the Panama Canal situation, these conclusions seem justified:

(1) There should be a new treaty.

(2) The problem of our relations with Latin America vis-à-vis the Canal relates solely to the matter of Panamanian sovereignty over the Canal Zone. If this matter were cleared up, that problem would be solved.

(3) The problem of our relations with Panama vis-à-vis the Canal relate primarily to three matters: sovereignty over the Canal Zone, a fixed duration for any new treaty, and money. As far as commitments for ultimate control and defense of the Canal by Panama are concerned, those are matters that might, if they could be worked out satisfactorily, enhance the foreign relations value of an overall settlement. But they are *not* essential to the solution of the problem.

The foreign trade interest of the United States as regards the Panama Canal must be measured in terms of the future economic value of the Canal to the United States. Most indications are that although that value is declining and will probably continue to do so, the Canal will be of considerable economic importance to the United States throughout the foreseeable future— 50 years, at least—probably longer.

The United States now has the right and the capability of realizing that future economic value by continuing its control and operation of the Canal. The sole question, then, from a foreign trade standpoint, is simply this: Would the United States be assured of realizing that future economic value if at some time during the foreseeable future control and operation of the Canal were turned over to Panama?

The answer to that question turns on whether or not Panama can be expected by the time of such transfer to have achieved the capability of operating the Canal as well as the United States does now—for the benefit of the United States, Panama, and the rest of the world. Certainly from the standpoint of U.S. foreign trade interest in the Canal there is no reason why the United States should accept a Panamanian capability any less than that as a basis for relinquishing control.

It can be conceded that over the years Panama, with the help of the United States, could acquire a technical capability of her own equal to that of the United States. In fact, there can be little doubt, witness the example of Egypt and the Suez Canal, that Panama could achieve that capability almost immediately by hiring foreigners, chiefly Canal-experienced Americans, to fill the key jobs. There must, however, be some reservations with regard to maintenance capability for reasons discussed earlier.

As for Panama's achieving, during the foreseeable future, the necessary financial capability, it seems obvious that without the occurrence of some economic miracle in Panama there is no possibility of that happening. The capital outlays that will be necessary during that period to maintain the Canal and to bring it up to maximum capacity, to say nothing of defraying operating losses if they continue to occur, will be far beyond any current potential of the Panamanian economy. And if Panama had to turn to others for financial help, as it would, whoever undertook to furnish that help would naturally insist on controlling the Canal's operations until the investment was paid off. Right now, the only prospects for that role, aside from the United States (a rather ridiculous thought), seem to be the Soviet Union, the OPEC countries, and possibly Japan. From the standpoint of U.S. foreign trade interest in the Canal, the first two of these, at least, would appear to be wholly unacceptable—in fact, fatal.

The political capability of Panama to operate the Canal as the United States does—impartially, unexploitingly, efficiently and, to the extent possible, economically—can scarcely be expected to be achieved in the foreseeable future. The present government's performance during recent years in other areas of Panama's economy make it probably the most unlikely candidate for such achievement that can be imagined. One can only guess whether or not there will be a change in government, or in the leadership of the present government, and whether, if there were, the prospect in this regard would be any better.

It is all very well to say that no government of Panama would be so foolhardy as to exploit the Canal for the personal gain of its leaders to the point of killing the goose that lays the golden eggs. Maybe so, but past performance in other Panamanian economic enterprises makes even that assumption doubtful. At any rate, it is almost a certainty that any government of Panama would use the Canal's economic potential to shore up other areas of the economy for political reasons and thus produce the same result. Given the prospects for the economy of Panama during the foreseeable future, the Canal appears to be too great a political temptation for any Panamanian government.

Summing up with regard to the United States' foreign trade interest in the Panama Canal, the conclusion seems inescapable that that interest is too important to be jeopardized by a commitment to transfer control and operation to Panama within the foreseeable future.

The value of the Canal to the United States as a defense waterway and the importance of continuing a U.S. military presence in Panama for the security of both the United States and the Western Hemisphere were developed in chapter 15. They compel the conclusion that the Canal is crucial to the United States' national security interest and will probably remain so indefinitely. Therefore, with respect to that interest there can be no justification for even suggesting that Panama might someday be capable of meeting those defense responsibilities—certainly not so long as the Soviets harbor thoughts of world domination.

The conclusions regarding all three basic U.S. interests, foreign relations, foreign trade and national security, add up to these:

(1) There should be a new treaty.

(2) Panama's sovereignty over the Canal Zone should be recognized.

(3) Any new treaty should have a fixed term duration.

(4) Panama should receive more money.

(5) The United States must retain the right to control and operate the Canal for the foreseeable future.

(6) The United States must retain the right to defend the Canal and maintain a military presence in Panama indefinitely.

A mere glance at this list indicates an apparent conflict between the conclusion regarding Panama's sovereignty over the Canal Zone, on the one hand, and those calling for continued U.S. control and defense of the Canal, on the other. There also seems to be a conflict between the conclusion regarding a fixed term duration for a new treaty and, again, those dealing with continuing U.S. control and defense rights.

Are these actual conflicts or can the conclusions involved be reconciled? If they cannot be reconciled, which ones should prevail? These questions deserve careful consideration.

There are many people in the United States who believe sincerely and intensely that the moment the United States concedes sovereign rights to Panama over the Canal Zone, the ball game will be over; that, in the face of such a concession, treaty provisions reserving to the United States the rights to control and defend the Canal would be worthless; and that Panama would at the earliest opportunity expropriate all U.S. property in Panama and order the United States out.

Because of the prime significance of the sovereignty question to both Panama and all of Latin America, it is probably not an exaggeration to say that the whole question of whether or not there will be, or even should be, a new treaty could turn on the validity or invalidity of this belief. Clearly, if it is valid, a new treaty that recognizes Panamanian sovereignty over the Canal Zone cannot, and should not, be accepted by the United States, regardless of the consequences.

A look at the Cuba–Guantanamo Bay situation furnishes an enlightening perspective for the resolution of this vital question. The U.S. naval base at Guantanamo Bay, at the southeastern tip of Cuba, consists of an area of about 45 square miles, of which approximately one-third is water. The land area of the base is enclosed by a perimeter fence. Behind the fence, on the U.S. side, are minefields and watchtowers. Behind the fence, on the Cuban side, there is a mined barbed wire barrier manned by Cuban troops and, behind that, artillery emplacements that, if guns were installed, could cover the entire U.S. base.

The base is used by the United States primarily as a naval training facility and a refueling station for naval ships. The population of the base is a little over 7000, including Cubans who come in each day to work. United States defense forces total about 900.

The United States occupies the base under a treaty-derived *lease* agreement, entered into in 1903 for an indefinite term. Title to all the land in the base belongs to Cuba. The U.S. "recognizes the continuance of the ultimate sovereignty of Cuba." In exchange, Cuba "consents" that the United States shall exercise complete jurisdiction and control over and within "the area."[2] Thus Cuba has both legal title to all the land and sovereignty over it.

On the island of Cuba there are tens of thousands of Soviet-trained, Soviet-equipped Cuban combat troops—including highly mobile tank and paratroop units—with strong air support. The fact that Castro, over a period of almost 20 years, and particularly during the more recent years of substantial Soviet-built military strength, has made no move to oust the United States, even under circumstances of extreme hostility and an absence of diplomatic relations between the U.S. and Cuba, is a matter of considerable significance. It makes it seem highly unlikely that a militarily powerless country such as Panama, under totally dissimilar and less compelling circumstances, would seize upon the cession to it of sovereignty over the Canal Zone as the basis for an attempt to oust the United States from Panama.

There is nothing but disadvantage to Cuba—and to Moscow—in having the continued presence of the United States in Guantanamo. On the other hand, there are innumerable advantages to Panama, not the least of them the U.S.-operated Canal, in having the United States presence in Panama. If Cuba does not see fit to make a move, why would Panama?

The Cuban situation points up the realities that govern the actions of nations in circumstances of this sort. It also indicates that the concern over the possible effect of the relinquishment of U.S. sovereign rights in Panama may be based more on questionable legal technicalities than on sound reasoning.

In the case of Cuba, it is obvious that Castro has not moved to oust the United States because he does not have the military strength for the ultimate success of such an effort and because the mere attempt to do so would result in the invasion of Cuba by the United States.

What about the legal technicalities in the Cuban situation? Cuba retains legal title to all land in the Guantanamo base area, so she would have no need of even going through the motions of expropriation. Furthermore, Cuban sovereignty over the base area is recognized by the United States. All Cuba needs to do from a technical standpoint is to unilaterally abrogate the 1903 treaty-lease agreement with the United States and tell the U.S. to get out. But that would be a violation of international law. "Que le hace?" Castro might say to that. But whether it matters or not, he still would be right back where he started. From a practical standpoint, he simply cannot afford a military showdown with the United States.

In the case of Panama, if by a new treaty Panama's sovereignty over the Canal were to be recognized by the United States, the situation would be quite similar. In attempting to oust the United States by force, assuming, of course, a continuing U.S. military presence, as would be the case under the proposed new Panama Canal Treaty, Panama would be undertaking the impossible. And, from a technical standpoint, she would be even worse off than Cuba, because the United States, not Panama, has the legal title to all the property essential for Canal operations and defense. Therefore, before the U.S. was told to get out, Panama would, from a technical standpoint, have to go through the motions of expropriation. Even that might involve a legal barrier because there is a question in international law of whether the right of expropriation is available in a government-to-government situation. The usual case is where a government expropriates privately owned property. In any event, even if expropriation were in order, Panama as her next move would have to unilaterally abrogate the new treaty with the United States. And that would be a violation of international law. Again, *"Que le hace?"* Torrijos or his successor might say. But, just as in the case of Cuba, Panama would be right back where she started—facing an impossible military showdown with the United States.

With all due respect to the sincerity of those who believe that recognizing Panama's sovereignty over the Canal Zone would be the end of everything for the United States in Panama, such a belief seems to be totally unrealistic and even to lack any technical, legal, foundation.

Short of the belief that recognizing the sovereignty of Panama would end everything, there is, at least at first blush, a perhaps more justifiable concern that, as a practical matter, the U.S. could not effectively operate or defend the Canal if it relinquished its rights of sovereignty over the Canal Zone for those purposes. But this concern overlooks the distinction between sovereignty, on the one hand, and jurisdiction and control, on the other, and the fact that the two are separable. The U.S.-Cuban lease agreement is a good example of that very distinction and separability.

In any new treaty with Panama involving recognition of Panama's sovereignty over the Canal Zone, it would be extremely important to limit Panama's jurisdiction and control over the area in such a manner and to such an extent as to assure the ability of the United States to operate and defend the Canal without interference. In addition to limiting Panama in this regard, it would also involve spelling out with great care the extent of the jurisdiction and control being retained by the United States for those purposes. This is a difficult, but not an insoluble, problem. It is the problem Congress faces with the proposed new Panama Canal Treaty.

The conclusions that the sovereignty of Panama should be recognized and that the rights of the United States to operate and defend the Canal should be retained are not in conflict as a matter of principle, and need not be as a practical matter—if carefully provided for.

The U.S. foreign relations interest in having a new treaty with Panama that would be of fixed rather than perpetual duration is at least in apparent conflict with the U.S. foreign trade interest in retaining control of the Canal *for the foreseeable future*. This apparent conflict would not, however, be in fact a conflict if the foreseeable future of the economic value of the Canal to the United States were susceptible of safe measurement and if by such measurement it were determined not to extend beyond a certain date.

Probably, from the United States' viewpoint, no one would quarrel if that date were determined to be at the end of a 100-year, or even a 75-year, period. Fifty years might even be acceptable. In those terms, then, there would be no conflict and the foreign relations and foreign trade conclusions could be reconciled in favor of a fixed duration. However, if such a determination cannot be made on a safe basis, there is a conflict that cannot be reconciled. In that case, the foreign trade interest outweighs the less pressing foreign relations interest and no commitment should be made to turn the Canal over to Panama by a certain date. Presumably the most that could be done would be to set the treaty up with regard to this matter on the basis of successive treaty periods of, say, 25 years, with a U.S. commitment to reexamine the situation at the end of each such period.

As far as the conclusion that any new treaty should be of a fixed duration and the conclusion that the United States should retain the right to defend the Canal indefinitely are concerned, it would be ridiculous even to suggest that there is no conflict, for the words *fixed* and *indefinite* are opposites. But in this situation the two conflicting conclusions do not have to be weighed against one another, because the interests from which they stem are, in fact, one and the same. The essential purpose of both foreign relations and national security is national survival. If placing a termination date on the right to defend the

Canal would jeopardize the survival of the United States, as chapter 15 tends to demonstrate it would, then both interests, foreign relations and national security, dictate the rejection of such a commitment. Here, again, perhaps successive treaty periods and a U.S. commitment to examine the situation periodically are the only practical solutions.

It is essential that a new treaty with Panama be one in the highest interest of the United States. At the same time it must be fair and just to Panama.

The time has come to develop a national policy with regard to the Panama Canal that will achieve these objectives as quickly as possible and to implement that policy with a new negotiating stance—one of dealing firmly and fairly from a position of strength. In effect, there was no policy at all during the 13 years of recently concluded negotiations—nothing but a servile effort to appease and please and a willingness to accept whatever may be left after Panama had been satisfied on every score.

Such a new policy and its implementation would go a long way toward resolving our Panama Canal dilemma, the seemingly inevitable clash between U.S. public opinion and U.S. official policy. But that dilemma will only be resolved when the will of the American people and the policy of their government coincide. And that can probably only happen when the American people, on their part, are ready to accept the principle of Panamanian sovereignty over the Canal Zone and the United States government, on its part, is ready to take a firm position on the retention of U.S. rights to control and defend the Canal.

Appendix A

Hay–Bunau-Varilla Treaty (1903)

The United States of America and the Republic of Panama being desirous to insure the construction of a ship-canal across the Isthmus of Panama to connect the Atlantic and Pacific oceans, and the Congress of the United States of America having passed an act approved June 28, 1902, in furtherance of that object, by which the President of the United States is authorized to acquire within a reasonable time the control of the necessary territory of the Republic of Colombia, and the sovereignty of such territory being actually vested in the Republic of Panama, the high contracting parties have resolved for that purpose to conclude a convention and have accordingly appointed as their plenipotentiaries,—

The President of the United States of America, John Hay, Secretary of State, and the Government of the Republic of Panama, Philippe Bunau-Varilla, Envoy Extraordinary and Minister Plenipotentiary of the Republic of Panama, thereunto specially empowered by said Government, who after communicating with each other their respective full powers found to be in good and due form, have agreed upon and concluded the following articles:

Article I

The United States guarantees and will maintain the independence of the Republic of Panama.

Article II

The Republic of Panama grants to the United States in perpetuity the use, occupation and control of a zone of land and land under water for the construction, maintenance, operation, sanitation and protection of said Canal of the width of ten miles extending to the distance of five miles on each side of the center line of the route of the Canal to be constructed; the said zone beginning in the Caribbean Sea, three marine miles from mean low water mark, and extending to and across the Isthmus of Panama into the Pacific Ocean to a distance of three marine miles from mean low water mark, with the proviso that the cities of Panama and Colon and the harbors adjacent to said cities, which are included within the boundaries of the zone above described, shall not be included within this grant. The Republic of Panama further grants to the United States in perpetuity the use, occupation and control of any other lands and waters outside of the zone above described which may be necessary and convenient for the construction, maintenance, operation, sanitation and protection of the said Canal or of any auxiliary canals or other works necessary and convenient for the construction, maintenance, operation, sanitation and protection of the said enterprise.

The Republic of Panama further grants in like manner to the United States in perpetuity all islands within the limits of the zone above described and in addition thereto the group of small islands in the Bay of Panama, named Perico, Naos, Culebra and Flamenco.

Article III

The Republic of Panama grants to the United States all the rights, power and authority within the zone mentioned and described in Article II of this agreement and within the limits of all auxiliary lands and waters mentioned and described in said Article II which the United States would possess and exercise if it were the sovereign of the territory within which said lands and waters are located to the entire exclusion of the exercise by the Republic of Panama of any such sovereign rights, power or authority.

Article IV

As rights subsidiary to the above grants the Republic of Panama grants in perpetuity to the United States the rights to use the rivers, streams, lakes and other bodies of water within its limits for navigation, the supply of water, or water-power, or other purposes, so far as the use of said rivers, streams, lakes and bodies of water and the waters thereof may be necessary and convenient for the construction, maintenance, operation, sanitation and protection of the said Canal.

Article V

The Republic of Panama grants to the United States in perpetuity a monopoly for the construction, maintenance and operation of any system of communication by means of canal or railroad across its territory between the Caribbean Sea and the Pacific Ocean.

Article VI

The grants herein contained shall in no manner invalidate the titles or rights of private land-holders or owners of private property in the said zone or in or to any of the lands or waters granted to the United States by the provisions of any Article of this treaty, nor shall they interfere with the rights of way over the public roads passing through the said zone or over any of the said lands or waters unless said rights of way or private rights shall conflict with rights herein granted to the United States, in which case the rights of the United States shall be superior. All damages caused to the owners of private lands or private property of any kind by the operations of the United States, its agents or employees, or by reason of the construction, maintenance, operation, sanitation and protection of the said Canal or of the works of sanitation and protection herein provided for, shall be appraised and settled by a joint commission appointed by the Government of the United States and the Republic of Panama, whose decisions as to such damages shall be final and whose awards as to such damages shall be paid solely by the United States. No part of the work on said Canal or the Panama railroad or on any auxiliary works relating thereto and authorized by the terms of this treaty shall be prevented, delayed or impeded by or pending such proceedings to ascertain such damages. The appraisal of the said private lands and private property and the assessment of damages to them shall be based upon their value before the date of this convention.

Article VII

The Republic of Panama grants to the United States with the limits of the cities of Panama and Colon and their adjacent harbors and within the territory adjacent thereto the right to acquire by purchase or by the exercise of the right of eminent domain, any lands, buildings, water rights or other properties necessary and convenient for the construction, maintenance, operation and protection of the Canal and of any works of sanitation, such as the collection and disposition of sewage and the distribution of water in the said cities of Panama and Colon, which in the discretion of the United States may be necessary and convenient for the construction, maintenance, operation, sanitation and protection of the said Canal and railroad. All such works of sanitation, collection and disposition of sewage and distribution of water in the cities of Panama and Colon shall be made at the expense of the United States, and the Government of the United States, its agents or nominees shall be authorized to impose and collect water rates and sewage rates which shall be sufficient to provide for the payment of interest and the amortisation of the principal of the cost of said works within a period of fifty years, and upon the expiration of said term of fifty years the system of sewers and water works shall revert to and become the properties of the cities of Panama and Colon respectively; and the use of the water shall be free to the inhabitants of Panama and Colon, except to the extent that water rates may be necessary for the operation and maintenance of sewers and water.

The Republic of Panama agrees that the cities of Panama and Colon shall comply in perpetuity with the sanitary ordinances

211

whether of a preventive or curative character prescribed by the United States, and in case the Government of Panama is unable or fails in its duty to enforce this compliance by the cities of Panama and Colon with the sanitary ordinances of the United States the Republic of Panama grants to the United States the right and authority to enforce the same.

The same right and authority are granted to the United States for the maintenance of public order in the cities of Panama and Colon and the territories and harbors adjacent thereto in case the Republic of Panama should not be, in the judgment of the United States, able to maintain such order.

Article VIII

The Republic of Panama grants to the United States all rights which it now has or hereafter may acquire to the property of the New Panama Canal Company and the Panama Railroad Company as a result of the transfer of sovereignty from the Republic of Colombia to the Republic of Panama over the Isthmus of Panama, and authorizes the New Panama Canal Company to sell and transfer to the United States its rights, privileges, properties and concessions as well as the Panama Railroad and all the shares or part of the shares of that company; but the public land situated outside of the zone described in Article II of this treaty now included in the concessions to both said enterprises and not required in the construction or operation of the Canal shall revert to the Republic of Panama, except any property now owned by or in the possession of said companies within Panama or Colon or the ports or terminals thereof.

Article IX

The United States agrees that the ports at either entrance of the Canal and the waters thereof, and the Republic of Panama agrees that the towns of Panama and Colon shall be free for all time, so that there shall not be imposed or collected customhouse tolls, tonnage, anchorage, lighthouse, wharf, pilot or quarantine dues or any other charges or taxes of any kind upon any vessel using or passing through the Canal or belonging to or employed by the United States, directly or indirectly, in connection with the construction, maintenance, operation, sanitation and protection of the main Canal, or auxiliary works, or upon the cargo, officers, crew or passengers of any such vessels, except such tolls and charges as may be imposed by the United States for the use of the Canal and other works, and except tolls and charges imposed by the Republic of Panama upon merchandise destined to be introduced for the consumption of the rest of the Republic of Panama, and upon vessels touching at the ports of Colon and Panama and which do not cross the Canal.

The Government of the Republic of Panama shall have the right to establish in such ports and in the towns of Panama and Colon such houses and guards as it may deem necessary to collect duties on importations destined to other portions of Panama and to prevent contraband trade. The United States shall have the right to make use of the towns and harbors of Panama and Colon as places of anchorage, and for making repairs, for loading, unloading, depositing or transshipping cargoes either in transit or destined for the service of the Canal and for other works pertaining to the Canal.

Article X

The Republic of Panama agrees that there shall not be imposed any taxes, national, municipal, departmental, or of any other class upon the Canal, the railways and auxiliary works, tugs and other vessels employed in the service of the Canal, storehouses, workshops, offices, quarters for laborers, factories of all kinds, warehouses, wharves, machinery and other works, property, and effects appertaining to the Canal or railroad and auxiliary works, or their officers or employees, situated within the cities of Panama and Colon, and that there shall not be imposed contributions or charges of a personal character of any kind upon officers, employees, laborers and other individuals in the service of the Canal and railroad and auxiliary works.

Article XI

The United States agrees that the official despatches of the Government of the Republic of Panama shall be transmitted over any telegraph or telephone lines established for Canal purposes and used for public and private business at rates not higher than those required from officials in the service of the United States.

Article XII

The Government of the Republic of Panama shall permit the immigration and free access to the lands and workshops of the Canal and its auxiliary works of all employees and workmen of whatever nationality under contract to work upon or seeking employment upon or in any wise connected with the said Canal and its auxiliary works, with their respective families, and all such persons shall be free and exempt from the military service of the Republic of Panama.

Article XIII

The United States may import at any time into the said zone and auxiliary lands, free of custom duties, imposts, taxes or other charges, and without any restrictions, any and all vessels, dredges, engines, cars, machinery, tolls, explosives, materials, supplies, and other articles necessary and convenient in the construction, maintenance, operation, sanitation and protection of the Canal and auxiliary works, and all provisions, medicines, clothing, supplies and other things necessary and convenient for the officers, employees, workmen and laborers in the service and employ of the United States and for their families. If any such articles are disposed of for use outside of the zone and auxiliary lands granted to the United States and within the territory of the Republic, they shall be subject to the same import or other duties as like articles under the laws of the Republic of Panama.

Article XIV

As the price of compensation for the rights, powers and privileges granted in this convention by the Republic of Panama to the United States, the Government of the United States agrees to pay to the Republic of Panama the sum of ten million dollars ($10,000,000) in gold coin of the United States on the exchange of the ratification of this convention and also an annual payment during the life of this convention of two hundred and fifty thousand dollars ($250,000) in like gold coin, beginning nine years after the date aforesaid.

The provisions of this article shall be in addition to all other benefits assured to the Republic of Panama under this convention. But no delay or difference of opinion under this article or any other provisions of this treaty shall affect or interrupt the full operation and effect of this convention in all other respects.

Article XV

The joint commission referred to in Article VI shall be established as follows:

The President of the United States shall nominate two persons and the President of the Republic of Panama shall nominate two persons and they shall proceed to a decision; but in case of disagreement of the Commission (by reason of their being equally divided in conclusion) an umpire shall be appointed by the two Governments who shall render the decision. In the event of the death, absence, or incapacity of a commissioner or umpire, or of his omitting, declining or ceasing to act, his place shall be filled by the appointment of another person in the manner above indicated. All decisions by a majority of the Commission or by the umpire shall be final.

Article XVI

The two Governments shall make adequate provisions by mutual agreement for the pursuit, capture, imprisonment, detention and delivery within the said zone and auxiliary lands to the authorities of the Republic of Panama of persons charged with the commitment of crimes, felonies or misdemeanors without said zone and for the pursuit, capture, imprisonment, detention and delivery without said zone to the authorities of the United States of persons charged with the commitment of crimes, felonies and misdemeanors within said zone and auxiliary lands.

Article XVII

The Republic of Panama grants to the United States the use of all the ports of the Republic open to commerce as places of refuge for any vessels employed in the Canal enterprise, and for all vessels passing or bound to pass through the Canal which may be in distress and be driven to seek refuge in said ports. Such vessels shall be exempt from anchorage and tonnage dues on the part of the Republic of Panama.

Article XVIII

The Canal, when constructed, and the entrances thereto shall be neutral in perpetuity, and shall be opened upon the terms provided for by Section I of Article III of, and in conformity with all the stipulations of, the treaty entered into by the Governments of the United States and Great Britain on November 18, 1901.

Article XIX

The Government of the Republic of Panama shall have the right to transport over the Canal its vessels and its troops and munitions of war in such vessels at all times without paying charges of any kind. The exemption is to be extended to the auxiliary railway for the transportation of persons in the service of the Republic of Panama, or of the police force charged with the preservation of public order outside of said zone, as well as to their baggage, munitions of war and supplies.

Article XX

If by virtue of any existing treaty in relation to the territory of the Isthmus of Panama, whereof the obligations shall descend or be assumed by the Republic of Panama, there may be any privilege or concession in favor of the Government or the citizens and subjects of a third power relative to an interoceanic means of communication which in any of its terms may be incompatible with the terms of the present convention, the Republic of Panama agrees to cancel or modify such treaty in due form, for which purpose it shall give to the said third power the requisite notification within the term of four months from the date of the present convention, and in case the existing treaty contains no clause permitting its modifications or annulment, the Republic of Panama agrees to procure its modifications or annulment in such form that there shall not exist any conflict with the stipulations of the present convention.

Article XXI

The rights and privileges granted by the Republic of Panama to the United States in the preceding articles are understood to be free of all anterior debts, liens, trusts or liabilities, or concessions or privileges to other Governments, corporations, syndicates or individuals; and consequently, if there should arise any claims on account of the present concessions and privileges or otherwise, the claimant shall resort to the Government of the Republic of Panama and not the United States for any indemnity or compromise which may be required.

Article XXII

The Republic of Panama renounces and grants to the United States the participation to which it might be entitled in the future earnings of the Canal under Article XV of the concessionary contract with Lucien N. B. Wyse, now owned by the New Panama Canal Company, and any and all other rights or claims of a pecuniary nature arising under or relating to said concession, or arising under or relating to the concessions to the Panama Railroad Company or any extension or modification thereof; and it likewise renounces, confirms and grants to the United States, now and hereafter, all the rights and property reserved in the said concessions which otherwise would belong to Panama at or before the expiration of the terms of ninety-nine years of the concessions granted to or held by the above-mentioned party and companies, and all right, title and interest which it now has or may hereafter have, in and to the lands, canal, works, property and rights held by the said companies under said concessions or otherwise, and acquired or to be acquired by the United States from or through the New Panama Canal Company, including property and rights which might or may in the future either by lapse of time, forfeiture or otherwise, revert to the Republic of Panama under any contracts or concessions, with said Wyse, the Universal Panama Canal Company, the Panama Railroad Company and the New Panama Canal Company.

The aforesaid rights and property shall be and are free and released from any present or reversionary interest in or claims of Panama, and the title of the United States thereto upon consummation of the contemplated purchase by the United States from the New Panama Canal Company shall be absolute so far as concerns the Republic of Panama, excepting always the rights of the Republic specifically secured under this treaty.

Article XXIII

If it should become necessary at any time to employ armed forces for the safety or protection of the Canal, or of the ships that make use of the same, or the railroads and auxiliary works, the United States shall have the right, at all times and in its discretion, to use its police and its land and naval forces or to establish fortifications for these purposes.

Article XXIV

No change either in the Government or in the laws and treaties of the Republic of Panama shall, without the consent of the United States, affect any right of the United States under the present convention, or under any treaty stipulation between the two countries that now exists or may hereafter exist touching the subject matter of this convention.

If the Republic of Panama shall hereafter enter as a constituent into any other Government or into any union or confederation of States, so as to merge her sovereignty or independence in such Government, union or confederation, the rights of the United States under this convention shall not be in any respect lessened or impaired.

Article XXV

For the better performance of the engagements of this convention and to the end of the efficient protection of the Canal and the preservation of its neutrality, the Government of the Republic of Panama will sell or lease to the United States lands adequate and necessary for naval or coaling stations on the Pacific coast and on the western Caribbean coast of the Republic at certain points to be agreed upon with the President of the United States.

Article XXVI

This convention when signed by the Plenipotentiaries of the Contracting Parties shall be ratified by the respective Governments and the ratification shall be exchanged at Washington at the earliest date possible.

In faith whereof the respective Plenipotentiaries have signed the present convention in duplicate and have hereunto affixed their respective seals.

Done at the City of Washington the 18th day of November in the year of our Lord nineteen hundred and three.

JOHN HAY   [SEAL]

P. BUNAU-VARILLA [SEAL]

Appendix B

*Letter to
President Carter
from Admirals
Robert B. Carney
Arleigh A. Burke
George W. Anderson
and Thomas H. Moorer
June 8, 1977*

Dear Mr. President:

As former Chiefs of Naval Operations, fleet commanders and Naval Advisers to previous Presidents, we believe we have an obligation to you and the nation to offer our combined judgment on the strategic value of the Panama Canal to the United States.

Contrary to what we read about the declining strategic and economic value of the Canal, the truth is that this inter-oceanic waterway is as important, if not more so, to the United States than ever. The Panama Canal enables the United States to transfer its naval forces and commercial units from ocean to ocean as the need arises. This capability is increasingly important now in view of the reduced size of the U.S. Atlantic and Pacific fleets.

We recognize that the Navy's largest aircraft carriers and some of the world's super-tankers are too wide to transit the Canal as it exists today. The super-tankers represent but a small percentage of the world's commercial fleets. From a strategic viewpoint, the Navy's largest carriers can be wisely positioned as pressures and tensions build in any kind of a short-range, limited situation. Meanwhile, the hundreds of combatants, from submarines to cruisers, can be funneled through the transit as can the vital fleet train needed to sustain the combatants. In the years ahead as carriers become smaller or as the Canal is modernized, this problem will no longer exist.

Our experience has been that as each crisis developed during our active service—World War II, Korea, Vietnam and the Cuban missile crisis—the value of the Canal was forcefully emphasized by emergency transits of our naval units and massive logistic support for the Armed Forces. The Canal provided operational flexibility and rapid mobility. In addition, there are the psychological advantages of this power potential. As Commander-in-Chief, you will find the ownership and sovereign control of the Canal indispensable during periods of tension and conflict.

As long as most of the world's combatant and commercial tonnage can transit through the Canal, it offers inestimable strategic advantages to the United States, giving us maximum strength at minimum cost. Moreover, sovereignty and jurisdiction over the Canal Zone and Canal offer the opportunity to use the waterway or to deny its use to others in wartime. This authority was especially helpful during World War II and also Vietnam. Under the control of a potential adversary, the Panama Canal would become an immediate crucial problem and prove a serious weakness in the over-all U.S. defense capability, with enormous potential consequences for evil.

Mr. President, you have become our leader at a time when the adequacy of our naval capabilities is being seriously challenged. The existing maritime threat to us is compounded by the possibility that the Canal under Panamanian sovereignty could be neutralized or lost, depending on that government's relationship with other nations. We note that the present Panamanian government has close ties with the present Cuban government which in turn is closely tied to the Soviet Union. Loss of the Panama Canal, which would be a serious set-back in war, would contribute to the encirclement of the U.S. by hostile naval forces, and threaten our ability to survive.

For meeting the current situation, you have the well-known precedent of former distinguished Secretary of State (later Chief Justice) Charles Evans Hughes, who, when faced with a comparable situation in 1923, declared to the Panamanian government that it was an "absolute futility" for it "to expect an American administration, no matter what it was, any President or any Secretary of State, ever to surrender any part of (the) rights which the United States had acquired under the Treaty of 1903" (Ho. Doc. No. 474, 89th Congress, p.154).

We recognize that a certain amount of social unrest is generated by the contrast in living standards between Zonians and Panamanians living nearby. Bilateral programs are recommended to upgrade Panamanian boundary areas. Canal modernization, once U.S. sovereignty is guaranteed, might benefit the entire Panamanian economy, and especially those areas near the U.S. Zone.

The Panama Canal represents a vital portion of our U.S. naval and maritime assets, all of which are absolutely essential for free world security. It is our considered individual and combined judgment that you should instruct our negotiators to retain full sovereign control for the United States over both the Panama Canal and its protective frame, the U.S. Canal Zone as provided in the existing treaty.

Very respectfully,
(signed)
ROBERT B. CARNEY
ARLEIGH A. BURKE
GEORGE W. ANDERSON
THOMAS H. MOORER

Notes

Chapter 1

1. See, for example, polls by Opinion Research Corporation of Princeton, New Jersey, as recorded in the *Congressional Record,* June 18, 1976, p. H6176, and July 26, 1977, p. S12828.

2. Richard Hudson, "Storm over the Canal," *New York Times Magazine,* May 16, 1976, p. 18.

3. United States Senate Res. 97, 93rd Congress, 2nd Ses.

4. United States Senate Res. 97, 94th Congress, 1st Ses.

5. *Congressional Record,* June 26, 1975, p. H6236.

6. Steve Diamond, "The Panama Time Bomb," *New Times,* May 10, 1976, p. 23.

7. *Department of State Bulletin,* January 9, 1965.

8. *Ibid.,* October 18, 1965.

9. *Ibid.,* July 17, 1967.

10. *Congressional Record,* July 17, 1967, pp. S18940–48; July 21, 1967, pp. S19741–46; July 27, 1967, pp. S20471–77.

11. "Controversy over Panama Canal Treaty Revision," *Congressional Digest,* April 1976, p. 128.

12. *Department of State Bulletin,* February 25, 1974.

13. "Panama Canal," *Atlantic Monthly* ("Reports and Comments"), June 1976, p. 10.

14. *Time,* October 18, 1976, pp. 17–18.

15. Ellsworth Bunker, address to the World Affairs Council, Los Angeles, Calif., State Department News Release, December 2, 1975.

16. *Department of State Bulletin,* February 23, 1976.

17. Robert A. Pastor, "In the Canal Zone: Who Should Be Sovereign," *Harvard Magazine,* June 1976, p. 43.

18. *U.S. News and World Report,* April 26, 1976, p. 24.

19. Hudson, "Storm over the Canal," p. 18.

20. Thomas M. Franck and Edward Weisband, "Panama Paralysis," *Foreign Policy,* Winter 1975, p. 187.

21. David Reed, "Should We Give Up the Panama Canal?" *Reader's Digest,* May 1976, p. 218.

Chapter 2

1. The first American statesmen to have this dream were Benjamin Franklin and Thomas Jefferson. See Lawrence O. Ealy, *Yanqui Politics and the Isthmian Canal* (Philadelphia: Pennsylvania State University Press, 1971), pp. 6–7.

2. Ian Cameron, *The Impossible Dream* (New York: William Morrow & Co., 1972), p. 17.

3. Immanuel J. Klette, *From Atlantic to Pacific* (New York: Harper & Row, 1967), p. 5.

4. *First International American Conference, Reports of Committees and Discussions Thereon* (Washington, D.C.: Government Printing Office, 1890), vol. IV, p. 144.

5. Hunter Miller, ed., *Treaties and Other International Acts of the U.S.A.* (Washington, D.C.: Government Printing Office, 1937), vol. 5, p. 115.

6. *Ibid.,* pp. 671–75.

7. Cameron, *Impossible Dream,* p. 44.

Chapter 3

1. Gerstle Mack, *The Land Divided* (New York: Alfred A. Knopf, 1944), pp. 190–91; Miles P. DuVal, Jr., *Cadiz to Cathay* (Stanford, Calif.: Stanford University Press, 1940), p. 39.

2. Donald B. Chidsey, *The Panama Canal—An Informal History* (New York: Crown, 1970), pp. 90–93; Cameron, *Impossible Dream*, p. 106; Mack, *Land Divided*, pp. 219–21.

3. Mack, *Land Divided*, p. 223.

4. *Congressional Record*, July 18, 1902, p. 6984.

5. *U.S. Stat. at Large*, vol. 32, pt. 1, p. 482.

6. Philippe Bunau-Varilla, *Panama: The Creation, Destruction, and Resurrection* (New York: McBride, Nast & Co., 1914), pp. 246–47.

Chapter 4

1. Miller, ed., *Treaties*, vol. 5, pp. 125–43.

2. *Ibid.*, pp. 138–42.

3. U.S. Department of State Archives, "Unperfected Treaty" (manuscript), D4; Senate Document No. 474, 63rd Congress, 2nd Ses., pp. 277–88.

4. Mack, *Land Divided*, p. 443.

5. *Ibid.*, p. 450.

6. Roosevelt Papers, Roosevelt to Hay, August 19, 1903, quoted in Dwight C. Miner, *The Fight for the Panama Route* (New York: Columbia University Press, 1940), p. 345.

7. Mack, *Land Divided*, pp. 454–55.

8. *Ibid.*, p. 455.

9. *New York World*, June 14, 1903.

10. Mack, *Land Divided*, p. 455.

11. Bunau-Varilla, *Panama*, pp. 310–12, 317–18.

12. Miner, *Fight for the Panama Route*, p. 359 *n.*

13. Bunau-Varilla, *Panama*, pp. 320–23.

14. *Ibid.*, pp. 323–24.

15. *Ibid.*, pp. 328–32.

16. Mack, *Land Divided*, p. 460.

17. *Ibid.*, p. 468.

18. Bunau-Varilla, *Panama*, p. 378.

19. Appendix A.

20. *Ibid.*, art. II.

21. *Ibid.*
22. *Ibid.*, art. VII.
23. *Ibid.*
24. *Ibid.*, art. III.
25. *Ibid.*, art. I.
26. *Ibid.*, art. XIV.
27. Cameron, *Impossible Dream*, p. 114.
28. Bunau-Varilla, *Panama*, p. 429.
29. *San Francisco Examiner*, March 24, 1911.
30. Mack, *Land Divided*, p. 472.

Chapter 5

1. Mack, *Land Divided*, p. 497
2. Cameron, *Impossible Dream*, p. 162.
3. Mack, *Land Divided*, p. 498.
4. Cameron, *Impossible Dream*, p. 162.
5. *Ibid.*, p. 525.
6. Mack, *Land Divided*, p. 528; Cameron, *Impossible Dream*, pp. 136, 141.
7. Cameron, *Impossible Dream*, p. 134 *n.*
8. Mack, *Land Divided*, pp. 537–41.

Chapter 6

1. Appendix A.
2. *Black's Law Dictionary*, 4th ed. (St. Paul, Minn.: West Publishing Co., 1968), p. 1568.
3. See appendix A, preamble.
4. *Ibid.*, art. II.
5. *Ibid.*, art. III.
6. Spruille Braden, *Panama and the U.S.A.: The Real Story* (Calif.: American Educational League, Freedom Center), reproduced in *Congressional Digest*, April 1976, pp. 122, 124, 126.
7. *Congressional Record*, June 17, 1976, p. S9765.
8. James Lucier, "Panama Canal: Focus of Power Politics," *Strategic Review*, Spring 1974, pp. 34, 37.
9. Miller, ed., *Treaties*, vol. 2, pp. 498–505.
10. *Black's Law Dictionary*, p. 573.
11. William M. Malloy, comp., *Treaties, Conventions, International Acts, Protocols and Agreements Between the U.S.A.*

and Other Powers (Washington, D.C.: Government Printing Office, 1910), pp. 1521–24.

12. Bunau-Varilla, *Panama*, pp. 368, 410, 414; DuVal, *Cadiz to Cathay*, p. 380.

13. Helen C. Low, "The Panama Canal Treaty in Perspective," Communique No. 29, April 1976, Overseas Development Council, p. 3.

14. *Ibid.*

Chapter 7

1. Mack, *Land Divided*, p. 489.

2. Jules Dubois, *Danger over Panama* (New York: Bobbs-Merrill, 1964), p. 39.

3. U.S. Department of State, *Foreign Relations of the U.S. 1926*, vol. II (Washington, D.C.: Government Printing Office, 1941), pp. 833–49.

4. *Treaties and Other Obligations of the U.S.A.* (Bevans), vol. 10, pp. 742–52.

5. Dubois, *Danger over Panama*, p. 123.

6. *Treaties and Other Obligations of the U.S.A.*, vol. 10, pp. 809–14.

7. Dubois, *Danger over Panama*, pp. 211–14.

8. *U.S. Treaties and Other International Agreements, 1955*, vol. 6, pt. 2 (Washington, D.C.: Government Printing Office, 1956), pp. 2273–89.

9. Dubois, *Danger over Panama*, pp. 211–12.

10. *Ibid.*, p. 209; Ealy, *Yanqui Politics*, pp. 112–13.

11. Dubois, *Danger over Panama*, p. 213.

12. *Ibid.*, pp. 291–313.

13. *Department of State Bulletin*, January 9, 1965.

14. *Ibid.*, October 18, 1965.

Chapter 8

1. *Arizona Republic*, December 6, 1975.

2. Report by the Commission on United States–Latin American Relations (Center for Inter-American Relations, 680 Park Ave., New York City), October 29, 1974.

3. Report by the Commission on United States–Latin American Relations, December 20, 1976.

4. *Congressional Record,* February 22, 1977, pp. S2819–23.
5. American Legion Bulletin No. 2-77 (National Security–Foreign Relations), February 11, 1977 (Washington, D.C.), pp. 3-4(A).
6. Hudson, "Storm over the Canal," p. 19.

Chapter 9

1. White House press release, December 18, 1964.
2. Atlantic-Pacific Interocean Canal Study Commission, *Interoceanic Canal Studies 1970* (Washington, D.C.: Report to the President of the United States, December 1, 1970), ch. X, p. 106.
3. *Ibid.*
4. *Los Angeles Times,* July 23, 1977.
5. U.S. Department of State, *Current Policy No. 9,* November 1975.
6. Address of Counselor John D. Blacken, U.S. Embassy, Panama, *Congressional Record,* September 25, 1975, p. S16743.
7. *Congressional Record,* December 5, 1975, pp. S21152–53.
8. *Ibid.,* p. S21153.
9. *Ibid.,* pp. S21153–54.
10. *New York Times,* July 29 and August 2, 1977.
11. *Ibid.,* August 11, 1977.

Chapter 10

1. The following are the principal sources of the statistical material in this chapter: "Foreign Economic Trends and Their Implications for the United States–Panama," U.S. Embassy, Panama, FET-76-010, January 1976, and FET-75-084, August 1975; Department of State Airgram, May 17, 1976, U.S. Embassy, Panama, to Secretary of State, Subject: Government of Panama—Consolidated National Budget—1974–76; miscellaneous statistical information furnished by USAID Panama, Panama City; Information Memorandum, Prospectus $80,000,000 Floating Rate Loan, April 1976, issued by Panamanian Ministry of Planning and Political Economy; "Finance, Banking and Development in Panama, A *Financial Times* Survey," March 11, 1975, the *Financial Times,* Panama City; address of Counselor John D. Blacken, U.S. Embassy, Panama, *Congressional Record,* September 25, 1975, S16743–46; *Panamanian Committee*

for Human Rights, vol. I (Panama: September 1976), vol. II (November 1976), vol. III (December 1976); *Daily Report— Latin America,* Foreign Broadcast Information Service, July 1975–August 1976.

Chapter 11

1. The statistical, much of the other factual, and some of the descriptive material in this chapter is derived from the following: *Panama Canal Company/Canal Zone Government Annual Report—FY 1975;* Government Accounting Office Report No. B-114839, May 28, 1975; Klette, *From Atlantic to Pacific;* miscellaneous briefing material, Panama Canal Information Office, Balboa Heights, Canal Zone; U.S. Department of Defense, *Commanders Digest,* vol. 14, no. 16 (1973); United States Southern Command, *Southcom Command Briefing* (updated to May 18, 1976).

Chapter 12

1. The statistical, much of the other factual, and some of the descriptive material in this chapter is derived from the following: briefing material (May 1976), Panama Canal Information Office, Balboa Heights, Canal Zone; Panama Canal Company–Panama Canal Zone Government annual reports, fiscal years ending June 30, 1975 and June 30, 1976; Government Accounting Office Report No. B-114839, May 28, 1975.

The treaty referred to on p. 143 is the Chapin-Fabrega Treaty of 1955 (*U.S. Treaties and Other International Agreements, 1955,* vol. 6, pt. 2 [Washington, D.C.: Government Printing Office, 1956], pp. 2273–89). The quotation appearing on p. 143 is from the "Memorandum of Understandings Reached," *Department of State Bulletin,* February 7, 1955, pp. 241–43.

Chapter 14

1. The principal sources of the statistical material in this chapter are the following: Panama Canal Company annual reports; Atlantic-Pacific Interoceanic Canal Study Commission, *Interoceanic Canal Studies 1970;* Leon M. Cole, "Economic Ramifications of Future Panama Control and Use: A Survey," Congressional Research Service, April 3, 1975; Klette, *From*

Atlantic to Pacific; Norman J. Padelford, *The Panama Canal in Peace and War* (New York: Macmillan, 1942); Norman J. Padelford and Stephen R. Gibbs, *Maritime Commerce and the Future of the Panama Canal,* Report No. MIT5G 74-28 (Cambridge, Md.: Cornell Maritime Press, 1975); Ely M. Brandes and Randall Chun, *Impact of Panama Canal Closure: Effects on Regions in North America,* vol. I ("U.S. Gulf"), November 1975, vol. II ("U.S.-Canada West Coast"), January 1976, vol. III ("U.S. South Atlantic"), February 1976 (Palo Alto, Calif.: International Research Associates); James E. Howell and Ezra Solomon, *The Economic Value of the Panama Canal* (Palo Alto, Calif.: International Research Associates, December 1973); "Review of Sensitivity Estimates Contained in Panama Canal Toll Increases: Effect on U.S. Economy," *Letter Report,* February 1974, International Research Associates; Ely M. Brandes, *Critique and Evaluation of the Panama Canal in U.S. Foreign Trade (Impact of a Toll Increase and Facility Closure) MARAD, May 1974* (Palo Alto, Calif.: International Research Associates, June 1974); Ely M. Brandes, James E. Howell, and Ezra Solomon, *Critique and Evaluation of "Panama Canal Revenues and Estimates of Savings to Users, CEPAL, December 1971"* (Palo Alto, Calif.: International Research Associates, February 1974).

Chapter 15

1. The principal sources of factual material and the views of others presented in this chapter are, in addition to news reports, personal interviews, and correspondence, the following: Dubois, *Danger over Panama;* Klette, *From Atlantic to Pacific;* Ealy, *Yanqui Politics;* Cameron, *Impossible Dream;* Jon P. Speller, *The Panama Canal: Heart of America's Security* (New York: Speller and Sons, 1972); James L. Busby, *Political Aspects of the Panama Canal: The Problem of Location* (Tucson: University of Arizona Press, 1974); Isaac Don Levine, *Hands Off the Panama Canal* (Washington, D.C.: Monticello Books, 1976); Reed, "Should We Give Up the Panama Canal?"; Melvin R. Laird, "The Moscow-Havana Connection," *Reader's Digest,* August 1976; "If the U.S. Gives Up Panama Canal," *U.S. News and World Report,* May 24, 1976; Hudson, "Storm over the Canal"; Stephen G. Rosenfeld, "The Panama Canal Negotiations—A Close-Run Thing," *Foreign Affairs,* October 1975; Franck and

Weisband, "Panama Paralysis"; Vincent P. McDonald, "The Panama Canal for Panamanians: The Implications for the United States," *Military Review*, December 1975; V. H. Krulak, "Panama: Strategic Pitfall," *Strategic Review*, Winter 1976; Hanson Baldwin, "The Panama Canal: Sovereignty and Security," *AEI Defense Review*, August 1977; Panama Canal Company annual reports; the *Congressional Record;* various State Department releases; Atlantic-Pacific Interoceanic Canal Study Commission, *Interoceanic Canal Studies 1970.*

2. See appendix B, pp. 220–21.

3. *Ibid.*, p. 222.

Chapter 16

1. The texts of the proposed new treaties and associated documents can be found in U.S. Department of State, *Selected Documents*, nos. 6 and 6B (Washington, D.C.: U.S. Department of State, Bureau of Public Affairs, Office of Media Services, September 1977).

2. Canal Treaty, art. I, par. 1; Agreed Minute, par. 1.

3. *Ibid.*, art. II, par. 2.

4. *Ibid.*, preamble; art. I, par. 2; art. III, par. 1; art. XI.

5. *Ibid.*, art. VII, par. 1.

6. *Ibid.*, art. VII, par. 2; Agreement in Implementation of Article IV, of the Panama Canal Treaty (hereinafter referred to as Imp. IV), art. V.

7. Canal Treaty, arts. I, III (par. 10), VII, IX, XI.

8. *Ibid.*, art. XI, par. 1.

9. *Ibid.*, art. XI, pars. 1, 2.

10. *Ibid.*, art. XI, pars. 3, 4, 5.

11. *Ibid.*, plus Annex, par. 4(b).

12. Agreement in Implementation of Article III of the Panama Canal Treatry (hereinafter referred to as Imp. III), art. III, par. 8; Imp. IV, art. VI.

13. Canal Treaty, art. III, par. 6.

14. *Ibid.*, art. III, par. 5.

15. Imp. IV, art. VI, par. 6.

16. See chapter 9.

17. Canal Treaty, Annex, par. 4(a) (xii).

18. *Ibid.*, Annex, par. 4(a) (xiii).

19. *Ibid.*, Annex, par. 4(a).

20. *Ibid.*, art. XIII, par. 2(a); Imp. III, art. V.

21. Canal Treaty, art. XIII, par. 2(d).

22. *Ibid.*, art. III, par. 1.

23. *Ibid.*, art. IV, pars. 1, 2.

24. Imp. III, art. III, pars, 1, 2; Imp. IV, arts. I, IV.

25. Canal Treaty, art. XIII, par. 4.

26. Speech by Sol M. Linowitz, State Department Release, August 19, 1977, Denver, Colorado, p. 5; State Department "Draft Environmental Impact Statement for the New Panama Canal Treaty" (Washington, D.C., August 1977), tab B, p. 3.

27. See chapter 9.

28. Canal Treaty, art. III, par. 2(a).

29. *Ibid.*, art. III, par. 2(c).

30. *Ibid.*, art. III, par. 7; Imp III, art. II.

31. Canal Treaty, art. III, par. 2; Annex, par. 3.

32. *Ibid.*, Annex, par. 4(a).

33. *Ibid.*, Annex, par. 5(b).

34. *Ibid.*, art. III; Imp III, art. VI, pars, 1, 2.

35. Imp III, art. IV, par. 3.

36. Canal Treaty, art. X; Imp III, art. VIII.

37. Canal Treaty, art. X, pars. 3(c), 5, 7.

38. *Ibid.*, art. IV.

39. *Ibid.*, art. IV, par. 5.

40. Imp. IV, art. XI.

41. *Ibid.*, art. VI.

42. Canal Treaty, art. XII, par. 1.

43. *Ibid.*, art. XII, par. 2(a).

44. *Ibid.*, art. XII, par. 2 (b).

45. *Ibid.*, art. XII, pars. 3, 4, 5.

46. Neutrality Treaty, art. VIII.

47. *Ibid.*, arts. I, IV.

48. *Ibid.*, art. I.

49. *Ibid.*, art. II.

50. *Ibid.*, art. III, par. 1(a), (b), (c).

51. *Ibid.*, art. III, par. 1(e).

52. *Ibid.*, art. VI, par. 1.

53. *Ibid.*

54. *Ibid.*, art. VII.

55. In May 1977 President Carter removed Maj. Gen. John K. Singlaub from his command position in South Korea for his publicly expressed disapproval of the president's policy of troop withdrawals from that country. See *Time*, May 30, 1977, p. 14; *Newsweek*, May 30, 1977, p. 17.

Chapter 17

1. "Controversy over Proposed Revision of the Panama Canal Treaty," *Congressional Digest*, April 1976, p. 128.

2. *Treaties and Other International Agreements of the United States, 1776-1949* (Washington, D.C.: Department of State, 1971), vol. 6, pp. 1113-14.

Index

235

Hull-Alfaro Treaty of 1936, 81–82, 83, 132, 179
Humphrey, Senator Hubert, 171

Industrial Revolution, 32
Interoceanic Canal Studies 1970, 164, 172
Isthmian Canal Commission, 77

Johnson, President Lyndon B., 20, 23, 24, 26, 87–88, 90, 94–95, 100

Kennedy, President John F., 86, 176
Kissinger, Secretary of State Henry, 25–26, 27, 28, 95, 97, 103; Kissinger-Tack Statement of Principles, 90, 91, 97, 99, 101, 103, 179, 180, 182, 183–84, 186
Krulak, Lt. General V. H., 168

Linowitz, Sol, 95–96, 98, 110
Lucier, Dr. James, 70

McDonald, Lt. Colonel Vincent P., 172
McKinley, President William, 42
Marine-Midland Bank, 96
Martinez, Boris, 119
Military Review, 172
Monroe Doctrine, 32, 176
Moore, Professor John Bassett, 53
Moorer, Admiral Thomas H., 168, 172, 220, 222
Morgan, Senator John Tyler, 41–42, 50; Morgan bill, 42–43, 44, 57

Nashville, U.S.S., 54
New York Times Magazine, 170
New Yorker, 21, 22, 23, 24, 26, 194, 195
Nicaragua: as a canal site, 32, 33, 34, 38, 43, 44–45, 50–51, 52, 58, 187
Nixon, President Richard M., 20, 24–25, 26, 90, 95, 99, 161

"Operation Sovereignty," 85
Oregon Territory, 33
Oregon, U.S.S., 41, 42, 165
Organization of American States, 87, 178

Padelford, Norman J., 163
Panama: area of, 112; attitude toward Americans, 114–15; average temperature of, 112; balance of payments, 119; banking in, 116–17; Cerro Colorado Project, 117–18; Colon Free Zone, 117; and communism, 93, 122–23, 124, 175–77, 198; and Cuba, 30, 174, 175–77; and deficit spending, 118; government crisis in, 195; gross national product of, 115–16, 119; literacy rate of, 112; national debt of, 118, 148; per capita income of, 112, 116; physical contour of, 35, 37, 112; population of, 112–14; as a province of Colombia, 45–47, 50, 52, 53; resources of, 19, 117–18; becomes a republic, 55; and security position system, 144–45; slums in, 128; and socialism, 121, 124; a Third World nation, 21, 27, 111; unemployment in, 118; violence in, 22, 23, 29, 84, 85–86, 87, 88, 94, 123; and World War

II, 82, 111; and post-World War II, 88–89, 111, 113